DATE DUE			

THE CENTURY PSYCHOLOGY SERIES

RICHARD M. ELLIOTT, GARDNER LINDZEY,
AND KENNETH MACCORQUODALE

EDITORS

ALAN C. KERCKHOFF
KURT W. BACK
BOTH OF DUKE UNIVERSITY

THE
JUNE
BUG: A STUDY OF HYSTERICAL CONTAGION

NEW YORK

APPLETON-CENTURY-CROFTS
DIVISION OF MEREDITH CORPORATION

Preface

Collective behavior is a term used by sociologists and psychologists to refer to a rather large number of different kinds of phenomena. Crowd behavior, panics, fads, crazes are all forms of collective behavior. The common definitive characteristic of such phenomena is a spontaneous response of a number of people in a situation in which there is no common cultural definition of what is appropriate. What occurs, therefore, is an emergent social form whose qualities can often be specified only after they develop. In most cases, the response is an active one, the collectivity *does* something with reference to some element in the situation—they lynch the prisoner, run from the fire, buy the presumed valuable commodity, and so on.

The form of collective behavior represented by the case analyzed in this volume is somewhat different from most other forms. It is generally called "hysterical contagion," and it consists of the dissemination within a collectivity of a symptom or set of symptoms for which no physical explanation can be found. In such cases, people get sick from "gas" but no gas can be found; they get "food poisoning" but no toxic element can be found in the food; or, as in our case, they suffer from "poisonous insect bites" but no poisonous insect can be found. The noteworthy phenomenon, therefore, is not an active response to some element in the situation; it is a passive experience. The actors do not *do* something so much as something happens *to* them. In fact, we are more likely to think of them as victims rather than actors.

Although it can safely be said in general that there have not been many empirical studies of collective behavior, it is even more true that studies of hysterical contagion are hard to find. This fact made the prospect of carrying out the study reported here both more exciting and more fearsome. There was little to go on, and there was even basis for doubting that anything of value *could* be done. Since the study could be made only after the event occurred, and since there seemed to be little order to the series of events that constituted the contagion, the usual tools of behavioral science seemed less than adequate for the task. And yet the challenge of coming to grips with such an amorphous but significant social phenomenon is great, and we present the analysis of this single case in the hope that it will stimulate further research in this area of inquiry. It will be apparent that we have not solved all of the problems of such research, but if what follows indicates that these problems are worthy of continued systematic investigation, the effort will have been justified.

The book has been organized to reflect the kind of problem faced in undertaking this study. Part I consists of two chapters which report what was "given" at the time the study got under way. Chapter 1 provides an outline of the external facts of the epidemic as reported by the various mass media and as reconstructed during our initial contacts with officials who had been involved. It thus relates what we knew about this particular case when we planned the field work. Chapter 2 is a summary of what we saw as the most relevant ideas current in the literature at the time and represents the conceptual framework with which we approached the investigation. Part II reports the outcome of our efforts within this context. It consists of seven chapters which present our solutions to the problems of research design and analysis (Chapter 3), the findings relevant to the major dimensions investigated (Chapters 4 through 7), and summary and concluding statements (Chapters 8 and 9).

This book owes its existence to the generous support of two organizations. Funds from the Office of Naval Research (Group Psychology Branch) through Contract Nor 181 C11 (Project NR177-470) made it possible to act promptly when our suspicion of extensive hysterical contagion was aroused through local newspaper reports. A grant from the National Science Foundation (NSF GS-89) enabled us to carry out the study. We want to express here our special appreciation to the responsible administration, Luigi Petrullo of ONR and Robert L. Hall of NSF, for the flexibility and promptness with which they responded to our needs and without which it would not have been possible to take advantage of this unique situation for scientific purposes.

Like other research projects of this magnitude, this study owes much to help of colleagues, staff, and participants in the field. We recognize especially the contribution of Norman Miller in the early stages of the research, in the initial contacts with plant management, the design of the study and construction of the questionnaire.

We appreciate the excellent interviewing by the field staff of the National Opinion Research Center under the direction of Galen Gockel. The further processing of the data was aided materially by a group of research assistants at Duke: A. Clarke Davis, Carl Hirsch, Patricia B. Frazer, Robert H. Roth, and Frank D. Bean, assisted in coding by Frances Anderson and Mary Sargent. The computations were conducted by Duke University Computation Center which is supported by a grant from the National Science Foundation.

Mary L. Brehm undertook the demanding task of the final editing of the manuscript and preparation of the index, and we are grateful for this essential contribution. We also wish to acknowledge the skillful typing of the manuscript by Ann Boneau and Susan Wright.

We have also profited from comments on earlier versions of the manuscript by Arlene Daniels, Kurt Lang, and Guy E. Swanson.

Finally, we must acknowledge, by necessity anonymously, our gratitude to the workers and officials of Montana Mills (especially "Hiram L. Lamont," the personnel manager who cooperated so splendidly with the research group), to "Dr. Joseph R. John" of the Communicable Diseases Center who gave us valuable first-hand medical information, and to those associated with the various media of mass communication who have permitted us the use of their reports in order that the immediate impact of the incident can be portrayed.

A. C. K.

K. W. B.

Contents

"If men define situations as real,
they are real in their consequences."

W. I. THOMAS

Part I

The social phenomenon analyzed in the following pages had the qualities which are characteristic of most cases of hysterical contagion. It was unexpected, it was newsworthy, it was disruptive, it was short-lived. The decision to study it could only be made after it was over. There was some real doubt about what had "really" happened. Even if we assumed, as we ultimately did, that the official statement of what had occurred was correct, there was no very clear basis for deciding what kinds of data to collect.

The two chapters which constitute Part I provide a picture of where we were when the study began. Chapter 1 presents selections from the news reports on the epidemic and a summary statement of the information originally available to us from official sources. It reconstructs the events of the epidemic as reported to the public and as seen by those who had investigated it before us. Chapter 2 turns to the problem of conceptualizing the epidemic in light of the literature on collective behavior and in a form that would make an empirical investigation possible. Thus, Part I reports what was "given" at the time the study began.

To the experienced researcher it will be obvious that the picture was not as well-organized as these two chapters suggest, however. They have been written, after all, after the study was completed, and they would be too cumbersome if they included *all* of the bits and pieces of evidence and ideas with which we were originally faced. Chapter 2 even refers to literature published after our field work ended. The attempt is made, however, to provide the reader

1

with a view of the *kinds* of information and ideas available at the time so that he may move with us through the process of design and execution of the study.

1

THE "BUG" AND THE
EPIDEMIC

Word first reached the public on the six o'clock news. The report was brief, and an air of mystery was already evident:

Officials of Montana Mills [1] shut down their Strongsville plant this afternoon because of a mysterious sickness.

According to a report just in from Strongsville General Hospital, at least ten women and one man were admitted for treatment. Reports describe symptoms as severe nausea and a breaking out over the body.

Indications are that some kind of insect was in a shipment of cloth that arrived from England at the plant today. And at the moment the bug is blamed for the outbreak of sickness.

Later that night, on the eleven o'clock news, further details were supplied. Some of them varied from the original report, but the melodramatic tone remained:

During the past three weeks a number of the 200 employees have been stricken with a mysterious illness, apparently caused by an insect

[1] All of the names used in this report are fictitious. In no case, however, has this failure to disclose the identity of persons or places involved a distortion of the essential information about the incident or those involved in it.

3

bite. Today about ten women and one man were stricken. Several were admitted to the hospital for treatment and observation. Company officials say they are fumigating the building.

The plant is scheduled to reopen tomorrow morning at six o'clock.

This station learned tonight from a company employee that the small insect attacks the skin, the bites leaving a wound similar to a gnat bite. In about twenty minutes the victim is struck with severe nausea. The company doctor informed us tonight that an entomologist is studying the problem. A report is expected later this week.

It was a Wednesday night in June, 1962. There was not much else worth reporting that day in Strongsville, a relatively small city in the South. But such strange happenings would be newsworthy in any event. In fact, the story was soon picked up by the news services, and reports of the Strongsville epidemic were seen and heard throughout the country. Before it ended, the story became considerably more complex and the cast of players grew markedly. Some feeling for the event and the reactions to it can be derived from a brief sampling of the reports of the various news media over the next few days:

Thursday—The dressmaking division of Montana Mills opened for business this morning after a night of debugging. But the reason for a mysterious illness that has stricken 40 employees is unsolved. The outbreak of the illness had been confined to females in the sewing and stitching room at the plant, where 200 women work side by side, until yesterday when a man in the warehouse area suffered an attack. Reports that the insect might have entered the plant in an overseas shipment of cloth from England have been discounted. Last night the plant was fogged with Pyrethrum in an effort to rid the premises of a possible insect.

A plant physician treating the victims—all women except one—is quoted as saying that the diagnosis is still hanging fire, and that no one afflicted by the malady could give a specific description of the insects which many said they saw. A State College entomologist called into the case said that what caused the illness cannot be confirmed, but they are working on several theories.

Hiram L. Lamont, plant personnel director, said a number of women reported for work today, when the plant resumed operations, in a highly nervous state. At least six were treated by the company physician and sent home.

Dr. C. H. Foreman, Strongsville County Health Officer, reports tonight, however, that there is nothing present in the community to get excited about. The investigation continues, but Dr. Foreman said, "We haven't been able to put our fingers on a thing." And, he emphasized, although some of the women employees at the plant have been very sick, nobody is seriously ill. The predominating symptom according to physicians and company officials is anxiety. Doctors are keeping several of the stricken women at the hospital for observation in an effort to diagnose the ailment. Dr. Foreman says the doctors have ruled out a virus—since none have fever—and food poisoning. All are in good condition.

Friday—Two experts from the U.S. Public Health Service Communicable Disease Center arrived today in Strongsville to assist local health officials trying to determine the cause of the sudden outbreak of sickness which has hit employees of Montana Mills. These two physicians, along with Dr. C. H. Foreman and Dr. Daniel Gerard of the State Board of Health searched the plant today for the cause of the illnesses. Also on the premises were several plant officials, representatives of the plant's insurance company, two State College entomologists, representatives of the Strongsville Exterminating Company, and an engineer from the State Board of Health. All theories are being investigated, including the possibility that the air conditioning system in the plant could have been at fault. A thorough search was made of the vast textile plant, one of the most modern in the South, and several specimens were collected with the aid of a vacuum cleaner. The total catch consisted of one black ant, a housefly, a couple of gnats, a small variety of beetle—none with an attraction for human flesh—and one mite (a chigger) that could cause a reaction.

Nine persons remained hospitalized last night and two more have been treated in the hospital emergency room. There were unconfirmed reports this morning that at least four more persons have been hospitalized. About fifty persons have been affected.

We talked with one lady who suffered symptoms today—Mrs. Wilma Evans, a 29-year old resident of Pottsville. She said she felt a bite on her leg, then felt dizzy about thirty minutes later. She said her left arm became numb, and she felt weak all over. "I broke out in a cold sweat," Mrs. Evans said. But she could not find any evidence of a bite.

Dr. Foreman said that the cause of the illness is still unknown. The two Public Health Service doctors are returning to the Communicable Disease Center tonight with several specimens found today. The specimens are identified as small insects about the size of a mite.

Baffled physicians are pursuing a theory of mass hysteria in the search for the cause of the mysterious sickness. Medical spokesmen say the symptoms are "far beyond what should be, because of fear of the unknown." Dr. Joseph R. John, one of the specialists from the Communicable Disease Center said, "We never heard of anything like this before."

However, Dr. Foreman says there is no cause for alarm. Both he and plant officials point out that only one percent of the employees have been affected and that, they say, is just about normal for a textile plant where nearly 1,000 employees work.

Saturday—Today Dr. C. H. Foreman and the experts from the U.S. Public Health Service conferred on the findings of the laboratory tests on several insects taken from the Montana Mills plant to be analyzed at the Communicable Disease Center. Among the specimens examined was a small chigger-like bug, known as a bird mite, which could be the insect causing the skin abrasion found on many of the afflicted employees. But, Dr. Foreman emphasizes that they are only saying the insect *could* be causing the extreme symptoms in evidence by most of the patients—that is, the stomach pains and dizziness. All the physicians feel that a great deal of anxiety enters the picture. They also feel that the press has played the "mystery malady" angle too much, thus increasing the anxiety in the plant and in other areas of the state.

Said Dr. Foreman: "We don't question that some of these people have been bitten . . . but certainly there is a great deal of anxiety. Fear has ballooned it out of proportion."

The physicians have advised the company to fill the building with a residual spray that would kill off the bird mite. Officials said they would take this precaution over the weekend. But the investigation continues, say the experts, because nothing specific has been found as yet.

There was one more case of the unknown sickness at the plant today. A woman employee was sent home after she complained of being bitten by a bug, causing her to feel weak and dizzy. There are still three women from the plant bedded down at the Strongsville General Hospital who were stricken last Wednesday. Others went home yesterday.

Sunday—Nervous disorder, publicity and lastly a bug's bite caused the outbreak of a "very real" and mysterious sickness at Montana Mills. That's the opinion of physicians who carried out extensive investigations. The illness was characterized by nervousness, nausea, weakness, numbness and insect bites.

They summarized it like this: The sickness was definitely real but related to overtones of anxiety and nervousness. They hesitated to use the word "hysteria." The least important factor was the bite of an insect.

Insect bites were found, but only one bird mite was found. Dr. John said it could have come in on somebody's clothing or in their hair. Dr. Foreman said the bite may have been a stimulant to incite the sickness—but it was not the cause.

Monday—Business was back to normal at Strongsville's Montana Mills plant today. The elusive bug apparently is a thing of the past. And, according to all the experts the rashes and other ailments which caused the trouble can be traced to a bug all right—but a mental one rather than one which crawls or flies.

After exterminators spent all day yesterday completely spraying the building inside and out, Dr. C. H. Foreman, plant officials, and two experts from the Communicable Disease Center voiced the opinion that most, if not all, of the fifty-seven employees afflicted were victims of nothing more than extreme anxiety. They said the illness could not be blamed on any insect.

In any event, as one exterminator put it: "Whatever has been here ain't here now."

And so it ended. No more cases were reported after Monday, and the plant returned to normal operations—though a sense of uneasiness was noticeable for some time afterward. It had come and gone in less than a week. A large number of people had been affected, and an impressive array of technical personnel had been brought in to help cope with it.

But what *was* "it"? The experts seemed to reach the conclusion, in effect, that it was "nothing," just anxiety. This, to them, seemed to be the only possible conclusion since they could find no evidence that any kind of insect was present which could have caused the symptoms recorded. They recommended the last spraying of the plant, we are told, simply as a means of reassuring everyone that there was nothing to worry about—if there ever was. Certainly, the newsmen accepted the experts' interpretation.

The experts were not very successful in convincing the women involved in the epidemic, however. We interviewed many of them two months after the whole thing was over, and even at that late date, most of them said they thought an insect had caused the symptoms, and very few suggested that the insect theory was not at least partially correct. Not only did they *believe* in the insect theory; many of them felt they had very impressive evidence of its validity.

In some cases, this consisted of having actually *seen* the insect responsible for their symptoms:

Well, I got bit, I caught the bug on my arm and I showed it to my supervisor, and we took it in the office. They put it in a jar. It looked like a little black gnat to me. It made me sick and I went home. They gave me a shot. I was out of work a day.

Well, they said it was my imagination, but it couldn't have been. I felt something bite me on my leg and when I scratched my leg, the little white bug came up under my fingernail. I got weak in the legs and got sick.

We even found some of those who had not been bitten who insisted that they had seen the insects which had bitten other women in their section of the plant:

I could see places on their arms and neck where little black bugs had bitten. We could see the bugs hop away. Then I would see the people being carried out.

These are rather graphic descriptions. It is difficult to charge that all of these women simply imagined they saw these insects. In fact, of course, the experts would make no such charge. They would say, as they did during their investigations, that there were certainly insects in the plant, and it is very likely that some of those affected were actually bitten by these insects. But, they would insist, the insects alone could not possibly have caused the dramatic reactions exhibited by the victims.

Here again the testimony of the victims would seem to contradict this type of interpretation. Many of them were very certain that there was a direct connection between the bite and the symptoms:

I was working and I felt a sting on my arm and I looked down and had a place on it. I scratched it, and my arm began to get numb. I got nauseated and they took me to the first aid room.

I was bit by the bug and it was such a sudden and sharp bite, you really didn't know what happened. It felt like a pin sticking me. Then the pain went down and up my arm and into my neck. I walked about six steps, and my legs started getting weak, and I just passed out.

And again we find women who were not themselves bitten who offer similar testimony:

Well, I think they got bit, 'cause I saw the bites on them. And I don't think anybody is going to pass out on that hard floor and vomit unless they did get bit.

The girl who rides with me got bit and had a place on her arm. She was real sick all night.

There were two different kinds of bites. One was a hole and it would bleed, and the other one looked more like a sting. The ones who had the hole were sicker than the ones with the sting-like bite, and they had to go to the hospital.

That is actually what I believe it was—an insect bite. I could see the girls as they fell over. I saw one girl's head draw back. She had convulsions. I saw the large areas where they were bitten, and the area got right hard.

There is little doubt in the minds of these women that there *was* a bug and that it *was* responsible for the symptoms from which the victims suffered. The experts, of course, would point out that, although many of the women were undoubtedly bitten, the reactions were too extreme and can only be explained by recourse to other factors, factors which they tended to lump together as "anxiety" or "nervousness." But such factors were not acceptable to most of the women. To them such an explanation meant the experts were saying they were "crazy," or were "putting on," and it is understandable that those who were bitten resisted this interpretation:

They brought this big doctor here, and he said we were crazy. But we *did* get bit.

I've got two little places on my arm where something bit me. They told us it was our imagination, but I don't think it was. One girl had convulsions so bad we all had to help hold her on the bed. She even foamed at the mouth.

I got bit on my finger. It left a stinger in my finger. They said it was all imagination, but they are crazy. I can understand that, though, because it would have been bad for the company if people thought it was an insect.

Similar rejections of the psychological interpretation were heard from those who had not been bitten:

Some said it was imagination, but I think it was a bug that came in the material.

Well, the only thing I know is that they say they got bug bit. I think something bit them. I don't think they were going on like that for nothing.

I feel that if there was not somethin', the girls would not have been sick like they were. I don't think people should make remarks about someone unless they really know about their sickness.

Not all of the women we talked with were so certain about the matter, however. Some of them, even some of them who were bitten, expressed doubt about the "real cause" of the epidemic. Yet in almost all of these cases their doubt was less than complete. They did not *fully* reject the significance of the insect as a cause. They viewed it as a cause of greater significance than the experts did:

I don't know, but I strongly believe that they were bitten by something. Some of it might have been hysterical, but I don't think all of it was.

A lot of them believed it was hysteria, but I don't think all of it could have been. It seemed like those that took medicine got sicker than the others. The medicine may have made them sicker.

I do think some of them did get bit, but not all of the ones that got sick were bitten. When you get frightened, you get sick.

Some really got bit and some really got sick. I think they got sick because they already had a virus.

I think some people really were bitten. Then other people who saw bites on themselves really got sick, maybe from fear or maybe from the bite.

My heavens! I've been told so many things, I don't know what to tell you. They said it was bug bites, but I didn't see any bugs. Some said it was nerves. Some of those women were deathly sick. They were passing out and they were taking them out of there like flies. I don't know what happened to me. I guess it was my nerves, but when I saw all that happening, I just got scared and I clocked out of there and came home.

There were the full-fledged skeptics also, of course. Some of those we interviewed completely rejected the idea that an insect was a significant cause of the epidemic. They had little sympathy for those affected and were sometimes quite sarcastic:

I think they got hysterical. I think it was all hysteria. I think all of them worked long hours and when you do that a lot of things will bother you. You know the power of suggestion. This one got sick, so this one said, "Well, I'm sick too."

I think it was an epidemic of panic for several different reasons. Most of the people in my department were new hands. Seems like it would have happened to old hands also. Some was "panic" and some was "put-on act." The mind plays tricks on us. Some did it for attention. . . . I got a lot of bites, but they did not make me sick. Although my body fights off germs easily, if it had been anything strong enough to affect that many people, surely I would have become ill too.

They said they only found one chigger. He shore had some visiting to do if he bit all those people.

But the complete skeptics were few in number. Even among those who had not been reported as bitten, less than 10 percent fully rejected the role of the insect bite, and almost half subscribed to a pure insect theory. The rest either thought that "some of it" was something else or simply expressed puzzlement. Of course, very few of those who had been bitten expressed any doubt, although a few thought that perhaps fear or excitement may have been involved as well. Thus, whatever the official "scientific definition," the clearly dominant "social definition" was that there was a rash of insect bites, and, although some other factors may have entered in too, the bites did make a lot of people sick.

Yet, in spite of the undeniably impressive symptoms the women had (so impressive that a great array of professional talent was mobilized to cope with the problem), and the strength of the women's belief in the reality of "the bug," no acceptable medical explanation could be found. We are left with the assessment voiced by one of the medical experts called in: "We must conclude that the outbreak was almost exclusively psychogenic in nature. There were probably no more bites at the plant during that week than in any other normal period at that plant or at other Strongsville plants."

If we accept this expert opinion, and we seem to have no alternative in a case so well studied as this one, we must view this epidemic as an almost classical case of what has been called "hysterical contagion." In the next chapter we will discuss this general type of phenomenon and attempt to tie up the several possible conceptualizations of such contagion with the basic information we have about the situation at Montana Mills. It will suffice for present purposes, however, simply to indicate that by "hysterical contagion" we mean the dissemination of a set of symptoms among a population in a situation in which no manifest basis for the symptoms may be established.

Since some of our discussion of the dynamics of the dissemination of such symptoms will make reference to the setting of the epidemic, it is well at this point to put the subjective and sometimes emotional comments just reported into a more objective context. It may easily be seen that the mass media accounts of the epidemic were less than fully consistent, at least in part because their early reports were based on "unofficial sources." A comparison between their news releases, in any event, and the more rigorously controlled data collected by the several experts who studied the case makes evident a number of inaccuracies. The victims themselves, though willing reporters, may also be unreliable sources. Briefly, then, we will present an outline of the basic facts of the epidemic as they may now be reconstructed before turning to the matter of conceptualization and analysis of the dynamics of the contagion.

A SCHEMATIC OVERVIEW

Montana Mills is a rather large plant employing 965 workers. A subsidiary of a large northern concern, it was relatively new in the area, the sprawling one-story building being only two years old. It is an unusual company in that it carries out all operations from spinning raw fibers into thread to the manufacture and distribution of finished women's clothing. Thus, there are several different departments separated in the various parts of the one large building. The newness of the plant is reflected in its attractive appearance and cleanliness, the new equipment, and the presence of air conditioning and piped-in music. It is a union-organized plant, although it is not (and by state law cannot be) a closed shop. Wages are higher than those paid in other similar mills in the area. Many of the workers receive a piece rate in addition to their base rate which makes a relatively high income possible for many.

The distribution of the workers by sex, department, and shift is significant for our purposes. The data are reported in Table 1.1. The plant works three shifts. The vast majority of the workers (728) worked on the first shift (8:00 A.M. to 4:30 P.M.) at the time of the

TABLE 1.1
Distribution of Workers and Affected Cases by Shift, Department, and Sex

	Number of Workers	Number of Affected Cases	Percentage of Workers Affected
Total	965	62	6.4
Women	674	59	8.8
Men	291	3	1.0
First Shift	728	59	8.1
Women	576	58	10.1
Dressmaking departments	490	58	11.8
Other departments	86	0	0.0
Men	152	1	0.7
Dressmaking departments	—	—	—
Other departments	152	1	0.7
Second and Third Shifts	237	3	1.3
Women	98	1	1.0
Dressmaking departments	—	—	—
Other departments	98	1	1.0
Men	139	2	1.4
Dressmaking departments	—	—	—
Other departments	139	2	1.4

incident. Of those on the first shift, only about one-fifth were men, whereas the majority (59 percent) of those on the second and third shifts were men. This difference was largely due to the fact that the dressmaking operations were carried out only during the first shift, and these operations were carried out by women.

Because of the newness of the plant, its personnel were all relatively new to their specific jobs. Perhaps more important, the plant was still in a state of tentative organization. As the size of the operation grew, people and machines were moved, and the organization of supervision and the flow of work were altered. This was accentuated in the dressmaking departments due to seasonal changes and the introduction of new lines. At the same time, plans were being made for the building of another plant in another town, and the managers of the Strongsville plant were responsible for this planning as well.

The rapid growth of the operation had caused serious difficulties in the area of personnel management. These difficulties were compounded by the fact that the Personnel Manager was also the Production Manager and a major participant in the planning of the new plant. It is unlikely that any one man could have fully performed all of these duties. In any event, the personnel records of the company at the time of the epidemic were almost nonexistent. There was no easily accessible list of employees besides the current payroll. There were no organized records of such basic information as age, sex, race, marital status, and work experience. There were no well-established channels of communication between management and the workers.

Finally, it must be noted that June is a month of peak production in this plant. Given the seasonal nature of the basic product, women's clothing, time is of the essence, and June is a crucial month in the production of the fall line. Because of this, much overtime was worked by those in the dressmaking departments. Since there was only a single shift of these personnel, overtime was organizationally more possible in these departments than in those which worked on a three-shift basis. Normally the machines in the dressmaking departments stood idle after the first shift, but during the rush season the first-shift workers could be asked to stay longer hours to get the work out. It is also noteworthy that the seasonal nature of the business routinely led to slack periods after these production peaks which involved the layoff or cutting back in hours worked by most of the women in the dressmaking departments. In a business which consistently faced peaks and valleys, then, the epidemic occurred at a peak of production.

It is difficult to specify when the epidemic began. As some of the news releases indicated, workers had complained of insect bites for several weeks before the first group of serious cases brought the situation to the attention of the newsmen. In fact, sections of the plant in the dressmaking departments had been sprayed three times with Malathion the week prior to the outbreak. In spite of this, the complaints continued. Most of the complaints in this earlier period, however, did not lead to medical attention. Somewhat arbitrarily, therefore, we have followed the lead of the medical investigators in using the period from the Friday prior to the Wednesday outbreak through the Monday following that Wednesday as the period of investigation. This is a period of 11 days which includes two weekends.

Within this 11-day period 62 plant employees were known to have been seen by physicians either at the plant or outside. Of these persons, 57 visited the physicians specifically because of bites and associated symptomatology. Most of the other 5 had other assorted complaints which, while not specifically defined as due to insect bites, could be defined as associated with the epidemic. These included nervousness, a burning on the calf, fainting, numbness in an extremity, feeling "like a balloon ready to burst," and an inability to turn the head. Since the epidemic was presumably a function of factors other than insect bites, all of these 62 cases must be considered as "affected cases," even though some errors of classification seem almost certain.

Of the 62 cases, 59 were women (see Table 1.1). Of the 3 men affected, 2 worked on the third shift and 1 worked on the first shift. Of the women, all but 1 worked on the first shift, the 1 other case being a second-shift worker. Thus, about 9 percent of the female workers in the plant were affected compared with only 1 percent of the males. Also, 8 percent of the first-shift workers were affected in contrast with just over 1 percent of those on the other shifts. Women on the first shift accounted for all but 4 of the cases, and all of these 58 cases were women in the dressmaking departments or in a cloth-mending department adjacent to the dressmaking area (see Figure 1.1). Thus, about 10 percent of the women on the first shift were affected and about 12 percent of the first-shift women in the dressmaking departments were affected.

Of the 62 cases, 50 occurred on the Wednesday and Thursday referred to in the news reports. Five occurred on Tuesday, and 4 occurred on Friday of that week. The only earlier case was on the previous Friday, and 1 case occurred each on the Saturday and Monday following the first news release on the epidemic. Thus, within the 11-day period, 95 percent of the cases reported occurred in 4 consecutive days with 80 percent of them occurring on 2 consecutive days.

As can be seen in Figure 1.1, all but 1 of the cases which occurred on the first shift and all but 4 of the total number of cases were located in one large area of the plant. This represented less than half of the total area of the plant, but it contained about two-thirds of the first-shift workers. This area was concerned with the cutting, sewing, mending, pressing, inspecting, and packing of women's clothing. Except for supervisory personnel, all of the workers in this area were women. There was no second or third shift in these departments. The rest of the plant was concerned with the preparation of the cloth, the storage, shipping and receiving of goods, and the office work. A much larger proportion (over half) of the first-shift workers in these other sections were men.

Whatever our approach to this phenomenon, there are thus several basic facts which must be taken into account. The epidemic occurred during the peak production season. It came and went rather quickly, lasting for all practical purposes a week or less. It rose rapidly to a peak and just as rapidly disappeared. Those who were affected were almost all women, and almost all of them worked on the day shift. All but a very few cases were found in one functionally and spatially separate section of the plant. Whatever "it" was, it struck first-shift women in the dressmaking departments more consistently than anyone else. And, most important of all, "it" could not be explained in any "normal" way.

FIGURE 1.1. *Diagram of Location of 58 of 62 Cases at Montana Mills*

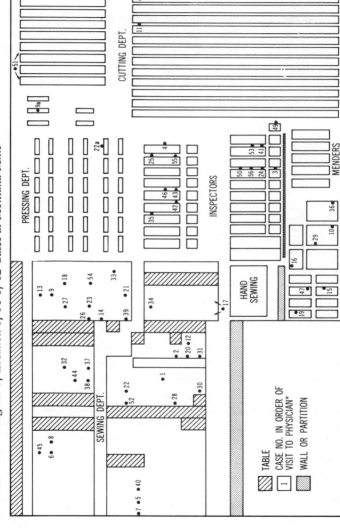

* Cases not in the "population at risk": 9a and 22a, Negro pressers; cases outside the sewing room: one each after cases 19 and 30 and two cases following 52.

17

THE RESEARCH PROBLEM

Given these facts, the "explanation" of the experts seems to make sense. However, to say that the epidemic "was mostly hysteria" or "almost exclusively psychogenic in nature" does not really explain the event. It simply labels it. It puts it in a category of events which, by definition, are not the usual business of the kinds of experts who investigated the case. In point of fact, it is not possible to define with any confidence whose business such phenomena are. There have been very few systematic attempts to investigate them, and, as we will see in the next chapter, the attempts to conceptualize them are at best variable and unsatisfying. The authors decided that, if this kind of event was anyone's business, it ought to be the business of the social psychologist.

As social psychologists, we felt that the experts' explanation basically posed our problem. If this was a case of hysterical contagion, if this epidemic was "almost exclusively psychogenic in nature," we needed to raise a whole series of questions about it. Why should such an epidemic occur at this time and place? What was there about this plant, these women, this period of time that brought about such an event? Why were only *some* of the people in the plant affected? Can we conceive of "susceptibility" and "immunity" to such epidemics much as we do with respect to epidemics of the flu or smallpox? If this was an epidemic, rather than a series of individual cases, what was the medium (or media) of transmission of the symptoms? If this was hysterical contagion, what can we say about the process of contagion? Is this whole business just so very mysterious that nothing short of a full psychoanalysis of all of the people in the plant will provide insight into its dynamics? What contribution can social psychology make to an understanding of such events?

These were some of the questions we had in mind as we approached the study of this epidemic. With no illusions about the probability of our being able to provide adequate answers for all such questions, we nonetheless felt we should use them as guides for our investigation. The rest of this volume reports the results of our endeavors.

2

COLLECTIVE BEHAVIOR AND HYSTERICAL CONTAGION

Once the basic facts of the epidemic of insect bites had become clear, it was evident that the careful medical investigation had with some certainty ruled out physically toxic elements in the situation as a major cause of the symptoms the workers had experienced. As a result, the event was made more directly relevant to the interests of the behavioral scientist. Here was a social event involving a delimited population of persons who interacted with each other, an event which was inexplicable through reference to the physical realm alone. But even as a social event, it was an unusual one. Most social events studied by behavioral scientists involve behavior which is in some rather direct manner associated with the characteristics of the situation. Such characteristics might be physical or cultural, but the usual form of explanation involves reference to situational conditions and makes the implied argument that the actors behaved as they did because of a logical connection between these conditions and their behavior. In the present case, however, there was no obvious logical connection between any of the facts of the case as we knew them and the fact that a large number of people got sick from the bite of an insect which did not exist.

Although such a state of affairs is in one sense a disadvantage because it gives the researcher less to build on, it has certain advantages which we saw as very attractive. If we are correct in defining this as a case of hysterical contagion, what we must argue is that the behavior in question is almost completely explicable in social and psychological terms. Some of the women got sick and went to the doctor, which is a physical fact, but that sickness cannot be understood by reference to the physical context. Certain modes of behavior evolved "as if" the physical reality they faced was of a particular type, but we know that this definition of reality was factually wrong. Thus, if such an event can be understood at all, it must be by reference to the characteristics of the social and psychological contexts of behavior, not the physical. In fact, such an explanation seems to be wholly dependent on social and psychological factors.

The fascinating and unsettling thing about such phenomena as fads, crazes, and rumors is their seeming disconnectedness from the points of reference usually used in explanations of behavior. They seem inevitably to lead to outcomes which the participants do not seek, outcomes which they would presumably carefully avoid if they could foresee them. They seem to involve behavior which is founded on unrealistic, false, or illogical assumptions. Because of this, they appear to be terribly disorderly, and most behavioral scientists have chosen to avoid them, or to refer to them only to make textbooks more colorful. Yet, such events come as close as any to being "pure behavioral events" in that they exhibit the social and psychological processes at work in relatively unconstrained conditions.

Most social responses to external reality can be understood quite adequately by reference either to the demonstrable qualities of the physical realm or to the traditional cultural system of the group in question. One can usually point out that a group took defensive action because there was a tangible threat in the vicinity. This is not only true of orderly behavior such as building stockades, but it is also true of some forms of spontaneous collective behavior such as panic in the face of a theater fire. When such a tangible threat cannot be located by the outside observer, the usual explanation is presented in terms of the culture patterns of the group. For instance, we explain behavior in reference to the threat of spirits and demons by pointing to the fact that certain people have a whole structure of such beliefs involving interpretations of natural events. We say simply that it is part of their culture. But in many instances of collective behavior such reference to the physical or cultural contexts does not provide an adequate explanation. Not only was there no evidence of a toxic insect (or any other physical source of sickness) at Montana Mills, there was also no evidence of an established culture pattern calling for the need to defend oneself against this kind of peril. In the face of such an epidemic, therefore, one's basic question is why such an event should occur at all.

There evolved a belief in a mysterious insect at Montana Mills, and the belief became very widespread within the population. Even more unusual was the fact that a sizeable number of these people actually experienced the bite of this imaginary insect and got sufficiently ill to require medical treatment. If there was no such insect, why was it "invented"? Given the fact that it was invented, why did so many people believe in its existence? And even given such a belief, what could lead to the experience of a bite from such an imaginary insect, an experience so real that sickness followed? If we strip away any possible reference to physical causality by accepting the investigators' report, and if we acknowledge that in Strongsville in June, 1962, such a phenomenon was defined as very unusual (and thus not "required" by cultural forces), what basis is there for a possible explanation? If this was a "pure behavioral event," what social or psychological factors are capable of helping us understand it? It is the task of this chapter to report what answers we were originally able to find to such questions.

The setting was almost ideal for the investigation of such an event. The epidemic had occurred within a delimited population, and we had potential access to all of the people in the population, both the victims and those not affected. This was unique in that most studies of epidemics focus almost completely on the victims. This, together with the fact that there was no evidence of physical causality, made this investigation much different from any carried out previously. In addition, we had knowledge of all the affected cases within the population including both their symptoms and when they were affected. Comparisons could thus be made between the affected and the unaffected and among those affected according to their symptoms or when they became sick. If this was indeed a case of contagion, social influence must have played some role in it, and knowing the sequence of cases should help to trace the channels through which the epidemic spread. Thus, not only was the kind of event of particular interest to behavioral scientists, but the particular setting and the opportunity it provided for following up leads to an understanding of such pure behavioral events was close to ideal.

There are very few such cases reported in the professional literature. The case that seems most similar is one reported by Schuler and Parenton (1943) in which a number of Louisiana high school girls became ill over a period of several weeks, and no legitimate physical cause of the illness could be determined. The authors speculate that there was a process of interpersonal influence involved and that the symptoms represented a means of escape from a distasteful situation and/or an attention-getting device. Another case which involved physical symptoms was that of "the phantom anaesthetist" reported by Johnson (1945). In this case, a number of women complained of being "gassed" by a mysterious prowler. The cases were distributed over a wide area, however, and the only known source of influence which might have tied them together was the newspaper. These two cases are particularly relevant since there was no known physical cause of the symptoms which the victims suffered. However, there was little information available on the victims and almost no basis for comparing them with those not affected by the malady.

In most other related studies, the lack of physical factors cannot be assumed. Some very interesting data, for instance, come from two studies by Imboden and his associates. In one study (1959) a comparison was made between patients with chronic brucellosis and those who had recovered from chronic and acute brucellosis. Medical evidence shows that chronic brucellosis is not a physical disease but a convenient way for patients to legitimize their desire to persist longer in the sick role, and therefore differences in personal characteristics could be expected between these kinds of patients. In the second study (1961), personality inventories were administered to a large sample of people before a winter in which there was an outbreak of influenza. Personality data differentiated between the chronic and recovered cases of brucellosis and between influenza victims who recovered quickly and those who did not. In both cases, those who recovered slowly or not at all were found to be "depression-prone." The difficulty in both cases, however, is that the patients had actually been sick with a medically recognized disease. Thus, although there were good systematic data available in these two studies, the relationship between the somatic and psychosomatic aspects of the cases is difficult to determine. Also, there was little attention paid to the difference between patients and those who did not get sick. These are common characteristics of studies reported in the medical literature.

In searching for answers to our preliminary questions, therefore, it became evident that there was little previous work which was directly relevant. In fact, there has not been any study conducted which is really comparable to this one. Similar events have been reported in the public press and in various professional journals, but in all cases the reports are too limited to permit a consideration of the kinds of questions we wished to raise. Either there was no systematic information about the victims, or there was no comparison of victims with those not affected, or it was not possible to rule out effects from physical causes. In practically all studies there was no delimitation of the population which could have been affected (what the epidemiologist calls the "population at risk") and it was not possible to compare the different groups within this population. The possibility of doing so made Montana Mills unique from our point of view.

In fact, most reports have not been very explicit. The logic has often been that since no physical explanation could be found, the problem "must have been" due to psychological causes, although evidence of these causes is seldom provided. Because of the dearth of directly relevant studies, we found it necessary (and profitable) to make reference to a somewhat broader body of literature than might at first have seemed relevant. We will report the findings of this review with reference to the major problems which guided the search.

DEFINING HYSTERICAL CONTAGION

If we are going to refer to the Strongsville epidemic as a case of hysterical contagion, our first task is to define the terms. Probably the most straightforward definition of contagion available is that

offered by Grosser, Polansky, and Lippitt (1951, p. 115). They refer
to "behavioral contagion" and define it as "a social interaction in
which a 'recipient's' behavior changes to become 'more like' that of
another person, and where this change has occurred in a social interaction in which the 'initiator' (other person) has not communicated
intent to influence the behavior of the recipient." The critical point
made in this definition (and in the study from which it is taken) is
that behavioral contagion differs from the usual concept of social
influence in that in contagion there is no indication that the initiator
intends to influence the other person(s). Also, in contagion the behavior of the initiator and recipient are always similar, whereas in
other kinds of social influence the recipient of influence may be
influenced to do something quite different from the behavior of the
initiator.

However, in most discussions of contagion, more is implied than
simple unintentional interpersonal influence to reproduce a form of
behavior. There is usually an indication that contagion involves a
more rapid and widespread dissemination of an act than would be
implied by the definition provided by Grosser and his associates. In
fact, the term "contagion" is not normally used in descriptions of
dyadic relationships, which is the type of experimental situation
these investigators studied.[1] Contagion, then, will be used here to
refer to the spread of a behavior within a collectivity [2] in which the
spread is rather rapid and in the nature of a geometric progression.

But why do we call this a case of *hysterical* contagion? We
should note to begin with that the term "hysterical" is not used here
in the technical clinical sense. We do not assume that all of the persons affected by the epidemic were "hysterics" as a clinician would
use the term. We find the term highly appropriate for several other
reasons, however. First of all, the persons affected by the epidemic
generally were hysterical in the more common sense, which refers

[1] The study reported by Grosser and his associates was only one part of a
larger research program, however, other parts of which dealt with larger groups.

[2] We use the relatively nonspecific term "collectivity" here because we do
not want at this point to limit our discussion to any particular kind of social
entity. The degree of organization of the individuals in the collectivity is, for
the present purposes, irrelevant. It will become clear later in our discussion,
however, that the structure of the social relations is a significant datum for any
analysis of contagion.

to highly emotional behavior. Second, the symptoms exhibited by most of those affected were closely allied to those found in many cases of clinical hysteria. Third, the epidemic fits very well the pattern of belief and behavior discussed under this heading by earlier students of collective behavior. This pattern involves the spread of physiological symptoms which are attributed to a fearfully mysterious and very threatening source.

A case of hysterical contagion, therefore, is one in which a set of experiences or behaviors which are heavily laden with the emotion of fear of a mysterious force are disseminated through a collectivity. The type of behavior that forms the manifest content of the case may vary widely from one example to the next, but all are indicative of fear, and all are inexplicable in terms of the usual standards of mechanical, chemical, or physiological causality.

THE CONDITIONS UNDER WHICH HYSTERICAL CONTAGION DEVELOPS

It is difficult if not impossible to identify *in advance* those situations in which hysterical contagion may occur. We will need to review some of the discussions on the matter in order to show that this statement is justified and to suggest why this is so.

In their chapter "Societal Conditions and Collective Behavior," Turner and Killian (1957, p. 21) note the importance of social organization, normative order, and communication to the carrying out of routine functions in a society, and they observe:

> Just as routine social behavior may be explained on the basis of these characteristics of social organization, collective behavior must be viewed as arising from changes in them. It has its roots in changes in these fundamental conditions for social cohesion and integrated group action.

Blumer's (1951) classical discussion of the field of collective behavior defines it as that kind of behavior which evolves in situations not adequately dealt with or controlled by the norms. In the Langs' (1961, pp. 16–19) discussion of the relationship between "collective dynamics and social structure" they make reference to "gaps" in the social structure and refer to these as "areas of chronic stress." Such gaps occur because of the existence of areas of discretion left by normative definitions, internal cleavages on some issue, tendencies toward alienation from social demands, and so on.

All of these discussions suggest that such conditions place people under pressure and present them with problems for which there are no fully acceptable solutions. In such situations forms of behavior evolve which are responses to strain. Some of these responses are directly problem oriented and are organized attempts to cope with the unstructured stressful situation. Others are more in the nature of collective expressions of frustration and discontent. They are expressive rather than instrumental, need fulfilling but not directly focused on the source of the problem. In most of the literature on collective behavior, hysterical contagion is thought to be this latter type of response.

When one seeks for explanations of why one form of collective behavior occurs rather than another, the answers are not very forceful. The dominant emphasis, however, is on the level of specificity of the source of difficulty or frustration and the degree of organization evolved to cope with it. It is usual to note the variation in organization of the various forms, ranging from such diffuse phenomena as fads and crazes to well-structured social movements. This variation in level of organization also generally parallels differences in the relevance of the behavior to the original source of frustration. Fads and crazes, which are wholly unorganized, are usually seen as a kind of mechanism for "draining off" the sense of tension without actually coping at all with the source of that tension. Social movements are, in contrast, usually more directly relevant to the source of dissatisfaction and thus more clearly a mechanism for problem solving.

The different forms of collective behavior, therefore, call our attention to the importance of preexisting and emergent forms of social structure in the collectivity. They also illustrate the importance of "a sense of problem" in the collectivity. These may be seen as differences in the clarity of ends (the goals to be sought, the definition of the problem) and differences in the availability of means for achieving those ends. As Turner and Killian (1957, p. 31) state in their discussion of mass hysteria in nineteenth-century Japan:

It is of particular significance that these instances of "mass hysteria" do not necessarily constitute true revolutionary or reform movements, but are primarily of an expressive nature, a means of giving vent to repressed feelings. Frustration and deprivation do not always lead quickly and surely to revolt; a revolutionary goal and an organization are needed.

In the absence of a goal (however vaguely defined) and a social structure for attempting to attain that goal, the frustration associated with the "gaps" in the social structure will generally be expressed in either individual aberrant behavior or some kind of collective emotional expression.

In one of the most ambitious attempts to date to organize and systematize our knowledge of collective behavior, Neil Smelser (1963) discussed hysterical contagion as a preliminary stage in the development of panic. A central concept in all of his analysis is the "generalized belief." He says (p. 8) that

. . . collective behavior is guided by various kinds of beliefs—assessments of the situation, wishes, and expectations. These beliefs differ, however, from those which guide other types of behavior. They involve a belief in the existence of extraordinary forces—threats, conspiracies, etc. —which are at work in the universe. They also involve an assessment of the extraordinary consequences which will follow if the collective attempt to constitute social action is successful. The beliefs on which collective behavior is based (we shall call them *generalized beliefs*) are thus akin to magical beliefs.

He sees generalized beliefs as the basis for all forms of collective behavior. They are the beliefs that prepare the participants for action, and they "arise when structural strain is not manageable within the existing frame-work of action." They form one essential part of the etiology of collective behavior, and their form and effect on the collectivity vary with the other conditions.

Cases such as the one we find in the insect epidemic, according to Smelser, are based on many of the same conditions as lead to panic. Both involve an hysterical belief which he defines (p. 84) as one "empowering an ambiguous element in the environment with a generalized power to threaten or destroy." Both involve conditions of strain, and both involve the possibility of communication among the participants.

There are a number of cases described in the literature which seem to be of this type and which clearly involve hysterical beliefs but in which panic does not occur (Schuler and Parenton, 1943;

Johnson, 1945; Medalia and Larsen, 1958). In each of these cases, Smelser says, one or more of the necessary conditions for panic was missing. There are some cases which are very similar to our own in that in addition to an hysterical belief and the report of an experience, there is evidence of the availability (and the presumed use) of channels of communication among those involved and the presence of physiological symptoms in those affected.[3] In these cases, the only factors which Smelser says are needed for panic which do not seem to be present are limited and diminishing avenues of escape and mobilization for flight.

If we accept his account of such events, therefore, we would say that cases of hysterical contagion occur in stressful situations in which there are channels of communication among those experiencing the stress. The hysterical contagion can develop, however, only if an hysterical belief is present (or evolves) and a precipitating event occurs to heighten the sense of immediate and tangible threat.[4]

We find that no one has very good advice on how we might *predict* when such cases of hysterical contagion (or panic) will occur. Condition of strain can presumably be observed in advance, but Smelser, along with all other students of such phenomena, indicates that "many different kinds of strain may give rise to one type of belief (and thus a particular type of collective behavior), and one kind of strain may give rise to many different types of belief" (p. 83). Thus, the kind of belief that develops is not easily predicted, and the precipitating event is basically unpredictable also. In most cases, it may be possible to perceive "reasonable" connections between the

[3] In the case discussed by Schuler and Parenton (1943) there are many parallels to the present case both with respect to symptoms and with respect to the possibility of communication among the participants. In the case discussed by Johnson (1945) the parallel is limited to the kind of symptoms, although the media of mass communications undoubtedly served some of the same functions as interpersonal communication presumably served in our case.

[4] With regard to the role of the precipitating event, Smelser (1963, pp. 146–147) says: "Most panics [and cases of hysterical contagion] are preceded by a build-up of what some observers have called a 'tense psychological state of mind'. . . . The place of a precipitating factor . . . is that it 'confirms' the generalized suspicions and uneasiness of anxious people. . . . Anxiety alone does not produce panic; it must be transformed into fear of a specific threatening agent."

situational characteristics, the hysterical belief, and the precipitating event *after* the fact, but any a priori statement about these relationships is not easily made.

Much will depend, of course, on the temporal relationship between the development of the hysterical belief and the precipitating event. Should the belief exist before the event, only certain events will be capable of being interpreted as relevant to the belief and thus as representing the kind of threat the belief validates. Should the event occur first, however, almost unlimited possibilities exist for the development of a belief which gives the necessary meaning to the event. We are thus left with a considerable amount of ambiguity with respect to this aspect of the etiology of hysterical contagion.

Equally ambiguous is the reason why some beliefs and events lead to cases of hysterical contagion and others do not. Examples of "precipitating events" and "hysterical beliefs" which do not lead to hysterical contagion must exist, although their existence is difficult to demonstrate because of their failure to lead to something. About all that can be said is that *some* events and *some* beliefs seems to "strike a chord" or "fit the situation" better than others, but this is certainly of little help, especially since which ones "strike a chord" can only be seen in retrospect. Even at that, some interpretations of the relationship between the situation and the precipitating event are based on rather involved reasoning. We cannot help agreeing with Brown (1954, p. 843) when he complains:

> We should like, first of all, to know why this kind of behavior "contages," rather than reasonable, cooperative action. In the second place, it is clear that even irrational and emotional behavior does not always diffuse through a collectivity. Under what conditions will it do so? The answer to this has too often been that contagion of emotion will occur in the mob, with the mob defined as a collectivity manifesting contagion. Something better than this must be found.

Smelser's analysis helps by suggesting the kinds of situations in which *some kind* of feeling or hysterical belief may "contage," but it does not offer much assistance in determining *what kind* of event or belief will have this effect in any given situation.

We can thus offer even provisional answers to only part of the questions relevant to a definition of the conditions under which hysterical contagion occurs. The most general statement that can be made is that it is likely to occur when a number of people are in a stressful situation for which no traditional forms of solution appear appropriate and within which develops a belief in an ambiguous threatening force. There are likely also to be channels of communication among the persons involved but no organized attempt to deal with the source of strain and no general mobilization for flight. Greater specificity as to what conditions lead to this form of collective behavior does not seem possible at present.[5]

THE CONNECTION BETWEEN THESE CONDITIONS AND PHYSICAL SYMPTOMS

It is one thing to note that various forms of collective behavior tend to occur when particular sets of conditions are found, but we need to move on to an even more refined question relevant to the case we are studying. Given that certain general conditions are the necessary if not the sufficient conditions for the development of a case of hysterical contagion, how are these conditions related to what actually occurs? If some kind of "imaginary" physical experience is the hallmark of hysterical contagion, what is there about these conditions which makes such an experience come about?

5 Brown (1965) has built on Smelser's analysis through a game theoretical treatment of collective behavior. He is able to show that, given a certain strength of communication and trust, mass behavior can be rational from the point of view of the individual participating, even if irrational from the point of view of the observer. Although his discussion provides an elegant analytic tool it would be difficult to use it to predict behavior in concrete situations and seems particularly deficient in treating an outbreak of hysterical symptoms which do not have any direct value even to the individual concerned (in contrast to panic behavior which may be of value to the first person to get out the door). In spite of these cautions it is striking how similar his definition of "crowd behavior" is to our analysis in the previous paragraph. "The basic situation is one of communication among persons having a similar conflict of mind, between an impulse that is socialized and one that is not, with the physical possibility of acting out the unsocialized impulse. . . . The outburst will occur because the total set of conditions produces a payoff matrix such that each person can act on his unsocialized impulse and be free of punishment or guilt" (p. 760).

To cope with such questions we need to make reference to a different part of the professional literature. For the most part, students of collective behavior have been largely concerned with the social aspects of their subject matter and have not dealt with questions relating to the specific content of the contagious experiences involved. To the extent that concern for content has been exhibited, it has been by way of noting that the symptoms were undoubtedly "symbolic" in some way of the "real" source of difficulty. Although this is a beginning and the place for us to start, it does not really help a great deal since the rules for determining the connection between symbol and reality are not specified.

There seem to be two approaches to this problem, one from the behavioral science side, the other from the medical side. Behavioral scientists have noted that there is always some kind of belief pattern which gives meaning to the physical experience. The hysterical belief Smelser refers to serves to objectify the source of a pervasive sense of discomfort and tension. It gives meaning to the dissatisfaction associated with the sources of strain. The belief serves this function because the strain involved is either too general to permit its identification or it is so closely associated with highly valued aspects of the people's lives that its identification would be too threatening. If some external source of threat is thus "invented," it can solve that part of the problem the people face. Since such a belief is motivated by strong needs for understanding and relief from tension, it is likely to be adopted avidly. Belief may then influence perception so that what is "imaginary" from the point of view of the outside observer can be "proven" by those involved through what they view as incontrovertible evidence. Perhaps the most impressive evidence that can be presented is the physical effect of the source of threat, an effect that seemingly can be explained only through reference to the imaginary threat.

But this only tells us how the belief and the symptoms can function to reinforce each other. Certainly no one would claim that the victims of such epidemics as the one we studied "figure out" such a relationship and then "decide" to get sick in order to prove that a frightening and toxic element really is among them. If it is not a conscious process, however, there are at least two further questions to raise. How does it happen that the new source of threat gets invented at all? What makes the people sick if the threat is imaginary?

There is little to be said in answer to the first of these questions. The connection between the experience of strain and the hysterical belief seems to be purely a matter of chance. Undoubtedly such an hysterical belief is invented by one or more individuals in the situation as a function of their own unique personalities and experiences. The precipitating event is likely to be the behavior of such a person based on the new belief. The belief is then adopted by others because of its functional significance in the situation. It seems almost certain that such beliefs are invented quite frequently in any population, but it is less common that the belief and a sense of strain that can easily be explained by it occur together. It would be very difficult, however, to demonstrate that this is so.

Medical investigators have become increasingly concerned with the fact that illness is not simply transmitted by physical vectors and organic injuries. This renewal of interest in medical ecology has been given an eloquent expression by Rene Dubos in his book *Man Adapting* (1965). He summarizes the section on determinants of microbial disease as follows:

> It is clear, in conclusion, that the type of relationship existing at any given time between hosts and their parasites is the outcome of many different factors, including past racial genetic experience, evolutionary adaptation through genetic changes and immunological processes, and transient disturbances in the external and internal environments. In the classical infections of exogenous origin, the determining event of the disease is exposure to the infective micro-organism. In endogenous microbial disease, the immediate cause is the environmental factor that upsets the biological equilibrium normally existing between the host and the microbial agents (persisters) (pp. 194–195).

This statement expresses the view that part of the etiology of any disease is the contagion mechanism which we have been deriving from the theories of social psychologists. The studies of disease we have discussed earlier in this chapter (pp. 22–23) are attempts to establish such relationships. On further search it becomes disappointing, however, how little definitive work has been done on any social conditions of illness. Dubos again states the case:

Successful physicians of all times have known that no disease state can be understood without considering the patient as a whole. But while this general truth is given lip service in medical schools, it is not taught with the thoroughness which comes from conviction, and it has not generated many research programs (p. 441).

Because of this paucity of concentrated research efforts on sociomedical problems we shall restrict ourselves to a critical discussion of a symptom which occurred prominently at Montana Mills, namely fainting.

Engel (1962a) has discussed the impact of psychological stress on the individual and notes that often such stress is adequately handled at the intrapsychic level. This he refers to as the "psychologically compensated state." However, in the "psychologically decompensated state," in which intrapsychic coping breaks down, "psychological stress acts to mobilize biological systems for the defense and protection of the body" (p. 367). Under these conditions, Engel points out,

. . . not only do affects become felt but also the neural system discharging into the body may be activated, meaning in essence that bodily systems are being mobilized to assure needs and to cope with stresses that cannot be handled through intrapsychic processes and controlled behavior. This, then, constitutes the most general and the most common avenue whereby somatic changes are brought about in response to psychological stress. On the psychological side this involves the experiencing of both signal-scanning affects of unpleasure and drive-discharge affects, felt as states of diffuse unpleasure, such as discomfort, distress or tension, or as their more definitive cognitive states, such as anxiety, fear, guilt, badness, shame, discouragement, anger, helplessness, or hopelessness. What is felt includes not only such vague to precise mental content (the cognitive part), but also the awareness of physiological changes, such as palpitation, sweating, flushing, muscle tension or "butterflies in the stomach" . . . The body, no longer buffered against the vicissitudes of the environment by an effectively operating mental apparatus, now is alerted to anticipate damage or exhaustion (pp. 383–384).

These physiological changes are exactly the kinds of symptoms found in all cases of hysterical contagion. In the most severe form, such physiological responses to psychological stress can lead to fainting, particularly in situations where the body has prepared for flight from a threatening danger but the individual is inhibited from carrying out the actual behavior of flight (Engel, 1962a, p. 390; Engel, 1962b).

What we find here, therefore, is not only an explanation of the connection between the experience of psychological tension and physiological symptoms. We find also a basis for understanding why an external "cause," which forms the core of the hysterical belief, would be so easily accepted. Not only does it place the explanation of the experienced discomfort in a socially acceptable etiological framework, it also provides a "cause" whose presumed "effects" correspond closely with the actual experience of those who are under stress.

A very interesting set of findings relevant to this matter has been reported by Schachter (1964) who has investigated the relationship between the cognitive and physiological elements of emotion. In a series of experiments he manipulated these two elements and was able to demonstrate that either could be influenced by the manipulation of the other. His significant theoretical contribution from our point of view is reflected in the following statement:

The key cognitive assumption underlying the human experiments described is that "given a state of physiological arousal for which an individual has no immediate explanation, he will label this state and describe his feelings in terms of the cognitions available to him." Obviously, this proposition implies that a drive exists to evaluate, understand, and label ambiguous bodily states. . . . Given a new, strange, or ambiguous bodily state, pressures will act on the individual to decide exactly what it is that he feels and to decide how he will label these feelings (pp. 76–77).

From this perspective, what occurs in cases of hysterical contagion is that physiological symptoms, which occur largely as a result of unresolved psychological stress, are explained (and thus responded to) in terms of a newly invented label which is provided by someone in the situation. To the extent that the new label "makes sense" and is thus easily accepted, it will be adopted readily by all those who have the experience but have been unable to conceptualize it satisfactorily. Schachter's work demonstrates that different labels can be successfully given to what must be assumed to be the same physiological experience and that the experience will correspond with the label in the view of those having the experience. The kind of physiological arousal which Engel describes, then, is evidently capable of a rather wide range of cognitive interpretations. For a case of hysterical contagion to occur, what is needed is a combination of a number of people who are so aroused and a belief in a credible source of such discomfort. Evidently the arousal is present beforehand and what "contages" is the new belief which gives meaning to the sense of arousal. One would also assume, however, that as the credibility of the new belief increases, relatively minor physiological cues might suffice to suggest a connection between one's experience and the source of threat.

THE PATTERN FOLLOWED BY HYSTERICAL CONTAGION

If one is interested in mapping the flow of hysterical contagion, a number of different kinds of questions might be raised. For instance: What is the rate of diffusion of the behavior? What kinds of people are likely to be involved? What is the channel through which dissemination occurs? What relationship does the contagion have to the characteristics of the collectivity and/or the larger social system? Suggestions have been made regarding all of these matters, and we will present a brief summary of them here.

As we noted in Chapter 1, the spread of the insect bite symptoms accelerated rapidly and just as rapidly diminished. The vast majority of the cases occurred on two days with a few days of build-up before and a few days of drop-off after. This is a familiar pattern, and it has been found in other such cases. We seem generally to find a kind of "snowballing" effect which evidently soon leads to a state of satiation. However, agencies of social control usually enter in to limit the spread of the behavior before any "natural satiation" occurs. Some of the rapid drop-off, then, is undoubtedly a function of outside forces being introduced into the situation. The pattern of rapid rise and rapid fall, however, is very common.

When we ask: "What kinds of people are affected?" the answer is far less simple. The easiest answer to this question is that only people in the situation are affected, but even this is not as clearly true as might be expected. Or, one might at least wonder how we decide who is "in the situation." Were those outside the dressmaking departments at Montana Mills in the situation or not? Another deceptively simple answer is to say that only people who have been exposed to the pre-contagion strain would be affected. But we have already seen that it is generally conceded that any number of sources of strain might lead to the "same" kind of hysterical behavior.[6] Thus, participation in an hysterical epidemic such as we have studied may somehow satisfy the various needs of persons under very different kinds of strain.

Most of the discussion of the kinds of participants, or the variations in susceptibility to contagion, however, focus rather directly on the more enduring personal and social characteristics of individuals. Some have focused almost exclusively on a personality type and claimed that participation in a whole range of types of collective behavior is a function of meeting the needs of such a personality (Hoffer, 1958). Also a common assumption is that women are more susceptible than men to the kind of contagion we are studying. Others assume that low intelligence is a good predictor. Many discussions have revolved around the questions of whether there is a trait of "general susceptibility" to contagion. We would agree with the general conclusion of the Langs (1961, Ch. 10) that there is good reason to doubt the adequacy of any of these sweeping generalizations.

However, it may well be that some kinds of people, under some circumstances, have a greater potential for participation in the contagious spread of unusual behavior. The Langs note, for instance, that the socially inadequate and insecure person will presumably be more dependent upon social cues for an indication of his own adequacy. He should, therefore, be more susceptible to almost any form of social influence. In contrast, those they define as "high ego-

---

[6] This position is defended very cogently at a much more general level by George Devereux (1961, p. 236). He points out that participation in *any* social activity may serve many different individual needs. "The real point to be stressed is that *both organized and spontaneous social movements and processes are possible not because all individuals participating in them are identically . . . motivated, but because a variety of authentically subjective motives may seek and find ego syntonic outlet in the same collective activity.* This is equally true of spontaneous revolutionary movements and of extreme conformity."

defenders," who project their own intrapsychic conflicts into the world, will be strongly susceptible to some kinds of influence but not others. Similarly, there is some appeal in the idea put forward by several authors that those who are "socially marginal" might be more susceptible than those closely integrated into a normatively controlled social structure (Turner & Killian, 1957, pp. 103–112). Since such marginal persons are less constrained by group norms, participation in the process of hysterical contagion should be more probable for them. This should be so because such contagion, by definition, is predicated on an unusual definition of the situation, one which is often outside the established normative system.

This last point brings us to a consideration of the third of our four questions: What is the channel of dissemination of the contagion? It also reveals some of the contradictions and ambiguities in the literature relevant to hysterical contagion. Since many conceptualize contagion as the result of a process of interpersonal influence, presumably the interpersonal relationship is a basic medium of transmission of the hysterical behavior. In their studies of behavioral contagion, Polansky, Lippit, and Redl (1950) found that, among the children they studied, those in less secure social positions neither initiated nor were susceptible to contagious influence as much as the secure children. On the other hand, these insecure children were much more subject to direct social influence. These authors also suggested that the less secure child may join in such contagious activity but do so relatively late in the process, after it has become clearly accepted by the group. Such an analysis adds to our understanding of contagion, but it also emphasizes some of the real complexities of the process.

The same authors note a related complexity when they interpret some of their experimental findings as indicating that "impulsive" children will be more active in contagion in situations in which there are strong normative constraints but also a strong pressure on the group toward deviation from the norms. We find here the suggestion that the significance of one's social position for the transmission of contagion may vary depending on the kind of behavior being diffused and the kind of situation in which the collectivity finds itself. Many other bases for such an ambiguous view could also be presented. Because of the complexities involved in such a view, we have found it difficult to state with any clarity a general relationship between social position and role in the transmission process. We thus postpone until Chapter 6 a more detailed discussion of the issues involved, and at this point we simply record that social position should presumably be an important factor in the transmission process.

Somewhat similarly, the question of what personality characteristics are most likely to lead to participation in a pattern of hysterical contagion can only be answered in a very tentative way. The answer must be given largely in terms of the relationship between the personal characteristics of the people involved and the kind of behavior which spreads through the population. One can more easily predict which kinds of people will be likely to be affected once one knows what kind of behavior those affected engage in and what kinds of beliefs legitimize that behavior.

All of this leads to the conclusion that there is undoubtedly some pattern of interaction among personality, social structure, and situational characteristics which influences how the diffusion of the pattern of behavior will occur. Although there seems to be general agreement that *some* kinds of personality characteristics and *some* kinds of social relationships may assume significance in *some* kinds of situations, it is difficult to specify with any degree of certainty what combinations are most likely to occur together.

Finally, we turn to our last question in this general area: What relationship does the contagion have to the characteristics of the collectivity and/or the larger social system? We again find some suggestions but little firm guidance. We have already noted the emphasis given to the role of strain or stressful conditions in the development of all kinds of collective behavior. The preceding discussion also suggests that level of organization of the collectivity may play an important part. These two factors are presumably related since a highly organized group will have fewer sources of strain of the type the Langs call "gaps in the social structure," and highly organized groups should have greater resources for coping with strain when it does occur. Earlier in this chapter we also noted the importance of external agencies of social control in the development and spread of contagion. The effectiveness of these agencies will be a function of the degree of organization of the larger system. There is reason to believe, therefore, that the degree and effectiveness of organization of both the participants and the larger social system of which they are a part will be important variables in determining the pattern and extent of dissemination of contagious behavior.

APPLICATION OF CONCEPTS TO THE INSECT BITE EPIDEMIC

Following Smelser for the moment, we can see that the insect bite epidemic included all of the ingredients for panic except "limited and decreasing access to avenues of escape" and the final "mobilization for flight." "Strain" was present in the fact of overtime work, the lack of clear organization of the plant, and the probable conflict between work and home obligations for many of the female workers. One can assume that under these circumstances many of the workers had at least vague feelings of frustration and discontent in the work situation. It may very well be that the persistent complaint of insect bites prior to the epidemic was an expressive means of giving vent to these feelings. The bites were at least tangible sources of irritation which could be defined as unnecessary, whereas the overtime could be seen as both necessary and desirable (for the income it provided), and the lack of effective organization in the plant was too vague a source of irritation.

It is difficult to say whether the precipitating event preceded or followed the development of the generalized belief in this case. Since the plant had been sprayed twice just prior to the epidemic, and the bites had continued, there had undoubtedly begun to develop some notion that these were unusual insects. However, it seems unlikely that they were defined as the sinister, mysterious, and potent force they soon became. Therefore, a precipitating event must have occurred which confirmed the vague worries about "the bug" and provided a tangible focus for the ambiguous sense of frustration and anxiety which had evolved. This precipitating event was evidently the extreme reaction of the first case (or first few cases) in the epidemic. Suddenly there was tangible evidence of a serious threat. Suddenly anxiety was replaced by fear as a real danger was found.

But what "caused" the first case, or the first few cases? It is interesting to note that the first case was a young woman of 22 who complained of a bite on the Friday before the first big day of the epidemic. Soon afterwards, she fainted. Most noteworthy, this woman had fainted approximately five times during the past year, the last time being one and one-half months before she fainted in the plant. (She also fainted again later in the epidemic.) The second case, which occurred on the following Tuesday, was a young woman who worked near the first case. She said she had been bitten the previous week, but she did not report to the doctor until that Tuesday when she complained that she felt "like a balloon ready to burst." On the same day four other women reported to the doctor. The third case passed out soon after having been bitten that afternoon. This young woman had been under a physician's care for the past several months for "nervousness." The fourth case complained not of a bite but of a crawling sensation on her thigh, and she almost passed out. Late that afternoon the fifth and sixth cases occurred when two women became emotionally disturbed, and one of them fainted. The next morning the epidemic developed with a rush. Eleven women reported to the medical authorities before noon, and the contagion began to snowball.

It may very well be that the first few cases (or at least some of them) were responding to conditions which were not extraordinary in the plant context but which seemed to them to be extreme because of their presumably unusual personalities. Their reactions may have been appropriate to the situation, therefore, only in the very special sense that their personalities made them so. As they were observed by others, however, the behavior they exhibited appeared to indicate an extremely potent force at work. Undoubtedly some of those who observed these first few cases simply shrugged the whole thing off as the strange behavior of "some crazy women." But others were more impressed by what they saw, and the hysterical belief began to evolve and spread. As the number of cases grew, the validity of the belief was increasingly strengthened and more widely disseminated, until almost everyone believed in the reality and potency of "the bug."

Returning to Smelser's discussion again, we may ask why panic did not occur and why this hysterical belief did not give rise to "pell-mell flight" in the face of such a potent danger. There seem to be several possible answers, although our evidence is less than adequate to provide convincing support for them. First of all, there evidently *was* some flight from the danger. As one of the women indicated in the interview, "I just clocked out of there." Management told us that there was an increase in absenteeism during this period, but they had no adequate records of the extent of it. Second, management acted on the afternoon of the big Wednesday in a way that precluded flight: they sent the workers home. This did not remove the threat from the situation (cases began occurring immediately the next morning), but it removed the workers from the threat at least for a while. Third, the *possibility* of "clocking out" was always open to the workers, although admittedly difficult to utilize because of general work norms. The avenues of escape were not limited, nor were they diminishing. Fourth, from the onset of the epidemic, forces of social control were at work. Management took control by clearing the plant and calling in the exterminators. Other experts were soon on the scene telling the workers that there was no reason for fear. The press was hinting broadly from the beginning that it was simply a case of some hysterical women (although they also played up the mystery involved). These forces of control were far from fully effective, but they undoubtedly reduced the seriousness of the epidemic. All of these factors, then, kept the epidemic from becoming a case of panic.

The hysterical forces, however, were effective—an epidemic did occur. Given the balance between the forces impelling the workers toward hysterical contagion and the forces operating to dampen this effect, some became more clearly affected by the contagion than others. What basis do we have for predicting which ones were affected and which were not? This seemed to be the most reasonable question for us to use in guiding our research. We cannot in any convincing sense "predict" the epidemic itself since it had already occurred and we have only the single case to analyze.[7] We can illuminate the case by reference to what are presumably the dynamics of such events, but there is no basis for testing any tentative expectations about a single case such as this. We can, however, even after the event, investigate the applicability of expectations about

---

[7] We did, however, collect similar data from another clothing manufacturing plant in which no epidemic had occurred to determine how atypical our subjects were. See the Appendix for a discussion of these data.

which kinds of people will be affected by such an event and which will not. There is a built-in control in the situation: all were exposed to many of the same forces, but only some were affected.

We already knew something about differences between those affected and those not. Almost all of the former were women, almost all of them were in one limited section of the plant, almost all of them had been exposed to a considerable amount of overtime on the job. Since there were men in the plant, since there were both men and women in other parts of the plant, and since there were those in the plant who had not worked much overtime, these are evidently important characteristics. But, also, since there were women in the dressmaking section of the plant who had worked overtime and had not been affected, these characteristics are not fully adequate for our purposes.

We have noted several other kinds of factors which may be involved in such cases. These may be classified under three general headings: personality, strain, and social relations.

PERSONALITY

Our earlier discussion of the personality variables presumably associated with hysterical contagion indicated that there is little consensus among students of collective behavior as to which kinds of personality are most susceptible to hysterical contagion, but most agree that personality is likely to be an important variable. The Langs emphasize the probable importance of the "socially inadequate" or "insecure" person in these cases. Such a person will be more sensitive to and dependent upon social cues and will thus be more easily influenced by such cues; they would be likely to conform whatever the behavior involved. The Langs also note, however, that some other types of persons, whom they call "high ego-defenders," will be susceptible to the extent that the behavior being diffused serves their particular psychic needs.

We also find in the collective behavior literature an acknowledgment of the fact that some persons have a lower tolerance for strain than others. This seems to be what is generally meant when we speak of a person as being "nervous." If the behavior involved in this epidemic was a function of fear of a threatening force as we have suggested, it seems likely that nervous or tense women would be more likely to exhibit the more extreme physiological reactions than would others. Thus, without claiming any general tendency to be susceptible, such persons would seem to be more susceptible to this particular type of contagion.

Closely related to this characteristic would be the general tendency to seek medical assistance when and if symptoms appear. We might surmise, for instance, that even given the "same" symptoms, some women would report to the doctor and others would not. Since our knowledge of who was affected by the epidemic was at least originally limited to the medical records, we have found it important to be aware of the difference between "experiencing symptoms" (and perhaps even "exhibiting symptoms") and being known by the doctor as an affected case. Because of this, it seems very likely that what has been called the "inclination to adopt the sick role" would be a possible basis for differentiating between those known to be affected and those not. This may be where the Langs' definition of the high ego-defender fits in. There are undoubtedly some people who are more likely than others to be responsive to "external" physical threats.

STRAIN

We have suggested that the heavy overtime worked by the women in the dressmaking departments would have been a source of strain on the job. All discussions of such forms of collective behavior indicate that physical fatigue is a predisposing condition. On the other hand, not all of the women had worked the same amount of overtime, so it is possible that variation in this source of strain might have been an important factor. There are, of course, many other sources of strain on the job which might vary among the workers. Their degree of skill, intelligence, and experience would seem to be important variables since the greater each of these is, the better able the worker would be to meet the demands of the job and the less strain he would experience on the job. If there are different levels of work load, a worker who had (or thought that he had) a heavier work load would be under more strain. We might also define the adequacy of the worker's relationships with others on the job as a possible source of strain.

Not all of the sources of strain experienced by the worker need be in the work situation itself. Since it would be impossible to investigate all possible sources of strain, however, it seems reasonable to focus only on those which have some clear connection with a presumed sense of strain while working. These would be largely the kinds of strain experienced because of conflict between demands of the job and demands of other roles carried out by the workers. Female workers might feel strain in family roles due to conflict with work obligations. If a woman works overtime, it will be difficult if not impossible for her to carry out her usual activities with respect to child care and the upkeep of her home. Her relationship with her husband would also be more limited and thus possibly less satisfying. Such sources of strain appear to be potentially significant.

SOCIAL RELATIONS

As noted earlier, we may view the adequacy of one's social relations in the plant as a source of strain. There is another way in which the structure of social relations might prove to be important, however. These relations may act as either means of transmission of the contagion or as means of obstruction to its transmission. We have discussed earlier, however, some of the problems involved in making a priori estimates of the role of social relations in the transmission process. There seem to be some grounds for making several different predictions.. Because of this, we were originally unable to go beyond the very general proposition that a person's position in the structure of social relations should make a difference in the probability of his being influenced by the contagion process.

We thus began our investigation sensitized to look for indications of variation in personality characteristics, strain on and off the job, and the structure of social relations on the job. Our specific areas of inquiry varied all the way from measures of "tenseness," to finding out how many children of what age the women had, to asking about friendship relations in the plant. Our guiding question was: Why were some of the workers affected by the epidemic to the point of requiring medical aid while others who were evidently in the same situation were not affected in this way?

Part II

The remainder of the volume presents a report of the results of our research efforts. In Chapter 3 we discuss the general research method and analyze the problem of specifying the dependent variable in the study. We have already noted that a belief, an experience of symptoms, and a form of behavior (reporting to the doctor) were all important aspects of the epidemic. All of these might be considered as legitimate variables, and all of them might be measured in different ways. Thus, a clarification of these variables and their relationships to each other is a necessary prerequisite to the later discussion.

The next four chapters present the findings in relation to the various factors we have discussed above as being potentially relevant to the pattern of distribution of symptoms and the development of the hysterical contagion. Chapter 4 focuses on the sources of strain experienced by the women both due to the job and the conflicts between the job and home. Chapter 5 reviews the data on the personality variables we were able to measure in the interview in light of the conceptualization suggested by previous discussions of such epidemics. Chapter 6 is concerned with the pattern of social relations among the women and the evidence we have of the relevance of such relations to the development and spread of the epidemic. In Chapter 7 we review the data of Chapters 4, 5, and 6 as they relate to each other and as they mutually contribute to an understanding of the epidemic. Whereas the previous chapters raise questions individually, Chapter 7 attempts to put them together in a

single complex question: Why did these individuals, faced with
these situational strains, in this social situation become participants
in the process of hysterical contagion represented by the insect bite
epidemic? Chapter 8 presents an abstract general conceptualization of
the phenomenon we have studied as well as a discussion of the
difficulties and possibilities of further research on such problems.
Finally, Chapter 9 consists of a discussion of three closely related
concepts—epidemic, contagion, and diffusion—in an attempt to clarify
the similarities and differences of these three processes of dissemination.

3

LIMITS AND KINDS
OF CONTAGION

In Part I we have posed the problem of this volume in two steps: in Chapter 1 we have described the incident the way it was perceived by the participants and by various functionaries in the community, especially the news media; in Chapter 2 we have discussed the conceptual framework which we decided to employ in studying this event. We must now describe our research operations and the general mode of investigation, after which we will present the results of our analysis.

We were not able to collect any formal data from the workers at the plant until almost exactly two months after the epidemic ended. This delay was in part a function of the time necessary to prepare the field operations. It was more a function, however, of the reticence of management to permit us to "stir up the waters." There was understandable concern that our presence in the plant too soon after the epidemic might be interpreted by the workers as spying on them. The delay thus provided a cooling off period. Because of this concern, also, we limited our questioning about the epidemic to the bare minimum and presented the study as part of a larger investigation of worker attitudes and opinions. In addition, the workers were assured of the confidential nature of their responses by both us and management, and management insisted that the workers be told that they could refuse to be interviewed if they wished.

Because of the degree of concentration of the affected cases, as discussed in Chapter 1, we limited our subjects to women working on the first shift, excluding all office workers. A systematic sample of one-fourth of these blue collar women was drawn using a payroll list for the week after the epidemic as the population definition. Since 85 percent of all the first-shift women worked in the dressmaking departments, we went back and oversampled those blue collar women who worked outside these departments, obtaining a one-half sample. We did the same for the Negro women in the dressmaking departments because they were so few in number and we expected them to be different from the whites in the same departments. Actually, all of the Negroes in the sample were pressers, and no white women did that job, so the Negroes were organizationally as well as racially distinct. Finally, we added all of the women who were known to have been affected during the epidemic and who had not been drawn in the sample by these means.

A total of 185 women were interviewed. Any woman, except those affected whose names were added at the end (and who were thus not part of the systematic sample), who could not be interviewed was replaced in the sample by the woman whose name appeared next on the payroll list. Table 3.1 presents the composition of the final sample, the number of replacements, and the location of the interviews. In all cases where it was possible, the interviews took place in small interviewing rooms in the plant. They were carried out during normal working hours, and the women were paid by management for the time spent in the interview. Sixteen of the women who had been affected were interviewed at home either because they refused to be interviewed at the plant or were unavailable there. All affected first-shift females were ultimately interviewed. All interviews were carried out by two experienced female interviewers associated with the National Opinion Research Center of the University of Chicago. A copy of the interview is presented in Appendix B.

TABLE 3.1
Characteristics of Sample, Refusal Rate, and Interview Location

Original sample (including 15 affecteds)	142
Affecteds added to sample	43
Total sample	185
In total sample, interviewed in plant	144
Nonaffected replacements, interviewed in plant	25
Affecteds, interviewed at home	16
Reason for failure to interview in plant	
Not there (vacation, layoff, sick, etc.)	27
Nonaffecteds	17
Affecteds	10
Refused to be interviewed	14
Nonaffecteds	8
Affecteds	6

In addition to the interview data and the information available from the medical officer's records and the news media, we were able to obtain copies of the personnel forms the company had for these workers. These forms, which were filled out only after the epidemic, included information about age, race, marital status, number and age of children, work experience, and date employed. Unfortunately, however, the personnel forms were not complete in all cases, and a number of them were missing. Thus, when analyses involving these variables are made, there is some loss of sample size.

THE DEPENDENT ATTRIBUTE

The structure of our sample reflects the fact that our basic distinction was between those women who were known to have been affected during the epidemic and all others. We had the total population of the former and a sample of the latter. However, it soon became clear to us that it was important to distinguish among three different aspects or phases which the previous chapter has suggested are involved in hysterical contagion. People come to *believe* certain kinds of facts (e.g., the reality of the threat of a poisonous insect), they *react* emotionally (e.g., develop physiological symptoms), and they perform some *act* (e.g., they go to the doctor or they faint). All three of these aspects of the process can be observed and described in various ways, and in different instances of hysterical contagion the cognitive, emotional, and action components may be salient to different degrees. The dominant characteristic of the present case seemed to be the strength of its emotional component, the occurrence of illness. However, our basic criterion for identifying cases who had had such an emotional experience was the listing of a woman in the medical records. If there was a lack of complete correspondence between the emotional experience and the doctor's records, it was possible for us to miss some of those who had had the experience.

There was a great advantage in using the medical records since they provided not only the information that a woman had been affected, but what her symptoms had been and when during the epidemic she had been affected. Going to (or being brought to) the doctor is a definite public act, and it is precisely this act which made the whole episode a public event and brought it to the attention of management, official agencies, and the news media. The women who were involved in such a public act left behind a permanent record of their act, and we used this record in defining our sample. The study was designed to compare these women, whom we shall call "affecteds," with a sample of those who did not seek aid, whom we thought of as a control group.[1]

As soon became evident, however, there was not a perfect correspondence between the emotional reaction and the act of seeking or receiving medical aid. The affecteds were not the only ones who felt sick. During the interview, most of our questions about the epidemic were open-ended ones. After asking the women generally what had happened, we asked: "Did anything like this happen to you?" Of the 58 affecteds, all but 4 acknowledged that something like that had happened to them. Of the 4 exceptions, 2 said they were frightened and ran away; 1 said she was sick for other reasons

---

[1] As this is not an experimental study, the term "control" (equivalent subjects not exposed to the crucial stimulus conditions) may seem inappropriate. We are using the term in the sense of a base line group with which the critical group can be compared.

and was checked to see whether it could have anything to do with the epidemic; and the fourth did not mention that anything had happened to her. Two-thirds (36 of 54) of those who admitted they were sick did so spontaneously during their description of the epidemic, the other third doing so only after being asked this more specific question.

Even more important for our later analysis was a number of women who did not receive medical aid during the epidemic but who said that "something like that" had happened to them. Of the 127 women whom we had thought of as controls, 21 (or about one-sixth) said this. We could only interpret this as an indication that a rather large proportion of the total population of women had reacted emotionally during the epidemic and had experienced some kind of symptoms. Of these 21 women, 7 mentioned their own symptoms spontaneously during their description of the epidemic, the others acknowledging their experience in response to the more pointed question. If we assume that this one-sixth proportion accurately represents the proportion of all those who were not affecteds who actually experienced symptoms during the epidemic, it is apparent that there were more such women than there were affecteds. Thus, even though they did not come to the attention of the medical or other authorities, it is very likely that they played some part in the development and spread of the epidemic. At least it seems likely that some of their associates in the plant knew of their experience, and to the extent that there was any kind of interpersonal influence involved in the spread of the symptoms, they undoubtedly had their effect. Also, since they experienced symptoms but did not come to the attention of the medical authorities, the further question is raised as to why some who experienced symptoms got to the doctor and others did not.

The correspondence between self-report and medical attendance might be used as evidence of the reliability of the interview. In situations of this kind it is usually assumed that an interview will understate incidence as the respondents might be ashamed to admit their gullibility (Cantril, 1940, p. 58). Only the four cases mentioned above would give evidence for understatement of this kind and for them the discrepancy is at least explainable. On the face of it, it is unlikely that respondents would claim having been exposed to the hysterical contagion, if in fact they were not. This is not an activity which confers prestige.

On further consideration we can find an incentive which would make respondents claim to have had symptoms. This would be the position like "See, I felt bad too, but I did not go and make a fuss about it." A feeling of superiority of this kind might make people exaggerate retroactively. Symptoms are so indefinite in any case that it would be hard to ascertain a definite borderline where a person would claim "legitimately" to be affected by the epidemic. Thus the important point is this self-definition of the experience and it is in this sense that we can treat them as a separate group.

Because of the conceptual significance of these women, we decided early in the analysis to consider them as a separate category. Although they were not very numerous in our sample, they could be considered to represent a rather sizeable category of women within the total population of the plant. We thus singled them out for separate analysis and called them "self-defined affecteds" because we would not have known of their having been affected if they had not told us. It is likely that others among the third category of women (whom we shall call the "controls") also experienced symptoms during the epidemic but did not tell us about them. However, we have no way of determining the identity of such women, whereas the self-defined affecteds are a distinct category.

The third aspect of hysterical contagion, a belief, is also of interest to a student of such phenomena, and the dissemination of beliefs has traditionally been an important part of the subject matter of collective behavior. Given the lack of perfect correspondence between the emotional and action aspects of the epidemic, it seems highly likely that the cognitive aspect would not correspond with either of them. Whereas the action aspect was recorded at the time, and the emotional aspect was determined on the basis of a later self-report of one's feelings at the time of the epidemic, the only measure of belief we had was one made two months later and given in answer to questions which clearly indicated that we were interested in what they believed *then* (two months later).

As the remarks quoted in Chapter 1 indicate, even two months later and even after experts and the news media had labelled the epidemic as largely psychological in nature, most of the women believed in the potency of a mysterious insect. Some of the statements quoted earlier were given spontaneously during the description of the epidemic, but we also asked a set of direct questions about this matter. The two most relevant ones are presented in Table 3.2 along

TABLE 3.2
Beliefs About the Epidemic According to Own Response During the Epidemic

Questions and Responses	Affecteds (N = 58) %	Self-Defined Affecteds (N = 21) %	Controls (N = 106) %
What do you think caused this to happen?			
Insect or other physical cause	86.2	71.4	50.9
Physical plus psychological causes	3.4	4.8	17.9
Psychological cause only	3.4	9.5	7.5
Don't know	6.9	14.3	23.6
Do you think that some kinds of people were more affected than others? In what way were they different?			
There was no difference	51.7	23.8	22.6
There were physical differences	27.6	42.9	27.4
Other (including "imaginative" and "nervous")	20.7	33.3	50.0

with the distribution of answers given by the three categories of respondents. The most striking thing about these data are the high proportions of all three categories who accept the insect as the sole or a major cause of the epidemic and the very small proportions who attribute the sickness to purely psychological causes. The most common form of deviation from the insect theory is the expression of doubt about the whole thing. Given this widespread belief in the significance of the insect, it is reasonable to wonder why some people were affected and others were not. In response to this question, the most common answer was that there was no difference between those affected and those who were not (i.e., it was just a matter of chance), but many of the women thought that there was some physical difference in the affected women which made them more susceptible to the effect of the bites. There is, of course, greatest skepticism among the controls and least among the affecteds, but no more than half of any category thought some nonphysical difference was involved.[2]

The fact that belief in the causal significance of the insect was so widespread, together with the fact that the measure of belief was so clearly a measure of belief after the epidemic rather than during it, made us unwilling to use belief as a basic independent or dependent measure in this study. We will discuss the distribution of belief in greater detail in Chapter 7, but it will not be used systematically in our analysis. The emotional and action aspects of hysterical contagion will be viewed systematically, however, by carrying throughout the analysis the distinction between the affecteds and the self-defined affecteds. In fact, for most of this report we will be concerned with differentiating among those who experienced symptoms, those who got medical assistance, and those who did neither.

THE PATTERN OF EXPRESSION

The difference between the affecteds and the self-defined affecteds suggests that the behavioral and emotional aspects of an epidemic

2 One reason for the widespread belief in the insect explanation and the rejection of a purely psychological explanation was undoubtedly the fact that so many of the women knew someone who had been affected. We asked them: "Did this happen to anyone (else) in the plant whom you know well?" Ninety percent of the affecteds, 76 percent of the self-defined affecteds, and 55 percent of the controls said "yes" and were able to name the person or persons affected. We considered the possibility of using this information as another means of identifying the affected cases, but we found that, within our sample, there were only two women named as affected who did not either report to the doctor or admit in the interview that they had been affected. Therefore, the answers to this question do not add appreciably to our ability to identify affected women.

such as this one may be quite variable both in intensity and extensity. Both during the epidemic and the interview the women had the opportunity to express their feelings on matters related to the epidemic. This was also true during the encounter with the physician for those who received medical aid. All of these settings can be viewed as providing opportunities for the expression of feelings or opportunities for communication, although they certainly vary in the degree to which the behavior involved explicitly and consciously transmits a message about the woman's feelings. In considering these various modes of expression together we also emphasize the close relationship as well as the differences between the perspectives of the physician and the social psychologist in cases such as this. The physician often interprets a patient's symptoms, even when clearly caused in part by a definite physical agent, as an attempt to communicate certain needs to the physician and/or other people.[3] In the same way, the social psychologist looks on hysterical contagion as an expression of some underlying problem within a group or among certain of its members.

The affecteds complained of various symptoms when they discussed their problem with the doctor, and there is no consistent pattern in these symptoms. There was no one symptom common to all cases. In fact, there were 5 patients who reported no recollection of a bite, although they felt pain which might have been related to one. Nausea was mentioned most frequently, 40 of the 62 affecteds reporting this symptom. Fainting was also rather common, 23 patients being recorded as having fainted, and an additional 19 patients reported that they "almost fainted." It is probably worth noting here that fainting was probably the most disruptive kind of response to the epidemic, and if one wished (at whatever level of consciousness) to express her dissatisfaction with her surroundings, this would be a very effective way to do so. Headache was reported by 22 patients, and other symptoms listed were weakness, nervousness, dizziness, and being in a daze. Some rather vague feelings are also reported with

[3] The Tavistock Clinic in London has been most explicit in pioneering this approach among physicians (cf. Bion, 1961; Balint, 1957). Also, Szasz (1967) defines a concept of pain which lies predominantly in the communication aspect, ". . . it may be a request for help or a complaint about being unfairly treated or an attack or retribution against a needed but unconsciously hated object" (p. 104).

considerable frequency. The most prominent of these was a feeling that some referred to as "swelling like a balloon," and this expression occurs so frequently that it suggests the spread of a verbal pattern of reporting. But there is no very consistent pattern or combination of symptoms, and this kind of distribution reinforces the impression that we are not dealing with a relationship between a specific physical cause and a symptom but with a vague, probably psychogenic source of tension to which all kinds of symptoms could be related.

The doctor's records also report the temporal sequence of cases, and a pattern emerges from that sequence that is worth reporting. We have noted that there was a gradual build-up of cases over a period of almost a week with the great majority of cases reporting to the doctor on two big days, and a few cases coming in after these big days. The early cases often reported having been bitten several hours or days prior to seeing the doctor, but as the epidemic developed, the lag between the experience of the bite and seeing the doctor practically disappeared. Some of the women who saw the doctor during the two big days said they had also been bitten at some earlier time, but only two who were bitten on or after the first big day failed to report to the doctor the same day they were bitten.

This time sequence confirms our impression that seeking medical attention was a significant act in itself and that it was not identical with the experience of any particular symptoms. There is also a consistent trend to suggest that, as the epidemic progressed, less severe symptoms sufficed to induce a person to seek medical attention. If we take as the most severe symptom the act of fainting, we find that of the 6 persons who received medical attention before the two big days, 3 fainted. Of the 26 seen by the doctor on the first big day, 12 fainted. Seven of the 22 cases treated on the second big day fainted; and only one of the 6 patients treated after the second big day fainted. There is thus a steady decrease in the percentage who fainted from 50 percent to 46 percent to 31 percent to 17 percent. Evidently, as it became more and more socially acceptable to seek medical attention for symptoms, less severe symptoms were sufficient to lead one to treatment.

We have only the data from the interview on which to base any judgment about the severity of the symptoms experienced by the self-defined affecteds, but from their report in the interview it would appear that their symptoms were not as severe as those experienced by the affecteds. Some of them said they felt bites and became faint; but there were quite a few who mentioned that they were bitten and nothing happened. Thus, although there is some overlap in the symptoms experienced by these two categories of women, the self-defined affecteds do not seem to have been as seriously affected. It is very likely that during the spring and summer in the southeastern states a person might get some insect bites, and therefore it may be meaningful that some of the workers associated these bites with the epidemic, while others did not get sufficiently concerned to make this association and to report to the doctor. But both the affecteds and self-defined affecteds felt sufficiently affected by the experience that they considered themselves to be the victims of the epidemic either at the time or afterwards during the interview.

If we view the epidemic and one's involvement in it as an expression of some sense of dissatisfaction (either personal or against the organization) which the individual could not express in some other way, there are several ways in which a person could express himself through the symptoms: by just having them, by using them as a basis for an act of social consequence (that is, by obtaining medical aid), or by mentioning them in the interview (which is a social act of less consequence). The degree of spontaneity of report of symptoms during the epidemic, therefore, is one index of the strength of feeling. This index also suggests that the affecteds were more deeply affected by the experience. Only one-third of the self-defined affecteds mentioned their own involvement in the epidemic spontaneously, whereas six-tenths (36 out of 58) of the affecteds did so. Of course, there were 4 of the affecteds who did not fully admit their involvement even when more direct questions were asked, but there might also have been many women like our self-defined affecteds (in the sense that they experienced symptoms) who never actually admitted to being affected.

Another measurement of the strength of feeling would be the amount of talking about the epidemic the women did in the interview. The most straightforward means of indicating this is by the average length of response to our general request for a description of what happened during the epidemic. We have presented these data in Table 3.3 organized according to whether the respondent

TABLE 3.3
Pattern of Expression and Length of Statement About the Epidemic

Type of Subject	Mean number of words in description of epidemic	
	Total	To first probe
No part in epidemic admitted in interview		
No participation observed (Controls, N = 106)	29.1	24.0
Participation observed (Affecteds who deny being affected, N = 4)	73.3	40.0
Participation acknowledged in interview		
No participation observed (Self-Defined Affecteds)		
Spontaneous mention in interview (N = 7)	46.2	37.5
Mention after direct question (N = 14)	35.0	28.9
Participation observed (Affecteds)		
Spontaneous mention in interview (N = 36)	52.2	37.8
Mention after direct question (N = 18)	29.4	25.8

spontaneously mentioned her own involvement and according to her position in the three major categories of respondent—affected, self-defined affected, and control. The longest average answer was given by the four affecteds who later said they felt that they had not actually been affected by the epidemic. Although they were not challenged by the interviewer about this inconsistency (the interviewers did not even know who had gone to the doctor and who had not), they apparently felt a great need to talk about the episode and to justify their own behavior during the epidemic—especially after the interviewer asked her routine probing question. By contrast, those respondents who were not affected by either criterion gave the shortest answers. Among the other four categories of women, there is a consistent difference between those who spontaneously acknowledge their participation and those who do not, the former giving the longer

TABLE 3.4
Participation and Belief in the Epidemic

	What do you think caused this to happen? "Insect" %	Why some people more affected than others? "Psychological" %
No participation in epidemic indicated (Nonaffecteds) (N = 106)	28.3	27.3
Participation is indicated		
No participation observed (Self-Defined Affecteds)		
Spontaneous mention in interview (N = 7)	57.1	42.9
Mention only after questioning (N = 14)	42.9	28.6
Participation observed (Affecteds)		
Spontaneous mention in interview (N = 36)	63.9	11.1
Mention only after questioning (N = 18)	66.7	11.1
None indicated in interview (N = 4)	25.0	25.0

replies. This difference is greater among the affecteds, those who do not spontaneously admit having been affected giving answers as short as the controls. It may be that the epidemic was not as significant an event for these women as it was for those who spontaneously acknowledged their own participation.

In concluding this delineation of the kinds of effects of the epidemic, it may be valuable to consider the interrelations of different kinds of action and belief. Table 3.4 shows the answers of the different groups which we have described to two questions on beliefs about the epidemic. The action during the epidemic itself relates to belief about the existence of the insect. With the exception of those four women who denied having been affected, the affecteds are most likely to express belief in the insect. The controls are least likely to do so, and the self-defined affecteds are in the middle. As expected, the affecteds are least likely to suggest that psychological factors were involved in the epidemic and the controls are more likely to refer to such factors. However, the self-defined affecteds are most likely of all to suggest a psychological explanation. When this is viewed in conjunction with their acceptance of the insect explanation, they seem to be saying that there was an insect and people did get sick, but this was no reason to panic.

The general impression one gains from this analysis is that there were different degrees of severity of response both during the epidemic and afterwards. During the epidemic these ranged from those affecteds who fainted, through those self-defined affecteds who felt sick but did nothing about it, to those controls who did not feel upset at the time. During the interview there was also a variation in the strength of response about the epidemic. Some mentioned immediately that they had themselves been affected and gave rather lengthy accounts of the event, while others acknowledged their participation only after a direct question and gave rather brief accounts of the event. We have suggested that all of these measures may be interpreted as indications of differing degrees of dissatisfaction or tension in the situation, and in general such indexes of dissatisfaction and tension are found more frequently among affecteds than controls, as we would expect. In later chapters we will turn to a more direct measure of these dimensions of tension and dissatisfaction. We will seldom be able to cope with the minor variations of response we have just noted, simply because there is too much variation to permit any systematic analysis. We will, however, return to a consideration of the rather gross categories of affected cases defined according to which women fainted, which said they almost fainted, and which did neither. Throughout, of course, we will also be concerned with the difference between the affecteds and the self-defined affecteds as well as the ways in which both of these categories differ from the controls.

THE POPULATION AT RISK

Up to this point our discussion has encompassed either all of the affected cases (4 of whom were not even in our interview sample) or our entire sample of 185 women. For the purposes of the central analysis of this study, however, we have found it useful to delimit the population under consideration even more narrowly than this. Our sample was originally chosen because we knew that all but 4 affected cases were women on the first shift. That population which we sampled included two relatively small subgroups, however, which we either knew or strongly suspected were rather different from the bulk of the population of first-shift women. These were the Negroes and those who worked outside the dressmaking departments. As Table 1.1 indicates, the great majority of first-shift women worked in the dressmaking departments. Also indicated is the fact that none of the first-shift affected cases occurred outside the dressmaking departments. Even though we oversampled the blue collar women outside the dressmaking departments, we still had only 20 of them in our sample. Since they not only worked in other departments in the plant but also worked outside the large room in which the dressmaking departments were housed and where all the first-shift cases occurred, it seemed likely that they had not been exposed to the epidemic in the same way as had those in that large room. We therefore did not feel justified in including them with the others, and since there were so few of them, it did not seem worthwhile to carry on a parallel analysis throughout this report. We thus chose to separate these 20 women and discuss them briefly in the Appendix.

There was a similar situation with the Negro women. We had only 18 of them in our sample even though we had also oversampled from those Negroes working in the production departments. (There were some Negro women in service jobs also, but they were not included in the definition of the population from which we drew our sample.) All of these 18 women were pressers, and no white women held that job. Although the pressers were in the large room with the other dressmaking departments, and although 2 of these Negro women were among the affected cases, we were hesitant simply to include them in the sample used in the basic analysis for this report. There was no doubt that these women were a separate part of the personnel in this part of the plant. The racial barrier could not be ignored by us any more than it was ignored by the women themselves. And again there were too few of these women to warrant carrying on a parallel but separate analysis. We thus decided to exclude these women also and discuss them in the Appendix.

Although this decision to separate these two special subsamples from the rest of our subjects is defensible on the grounds just noted, it is worth mentioning here that our analysis of these cases has also strengthened the case for their separation. Especially with respect to the network of sociometric relations, these two subsamples of women are so different from the others we interviewed that there is no doubt that their inclusion in the general analysis would have tended to obscure some of the facts of the situation in which the epidemic took place.

We need also mention at this point three other cases which had to be excluded from the analysis. Because the sample was based on a population defined according to the payroll of the week after the epidemic, there appeared in our sample four women (one of whom was a Negro) who were not actually working at the plant during the epidemic. This was not discovered, of course, until the interviews had been carried out. Since the characteristics of these women are of no consequence for our understanding of the epidemic, they were also dropped from the analysis.

For our purposes, therefore, the population at risk is defined as all those blue collar white women working at the time of the epidemic in the dressmaking departments, all of whom were housed in one large central room in the plant. These women were most fully exposed to the epidemic, and in regard to them it may most legitimately be asked: Since they were all equally exposed to the epidemic, why were some affected by it while others were not? We know, of course, that the line between being affected and not being affected is not easily drawn and that, depending on our definition of "affected," it may be drawn in different places. However, wherever it is drawn, it is with respect to subdivisions of this population of women that the question is most legitimately raised. Our sample included 144 such women: 56 affecteds, 17 self-defined affecteds, and 71 controls. The affecteds were the total population of such women, whereas the self-defined affecteds and controls were an approximate one-fourth sample of such women. These three sets of subjects, representing as they do three different kinds of response to the epidemic, will be the focus of our investigation from this point forward. After we have presented an analysis of the data available on these women we will return (in Chapters 7 and 8) to further consideration of the characteristics of the population at risk and the pattern of the epidemic within that total population.

THE LOGIC OF ANALYSIS

The nature of the sample of women we used in the study poses some problems of analysis. The fact that we have a population of affecteds and a sample of other women makes some of the usual methods of analysis inappropriate. For instance, if we wish to ask if it is true that those who were under more strain were more likely to become affected, it would be normal to compare the percentage of those with high and low strain who were affected. Some test of the significance of the difference of these percentages could then be made. If we had a legitimate sample of the population at risk, such a procedure would be defensible, because it would be reasonable to assume that we had simultaneously sampled the distribution of levels of strain and the distribution of "levels" of affectedness (affected or non-affected). In our case such an assumption would not be reasonable because we very carefully did *not* sample levels of affectedness but chose instead to include all relevant cases of affecteds. Thus, if there were any relationship between being under heavy strain and being affected, the usual kind of analysis would tend to inflate the amount of that relationship by oversampling the high strain-affected segment of the distribution (Zeisel, 1957, Ch. 2).

Instead of such an approach, therefore, we have chosen to compare the percentage of the affecteds who had a particular characteristic with the percentage of the other categories with that characteristic. (We are thus asking if it is true that those who were affected were usually under more strain rather than if it is true that those under more strain were more likely to be affected.) Since the percentages are based on separate categories within each of which the sample proportion is constant, comparisons across categories are more legitimate and informative. If we find that a higher percentage of affecteds than controls were under high strain, this is a noteworthy finding which is not put in doubt by the fact that we have complete information about affecteds and only a sample of the relevant information about the controls.

The fact that our categories of cases are based on different sampling proportions also makes it more difficult to justify the use of tests of significance. Only the findings for the nonaffected cases are subject to sampling variation since the affecteds are a population. We have chosen not to use tests of significance in any systematic way, but we have also been concerned that we avoid the pitfall of stressing only those differences which "make sense" to us in terms of a particular point of view. Thus, although we do not report levels of significance, we have used as a rough rule of thumb for those basic kinds of analysis using all of our cases a difference which would meet the .10 level of significance on a usual test.

We feel that there are other than purely methodological reasons for not using tests of significance in this case, however, and it is important to emphasize this point before presenting the findings. Given the general state of theory in this area of inquiry and the paucity of previous empirical research, we deemed it inappropriate to present a list of formal hypotheses which would then be carefully tested by means of the data we collected. Not only are the propositions which might be so tested very few in number, they are also often contradictory with one another. We found it necessary, therefore, to retain a very flexible view of the phenomena before us and to examine our data from a number of different perspectives, even when some of them contradicted others. We cannot claim, therefore, to have "tested a theory" or even to have provided a fully adequate basis for the general conclusions we have reached. What we have done is to provide a detailed analysis of a case of hysterical contagion, a case whose characteristics suggest the greater adequacy of some propositions than others. We believe that this analysis moves well beyond the previous discussions of such phenomena, but its ultimate value must be determined by further empirical investigations which use it as a point of departure. Because of the rather exploratory nature of the venture, therefore, a rigorous use of statistical tests appeared both inappropriate and potentially misleading.

4

SOURCES OF STRAIN

What little knowledge we had of such phenomena as the epidemic we were studying led us to be sensitive to indications that the women were experiencing some kinds of strain, either on the job or elsewhere. The underlying assumption was that hysterical contagion is a form of response to stress and that it tends to occur in situations in which nervous tension is high. We were particularly concerned with the matter of tension since the connection between the particular symptoms exhibited in this epidemic and the experience of unresolved tension seemed to be very close. Not only can it be argued that such unresolved tension leads to the kinds of tactual sensations one experiences when an insect is crawling on the skin, but the more extreme symptoms reported by the women were the same as those found in classical cases of hysteria. What evidently happened in this case was that a number of people who were experiencing these kinds of tension-related symptoms came to associate the symptoms with a mysterious poisonous insect. Thus, although a crucial part of the process was the introduction of this "explanation" of the symptoms, a high level of tension was presumably a prerequisite. We were therefore interested in attempting to delineate significant sources of tension. We also wanted to see if there were differences in the level of strain experienced by those who were known to be affected by the epidemic and those who were not affected. It has already been noted that there were *general* sources of strain in the plant that were presumably experienced by all of the workers, at least those in the dressmaking departments. Our interest, then, was in those sources of strain which were variables rather than constants.

We viewed the possible sources of strain on the job as being of three kinds: those associated with the actual work itself, those associated with worker-management relations, and those associated with relations among the workers. We also investigated the possibility of strain due to conflicts between the work role and family roles. This seemed to be a very likely source of strain since women are subject to clear responsibility in both environments. Finally, we have included here a discussion of some means of coping with these potential sources of strain.

THE JOB AS A SOURCE OF STRAIN

One of the factors noted in our discussion of the general stressful quality of the work situation was the fact that the epidemic occurred at the peak of the production cycle. A great deal of overtime was worked at this time, especially by those in the dressmaking sections of the plant. We had hoped to obtain from the management records information as to the amount of overtime worked by each of our subjects during the period just prior to the epidemic. This information was never made available, seemingly through a complication in the record-keeping rather than through any unwillingness on the part of management to cooperate in the study. We were thus forced to use the information obtained in the interview. The interview, of course, was designed to give the minimum amount of emphasis to the epidemic. Therefore, it was not possible to ask the most directly relevant question: How many times a week did you work overtime during the four weeks just prior to the epidemic? It was not even possible to ask about that particular period of time. We were assured by management, however, that the overtime patterns had not changed in the interim, and on this basis we have used answers to the question: About how many times during the last month have you worked overtime during the week? as our indication of this source of strain on the job.

In spite of the doubt we had in the adequacy of the question for our purposes, it proved to be one of the clearest differentiators between the affected women and the controls. Almost two-thirds (66 percent) of the affected women had worked overtime at least two or three times a week compared with only 41 percent of the controls (see first section of Table 4.1). Even fewer (29 percent) of the self-defined affecteds had worked that much overtime. This finding is clearly in keeping with the expectation that those who became affected were under more strain on the job than those who were not affected, although the position of the self-defined affecteds is less easily fitted into this pattern.

We also found that more of the affected women had been laid off since beginning work at Montana Mills than had the controls, although the difference is not great (36 percent versus 25 percent). Again, however, the self-defined affecteds raised a question for us. Over half of them had been laid off. Since our original logic was that the experience of being laid off would add an extra burden for the workers and make the strain of the job greater, this finding suggests that the self-defined affecteds were under greater strain from this source than either the affecteds or the controls, and they should then have had a greater probability of being affected than either of the other categories of women. This is another indication that these women were rather different from those who reported to the doctor. We have seen in the last chapter that they interpreted the epidemic in a different way. We now begin to see that they were different with respect to the situation they were in also. This will be a recurring theme throughout our analysis. Consistent with this greater tendency for the self-defined affecteds to have been laid off is their unanimous statement that their jobs were not "steady" ones, that they could not "count on working at least a full week all year." In contrast, sizeable minorities among both the affecteds and the controls viewed their jobs as steady.

Almost all of the other findings in this part of our analysis are rather inconclusive. The affecteds are not much more likely to see the work pace as variable, though variation in the pace was viewed by us as a probable source of strain. They also tend to respond at least as favorably toward their jobs as do the other two categories of subjects. They have relatively favorable scores on two scales we devised to measure attitudes toward work, scales on which the self-defined affecteds have the least favorable scores. When we asked them what they would prefer to do if they had their choice, "work

TABLE 4.1
Indications of Strain Among Affecteds, Self-Defined Affecteds, and Controls

Index of Strain	Affecteds (N = 56) %	Self-Defined Affecteds (N = 17) %	Controls (N = 71) %
Worked overtime at least two or three times a week	66.1	29.4	40.8
Have been laid off	35.7	52.9	25.4
Do not define job as "steady"	76.8	100.0	81.7
Do not mention supervisor as one to go to with a complaint	44.6	17.6	25.4
Mention the union steward	28.6	11.8	15.5
Are members of the union	78.0	86.7	66.1
The section varies in output	41.1	35.3	25.4
Often find themselves "trying hard to keep up with the others"	25.0	11.8	23.9
They work faster than the others	17.9	29.4	12.7
Are sole family breadwinners	21.4	23.5	9.9
Provide half or more of family income	43.4	37.5	22.4
Are separated, divorced, or widowed *	16.1	25.0	2.9
Have a child under six years old *	48.0	31.3	36.8
Have a child under six years old *and* work overtime a great deal *	33.9	6.3	14.1
Overtime interferes with something	50.0	70.6	59.2

* Data on marital status and family composition came from company records. Since these data were not complete, there are some cases missing, and the percentages are sometimes based on slightly smaller category sizes.

here, keep house, or do something else," their responses were not much different from those of the others. In fact, here again the responses of the self-defined affecteds were the most unusual, more of them saying they would prefer to "work here."

With respect to the original expectation that the affected women would report greater strain on the job, therefore, the only finding that was clearly in keeping with the expectation was that the affecteds had worked much more overtime than either of the other two categories of women. Although they had also been laid off somewhat more than had the controls, the self-defined affecteds had experienced layoff more than either the controls or the affecteds. On the more subjective measures of the women's attitudes toward the work situation, the picture is mixed, but there is no real indication that the affecteds are less satisfied than the others.

WORKER-MANAGEMENT RELATIONS

We asked the general question: How are workers treated here compared with other plants? and a number of other direct questions regarding the women's attitudes toward their supervisors. There were no very noteworthy differences among the three categories of women on these items. If anything, the affected and the self-defined affected women responded somewhat more favorably to such direct questions.

This pattern of response to direct questions is cast in doubt, however, since the affected women responded quite differently to a more indirect question about their superiors. We asked them: "If you had a complaint about your job, to whom would you go or to whom would you talk about it?" The affecteds were less likely than either the controls or the self-defined affecteds to mention their supervisor in response to this question (see second section of Table 4.1). Only slightly more than half of them mentioned the supervisor compared with about three-fourths of the controls and an even greater proportion of the self-defined affecteds. Only about one-tenth of each category explicitly denied that they would go to their supervisor when we later asked this more pointed question, but almost half of the affected women failed to mention the supervisor when faced with the original question. They evidently had less faith than the other women in the official channels of appeal in the plant, although they did not readily admit it.

This interpretation is strengthened by the fact that the affecteds were much more likely to mention the union steward as the person to whom they would turn if they had a complaint, and they were more likely than the controls to be members of the union. Although we would not wish to make any general claim that union membership is an indication of a lack of faith in management, in this particular plant such an interpretation is more easily justified. It was very apparent to us that the stature of the union, both in the plant and in the larger community, was not very high. Management did not have any consistent or effective dialogue with the union representatives and usually ignored them or treated them with a mixture of disdain and suspicion. Although the majority of the women in the dressmaking portion of the plant were union members, unions had made very little headway in the other plants in the area. In fact, during our field operations a union was picketing a local establishment in an effort to gain recognition. This activity was treated with derision by both the local press and many of the passersby on the street. The only reason for the presence of the union at Montana Mills, so far as we could determine, was that the union had a contract with the parent company whose operations were mainly in the North, and this contract automatically covered Montana Mills when it opened. To join the union in the face of such general community opposition and the union's own weakness in the plant would presumably require rather strong feelings on the subject.

The major outcome of this analysis, therefore, is a striking contrast between the verbal statements of the affected women with regard to their attitudes toward management and their behavior both in joining the union and in failing to designate the supervisor as the point of appeal. We interpret the less direct measures as an indication of a rather low level of faith in management and suggest that the verbal statements of attitude are thereby cast in doubt.

PEER RELATIONS AMONG THE WORKERS

The other workers in the plant could serve as either a source of strain (if a woman found them unattractive) or a source of strength (if she found them attractive and friendly). As we will discuss in greater detail in Chapter 6, it is also possible to view the fellow workers as a means of communication and interpersonal influence in such an epidemic as this. But at this point in the analysis we are only concerned with the possibility that such relations may constitute an additional source of strain.

We raised two kinds of questions in this regard. First, there was a series of questions about the general degree of favorableness with which the women responded to their fellow workers. Second, there was a series of questions regarding how they viewed themselves in the work context in comparison with the others in the plant. The findings in both cases are at best mixed. In general, the affected and self-defined affected women seem to have somewhat more positive attitudes than the controls toward their fellow workers, but the differences are neither very great in most cases nor are they fully consistent. Both the affecteds and self-defined affecteds are somewhat more likely to perceive variation in work output in their sections than are the controls (see third section of Table 4.1). However, the self-defined affecteds are least likely of all to say they often find themselves "trying hard to keep up with the others." Instead, the self-defined affecteds are more likely than the others to say that they "work faster than the other people" in their section.

We thus find only limited support for the general thesis that those who were affected were those who had stressful relations with their peers. In fact, we find that the affecteds do not differ appreciably from the controls on any of the attitude measures. They are more likely than the controls to perceive variation in output in their section, but they are not different from the controls in their report of their own position in this pattern of variable output. Again, the position of the self-defined affecteds on these measures is not clearly consistent with any simple explanation of their self-defined role in the epidemic. We will return to some of these findings again later in the chapter.

CONFLICT BETWEEN WORK
AND FAMILY ROLES

Workers may experience strain from sources other than the job and their fellow workers and management, and such strain can have a significant effect on their job behavior. Other potential sources are almost unlimited and can vary greatly from one person to the next, but we focused our attention on the possible strain caused by a conflict between the demands of the job and the demands presumably placed on a woman in the family situation. The fact that those who were affected by the epidemic were most likely to have worked a great deal of overtime may be interpreted both as an indication that they were physically tired from so much work and as an indication that they faced more conflicts between home and work obligations than did the other women.

Other indications of such conflict were also investigated. We thought, for instance, that those whose work was more important as a source of income to the family might be under more strain, and we found that there was a tendency for the affected and the self-defined affected women more frequently to be the sole breadwinners in the family (see last section of Table 4.1). The affecteds are also more likely than the controls to supply one-half or more of the family income. The job was thus more important to them than it was to the other women.[1]

The affecteds and self-defined affecteds were somewhat more likely to have larger families than the controls. More important, however, is the composition of those families. The great majority (about three-fourths) of all categories of women were married, but both affecteds and self-defined affecteds more frequently had disrupted marriages. (This means also, of course, that there were more single women among the controls.) The affecteds were more likely than either of the other categories of women to have preschool children. More significantly, the affecteds were more likely to have young children *and* to have worked a great deal of overtime. This should mean that these women faced a greater strain due to the demands of maternal and work roles. The fact that *none* of the self-defined affecteds faced this kind of role conflict again makes them very unusual.[2]

[1] It may also be worth noting here that a larger proportion of the self-defined affecteds and the controls had more than two incomes in the family. Eighteen percent of the former and 19 percent of the latter had more than two incomes compared with only 5 percent of the affecteds.

[2] We also found a larger proportion of the affecteds had preschool children *and* supplied at least half of the family income. Only 7 percent of the controls had these characteristics compared with 18 percent of the affecteds. Again, *none* of the self-defined affecteds had both of these characteristics.

Given such knowledge about the family situations of these women, their responses to another set of questions come as a surprise. We asked the women whether working overtime interfered with their other activities, and we specified such activities as "housework," "taking care of children," "being with husband," "being with friends," and "going to church" as well as asking them if there were any other activities it interfered with. Although the affecteds were slightly more likely than the controls to say that overtime interfered with taking care of children and being with their husbands, the differences are very small, and in both cases the self-defined affecteds acknowledged such interference even more frequently than the affecteds. When we raise the more general issue of whether the women see overtime as interfering with *anything,* the affecteds were least likely of all to say so. Although the difference between the affecteds and the controls is not very large, it takes on added significance when we recall that the affected women were more likely to have worked a great deal of overtime and more frequently had small children.

It is difficult to interpret this finding with full confidence. We might say that the greater importance of the job makes the acceptance of the "interference" of overtime easier, especially since the added income presumably is of more importance to the affected women, and therefore the affected women would not be so likely to complain about the overtime. We might also suggest that the affected women were more likely than the others to give only "pleasant" responses to questions, to have less tendency to complain, because they were different kinds of personalities. We will return to this point later on in this chapter.

To summarize this portion of the analysis, the most noteworthy findings with respect to home–work conflicts appear to be the greater tendency for affecteds to supply half or more of the family income and to work overtime even when they had young children. These findings suggest that they had more to cope with in the work situation than did the other women, even though they did not overtly object or complain about these burdens.

COMBINING INDEXES OF STRAIN

In the previous sections we have investigated several sources of potential strain and have found a number of these which discriminated between the affected and control cases in the direction one would expect if strain increased the probability that a woman would participate in the epidemic. Since the general expectation calls for increased strain to lead to increased probability of participation, however, we are interested not only in these individual measures but also in the total burden borne by the women. Within each type of strain we have found some measures which discriminated the affecteds from the controls. It therefore seems likely that the total burden of the affecteds was greater. However, this does not necessarily follow. It is quite possible that the distribution of these several types of strain is such that any combined measure would not discriminate between affecteds and controls any better than the individual measures. We thus turn to an examination of the distribution of combined strains.

It might be argued that we should combine *all* of the measures we have used in the previous analysis so that our resulting index will be composed of a wide range of sources of strain. We have chosen to do otherwise for three reasons. First, we have suggested that there is some reason to doubt the adequacy of some of our original measures. This is particularly true of measures based on evaluations made by the subjects themselves. Second, since so many of the measures do not show any noteworthy differences between the affecteds and controls, their inclusion in a summary measure would tend to obscure the effects of the measures which do discriminate. To say this, of course, is to acknowledge that we are not able with any confidence to define in advance *what* sources of strain might be significant in such an epidemic as we have studied. Thus, third, we recognize that our procedure is in the nature of an analog of the discriminant function technique. We are searching for that combination of strain measures which most clearly discriminated between the affecteds and controls.

We have therefore taken the most noteworthy measure from each of the four areas discussed thus far and combined them. By "noteworthy" we mean both that they discriminated between the affecteds and the controls (not necessarily between the affecteds and the self-defined affecteds) and they characterized a sizeable proportion of the affecteds. Some of the measures meet the first criterion but not the second. For instance, many more of the affecteds than controls were separated, divorced, or widowed (see Table 4.1), but this still represented only about one-sixth of the affecteds. In that same area, however, we find that there are many more affecteds than controls who supply at least half of the family income, and this attribute characterizes more than two-fifths of the affecteds. We thus chose the latter index from Table 4.1 rather than the former. The indexes we combined, therefore were (1) working overtime at least two or three times a week, (2) not mentioning the supervisor as one to go to with a complaint, (3) saying that the section varies in output, and (4) supplying half or more of the family income.

The distribution of the number of these strains experienced by the three categories of women is presented in Table 4.2. It is very

TABLE 4.2
Distribution of Four Sources of Strain* Among Affecteds, Self-Defined Affecteds, and Controls

Number of Sources of Strain Experienced	Affecteds (N = 56) %	Self-Defined Affecteds (N = 17) %	Controls (N = 71) %
0	10.7	35.3	18.3
1	25.0	23.5	56.3
2	32.1	29.4	21.1
3	26.8	11.8	4.2
4	5.4	0.0	0.0

* The four measures of strain are as follows: worked overtime at least two or three times a week, do not mention supervisor as one to go to with a complaint, the section varies in output, and provide half or more of family income.

striking that the differences between the affecteds and the controls which were seen when using these measures individually have been increased by the combination of the measures. The maximum difference between these two categories of women in any of the previous four tables was 24.2 percent (the difference in how many worked a great deal of overtime). If we combine the sources of strain, we see that 25.3 percent of the controls and 64.3 percent of the affecteds experienced at least two of these, a difference of 39.0 percent. Thus, by combining the measures of strain, we have greatly increased our differentiation between these two categories. This increases our confidence in the importance of the sources of strain as factors leading to participation in the epidemic. It also increases our confidence in the idea that combinations of very *different kinds* of strain may operate in some additive manner to increase the probability of participation.

Before leaving Table 4.2, it is worth noting that the self-defined affected cases are different from both the affecteds and the controls. The most striking feature of this group is the large proportion who faced none of the four sources of strain. This is in keeping with much of what we reported in the earlier sections. The fact that so many of them faced two or more sources of strain, however, suggests that this may be a rather mixed category of people, so far as their overall position is concerned.

MEANS OF COPING WITH STRAIN

It would be incorrect to interpret the previous literature as suggesting that objective strain per se is predictive of hysteria. Not only are there likely to be variations in the personal qualities of individuals which make any given objective situation more or less stressful for them, it is also true that individuals differ in the facilities available to them for coping with the strain, facilities which go beyond their personalities.

Both age and level of education have been noted in previous studies as variables which seem to distinguish persons affected in somewhat similar circumstances and those who are not affected (Cantril, 1941; Johnson, 1945). The suggestion from these earlier works is that relatively young persons (adolescents or young adults) and persons of relatively low levels of education are more likely to be affected. In both cases, these characteristics are interpreted as indicative of low levels of critical ability and thus limited ability to cope with new and/or stressful experiences. Both of these suggestions are supported by our data (see Table 4.3), but the differences among our three categories of women are not large. Thus, although the affecteds were both the youngest and the most poorly educated, we cannot make much of these small differences. (We will return later

TABLE 4.3
Indications of Means of Coping with Sources of Strain Among Affecteds,
Self-Defined Affecteds, and Controls

Index of Means of Coping	Affecteds (N = 56) %	Self-Defined Affecteds (N = 17) %	Controls (N = 71) %
Are high school graduates	17.0	31.3	23.4
Worked elsewhere before Montana Mills	85.7	94.1	70.4
Overtime can be refused	46.4	58.8	45.1
It is wrong to stay home when not sick	82.1	52.9	73.2
Average age	28.2	28.9	30.1

to the fact that the self-defined affecteds were the most highly educated.)

Using the same general logic which suggests that affecteds should be younger and more poorly educated, we might also expect that a worker's critical ability might be lower if she were relatively inexperienced in the role of industrial worker. We had hoped to obtain job histories through the plant personnel department to help with this issue, but, as we have noted earlier, the information obtained from that source was very incomplete. This was particularly true of the job-history information. We thus had to fall back on a single question used in the interview which simply asked if the woman had ever worked elsewhere before coming to Montana Mills. There were sizeable differences between the affecteds and the self-defined affecteds on the one hand and the controls on the other, but these were in the direction of the *controls* having had less work experience than the others. This is clearly contradictory to expectation if one views inexperience as a factor facilitating the spread of the epidemic. Unfortunately we do not know if the previous work experience these women had was in work situations or on jobs that were at all comparable to the ones at Montana Mills. The relevance of the experience cannot confidently be interpreted, therefore. It is possible that this finding reflects an opposite dynamic from the one we originally assumed. Since those who have the most work experience are also those who are most likely to belong to the union,[3] previous work experience may have operated in such a way as to increase the workers' fear or mistrust of management. If this were the case, previous experience might be an indication that the woman was working under an added strain. However, this kind of interpretation can be seen as no more than an attempt to give some meaning to what is a clear reversal from our original expectation.

Another source of variation in the available means of coping with strain, we reasoned, would be the women's belief in the *legitimacy* of some of the means of coping which might be assumed to be open to all of them. We asked them, for instance: "Is working overtime the sort of thing you can refuse if you feel like it, or is it something that's expected of you and that's hard to refuse?"[4] There was no difference in response to this question between the affecteds and the controls, but the self-defined affecteds were more likely to say overtime could be refused. We find, therefore, that those who work the least overtime (the self-defined affecteds) more frequently believe overtime can be refused, while those who work the most overtime (the affecteds) less frequently believe this. This may, of course, be one of the reasons why the former worked less overtime than the latter—they more often refused to do so.

We also asked the women if they thought there were those in the plant who sometimes took off from work for a rest when they were not sick. We then asked them if *they* did this and if they thought there was anything wrong with doing this. About half of each of the three categories of women said they thought some people did this, and almost no one in any of the categories admitted to doing it herself. More interestingly, there were noteworthy differences among the women with respect to their evaluation of this practice. The affecteds were most likely of all to see it as wrong, and

[3] Using all subjects, the two-by-two table relating union membership and previous work experience has a Chi square of 6.87, $p < .01$ with one degree of freedom.

[4] Management had already told us that "of course" a woman could refuse overtime if she wanted to, but we suspected that at least some of the workers had come to think otherwise.

the self-defined affecteds were much less likely to view it this way. Although there is not a great difference between the affecteds and the controls in their reply to this question, the former, who have the most to cope with, are the least likely to accept this means of doing so. In fact, 54 percent of them worked a great deal of overtime *and* rejected this means of getting a rest, compared with 34 percent of the controls and only 18 percent of the self-defined affecteds.

PROBLEMS OF INTERPRETATION

The most obvious source of strain faced by the affected women was the frequent overtime they worked. They were also less likely to suggest that their supervisor would be a suitable person to turn to if they had a complaint about their job and more frequently named the union steward, thus tending to reject the most effective channel of appeal in the plant. They also more frequently rejected the idea of staying home for a rest, and they were not very likely to think overtime could be refused. These affected women had more obvious obligations at home: they more frequently worked overtime in spite of having preschool children and more frequently supplied a large proportion of the family income. Evidently they had both a great "need" to work and a "need" to stay home. Even on the job, they were more likely to see variation in output in their sections. When four of these measures of strain are combined, the affecteds are much more likely than the others to have experienced two or more of these four strains.

In rather sharp contrast with the affecteds, the self-defined affecteds seem to have both a lower level of strain and greater resources for coping with strain. Their major sources of strain were due to their contribution to the family income and the fact that many of them had been laid off. They worked less overtime than anyone and more frequently thought it was permissible to refuse overtime. They also were most likely to think it was all right to stay home to get a rest. They were most likely to see the supervisor as the person to turn to with a complaint and least likely to define the union steward as such a person, in spite of the fact that they were most likely to belong to the union. They were generally more highly educated than the others.

It is puzzling at first glance that the affecteds and the self-defined affecteds often are most clearly different from each other. It may seem reasonable that the self-defined affecteds were different from the affecteds only in the extent to which they were affected by the epidemic. One could assume simply that they were affected less dramatically and thus with respect to those characteristics which differentiate the affecteds and the controls we should expect them to fall somewhere in between. In fact, however, they are often more clearly different from the affecteds than the controls are.

The picture that emerges here of the self-defined affecteds, especially as it is contrasted with the one we get of the affecteds, is of a number of women who generally face only a limited number of strains and who have the means of coping with these strains. They seem to be very "normal" and "sensible" in many ways. They willingly acknowledge that they have some problems even when the question makes it obvious that that is what is being asked. They do not see their jobs as steady ones, which is realistic, since seasonal layoffs are to be expected. They readily admit that working overtime sometimes interferes with other things they would like to do. They are evidently willing to discuss their problems with their superiors and, if that proves ineffective, to take action on their own (e.g., staying home) to deal with the problems they face. Although this description may tend to make them appear excessively admirable, the fact remains that they seem to be rather open and realistic women who are not easily threatened and who seem to feel personally secure in their relations with others.

This raises the question, then, of why they should have been affected at all by the epidemic. In the last chapter we saw that they did accept the existence of the insect but are skeptical of people who asked for medical attention. This might indicate that they are subject to stress and its symptoms, but like to deal with it in their own way. We also note that they may have a slightly marginal position in the plant, being more likely to be laid off and less likely to be asked to do overtime. On the other hand, they keep their independence, feeling free to reject overtime and not thinking absenteeism wrong. We shall return in the following chapters to other evidence on the self-defined affecteds.

This discussion of the situation of the self-defined affecteds illuminates two related problems we faced in this chapter. Although the self-defined affecteds are usually different from the other women with respect to the more objective measures of strain they faced, much of our interpretation of their situation and many of the differences we found earlier were based on their (and the other women's) verbal assessment of their situation. We have noted that the self-defined affecteds seemed more willing than either of the other two categories of women to acknowledge difficulties when they were specifically asked about them. We have also faced the problem of deciding what role certain presumed sources of strain played in the epidemic. For instance, the self-defined affecteds were more likely than either of the other types of women to have been laid off from their jobs at Montana Mills. Does this mean that they were under more strain from this source and thus should have been more likely to become affected, or does it mean that because of this experience they would be less likely to be affected? Are there different kinds of strain which affect the women's position vis-à-vis the epidemic in different ways? We must look more closely at such issues.

THE VALIDITY OF VERBAL STATEMENTS

In several cases the evaluations our subjects made of their situations seemed to be in direct contradiction to the evident "facts" of the situation. This seemed to happen more often with the affecteds than with either of the other categories. For instance, there were many of them who consistently said (in reply to several questions) that they had a great deal of confidence in their supervisor and thought the supervisor understood their problems very well but who did not suggest they would turn to their supervisor if they had a complaint about their job. Also, the affected women, who had worked the most overtime and who most often had preschool children, less often said that overtime interfered with their being with their children than did the self-defined affected women who less frequently had worked overtime and less often had young children.

How may one interpret such findings? Did the seemingly inconsistent women "really" like their supervisor and have confidence in her? Is it simply irrelevant to their feelings of security on the job that they did not suggest going to the supervisor with a complaint? Did the affected women with small children "really" not find overtime a problem? Would it thus be incorrect to define it as a source of strain? Or is the opposite true? Were those who would not go to their supervisor with a complaint so uncomfortable in their relations with their supervisor that they could not even acknowledge this discomfort in an interview for fear of reprisal? Were the affected women with small children so caught up in the cross-pressures of their dual role of worker and mother that they could not see any solution and thus considered it useless to complain?

There is some reason, of course, to suspect that some of the answers the women gave were distorted because the interviews took place in the plant with the clear approval of management. Even though management had given their assurance that the interviews were confidential and had almost urged the workers to refuse to be interviewed if they preferred not to be, it would not be surprising if a degree of suspicion and fear remained for at least some of the women. One might even suspect that such doubts would have been greater for the affected women since they had so recently been involved in such a disruptive event in the plant.

It is difficult to *demonstrate* that they had such doubts, but the pattern of findings is at least suggestive. We have noted that a number of indices of strain have been distributed as one would expect, the affected women more frequently exhibiting them than the controls, but that some of the other indices have shown a very different pattern. We find that the two kinds of indices are quite different in content. The vast majority of the measures of strain which support the general hypothesis (that those affected were under more strain) are of a factual nature: the amount of overtime a woman worked, the number and ages of her children, the amount of the family income that comes from the woman's job, whether she has a broken marriage, and so on. On the other hand, those measures which contradict the general hypothesis are almost all measures of attitude: the work satisfaction scales, saying that "workers are treated better here," rejecting the notion that "overtime interferes with" various activities, seeing the supervisor as "easygoing," and so on. There is only one item which could possibly be called an attitude item which supports the hypothesis: saying that it is wrong to stay home for a rest when you are not sick. And here the difference between affecteds and controls is not great.

We thus find that "the facts" tend to support the hypothesis, but the verbal evaluations generally do not. In spite of indications of a number of sources of strain, the affected women do not respond very negatively about their lot. Their answers are on the whole at least as "pleasant" as those of the other women, and sometimes they are more so. Particularly, they tend to give more pleasant answers than do the self-defined affecteds. Given the consistency of this pattern within the data discussed in this chapter, and given its agreement with the pattern of the personality measures reported in the following chapter, we have chosen to emphasize the possible significance of these differences rather than simply view them as inconsistent results. We therefore feel that, in the context of the general hypothesis that strain should operate to increase the probability of a person's participating in the epidemic, the several more objective measures we have reported should be given the greater emphasis.[5] But since there is such a striking pattern of "pleasant" or "socially desirable" responses by the affecteds, isn't it reasonable to see the present findings as additional evidence of some form of "denial"? If so, is this type of denial also related to the tendency of a woman to be affected?

In order to follow up this possibility, we need to be certain that the *same* affected women did in fact say *both* that they experienced a situation we would call stressful *and* that the situation was not troublesome to them. We focused on the strain due to conflict between family and work roles to see if the affected women did actually deny the significance of role conflict when it seemed to be

---

[5] There are two items which have been interpreted as supportive of the general hypothesis but are not clearly either attitudinal or factual in nature. The affecteds more frequently say they would go to the steward with a complaint and less often mention the supervisor. They also more frequently say the women in their section vary in output. These items presumably ask for rather "factual" statements, but they were expected to reflect both the situation and the respondent's response to it. The important thing to note about these items in contrast with those attitudinal items which do not support the general strain hypothesis is that they are not *obviously* attitudinal in nature. They do not openly ask the respondent how she likes her supervisor or if she finds variation in work performance disturbing. When we ask the more obvious evaluative questions, our results with the affected women are not very different from those with the other women. But rather consistently when we do not, in effect, warn them that we want their attitudes toward something, the results are in the expected direction.

manifestly present. We found that of the 19 affected women who had worked a great deal of overtime in spite of the fact that they had small children, 15 said they "liked to work overtime." Also, 10 of them insisted that overtime did not interfere with child care. Of the 10 controls who faced the same combination of conditions, 7 and 5, respectively, gave these responses. Thus, of the 56 affecteds, 27 percent and 18 percent were deniers by this definition, compared with 10 percent and 7 percent of the 71 controls. More generally, 29 percent of the affecteds are "role-conflict deniers" (as we will call them) by one or both of these definitions, compared with 10 percent of the controls. Thus, affected women are more likely both to have this kind of conflict and to deny its significance. Such denial is therefore an important correlate of becoming affected.

DIFFERENTIATING BETWEEN "STRAIN" AND "RESISTANCE TO STRAIN"

In several cases in this chapter we have been surprised at the findings even when they were based on the more objective questions of fact. In each of these cases, we have found that the presumed source of strain, though more frequently found among the affecteds than among the controls, was also found very frequently among the self-defined affecteds. This was true with respect to the questions concerning layoffs, which women were the sole breadwinners, which supplied half or more of the family income, and which were widowed, separated, or divorced. In each case, both the affecteds and the self-defined affecteds had the significant characteristic more frequently than did the controls. In fact, in all but the question of supplying half or more of the income, the self-defined affecteds had the characteristic more often than the affecteds.

We have suggested earlier that perhaps some of our measures could be interpreted in either of two opposite directions. For instance, the threat of being laid off presumably adds a strain in that it makes the woman very much aware of the possibility of a future layoff. Because of this, we could (as we did) view it as a factor leading a woman toward becoming affected in the epidemic. On the other hand, one might argue that this very threat of possible layoff would make a woman more fully devoted to her job and less likely to become influenced by strange activities going on around her. The same kind of double argument could be presented for the three other measures. These presumably indicate the great importance of the job to the woman, and though this means she is bearing an added burden, it also means she would be more likely to be conscientious about her work and to persevere in the face of adversity.

Such "two-edged" sources of strain would presumably make it more likely that a woman would eventually succumb to the added burden of the epidemic (particularly since she would be less likely than the others to want to leave the plant), but they would be expected to have their effect later than some other sources of strain. Since the self-defined affecteds were rather likely to experience such sources of strain and to experience few of the other sources of strain, it is not unreasonable to speculate that if the epidemic had continued longer many of them might have become affected cases. Needless to say, we cannot demonstrate the validity of such speculation, but the dual nature of some of these forces is a reasonable assumption. In Chapter 7 we will present other data which add greater strength to this argument.

5

QUALITIES OF THE PERSON

In the previous chapters we have discussed participation in the epidemic as a means of communicating or expressing one's sense of tension or dissatisfaction and we have looked for sources of tension and dissatisfaction as part of our investigation of the phenomenon. It is also likely, however, that individuals will vary in the degree to which they will be responsive to such sources of strain and in their tendency to express their feelings in the particular manner found during the epidemic. That is, there will undoubtedly be persistent patterns of behavioral tendency which will in part determine the type and extent of response a woman will exhibit under such conditions. We have purposely avoided using the term "personality" in this context because our data do not permit any clinical or psychodynamic interpretations of the women's behavior, but to the extent that such persistent behavioral tendencies may be called personality, that is the subject of this chapter.

We have limited ourselves to the investigation of personal characteristics which may be viewed as rather directly relevant to the particular kind of behavior which formed the manifest content of the epidemic, namely, the hysterical contagion of illness behavior. We thus selected the following kinds of measures:

1. Since the mode of expression was through illness behavior,

the meaning of health and sickness in the person's life is directly relevant. Especially important is the question of the emotional significance of sickness, whether it is viewed in a rather matter-of-fact manner or whether it occupies a central place in the life of the person. This should give us some basis for differentiating among the women according to their readiness to respond in the manner observed during the epidemic.

2. Closely associated with this question of the emotional significance of illness is the kind of self-report a woman gives of her own state of health and her report of her recent experiences with illness.

3. Another rather direct measure of the relevance of illness to the woman is the frequency with which she acknowledges having symptoms listed for her by the interviewer.

4. Another characteristic, not necessarily directly associated with those just noted, is the degree to which a woman is anxious or tense. This should indicate a tendency to develop those symptoms which could be defined as due to "bites."

5. Finally, as a factor which would presumably predispose a woman to be influenced by the contagion, we also attempted to measure the level of suggestibility or acquiescence.

HEALTH AND SICKNESS AS AN EMOTIONALLY CHARGED AREA

Two different but related issues were raised in the interview. One was the general inclination to adopt the sick role; the other refers to the instrumental use of illness, namely, claiming illness as a reason to stay home from work to get a rest. The inclination to adopt the sick role was measured by an index derived from the work of Mechanic and Volkart (1961). It is based on the following question: During the past year would you have reported to the doctor if the following situations had arisen: (1) You had been feeling poorly for a few days; (2) You felt you had a temperature of about 100 degrees; (3) You felt you had a temperature of about 101 degrees. Each question could be scored from 0 to 3 for responses ranging from "certainly" to "very unlikely." The total scores were dichotomized so that a score of 0 to 5 indicated a high tendency to adopt the sick role and a score of 6 or higher indicated a low tendency.

We have briefly discussed the other measure in the last chapter. It was derived from the following questions: Do you think that some people here in this plant sometimes take off from work when they aren't sick, just to get a rest? Do you think that there is anything wrong with this? The answer to the second question was used as an indication of the woman's attitude toward using illness behavior as a means of improving her situation. The responses to this question were related to the scores on the measure of inclination to adopt the sick role, those having a high inclination being less likely to see such instrumental use of illness as acceptable. Though not strong, this relationship held up for all three categories of women (see Table 5.1).

TABLE 5.1
Inclination to Adopt the Sick Role and Approval of Instrumental Use of Illness Among Affecteds, Self-Defined Affecteds, and Controls

Characteristic	Affecteds (N = 56) %	Self-Defined Affecteds (N = 17) %	Controls (N = 71) %
High inclination to adopt sick role			
It is wrong to stay home when not sick	60.7	41.2	52.1
It is not wrong	8.9	29.4	15.5
Low inclination to adopt sick role			
It is wrong to stay home when not sick	21.4	11.8	21.1
It is not wrong	8.9	17.6	11.3

All three categories of women scored rather high on the measure of inclination to adopt the sick role, over two-thirds of all the women being in the "high" category. If we compute the mean of the actual scores for each category of women, the affecteds had a somewhat greater inclination to adopt the sick role. Their average score was 4.1 compared with 4.6 and 4.4 for the self-defined affecteds and controls, respectively, a low score indicating a high inclination to adopt the sick role. As we have seen before, there was greater difference in the responses on the second measure with the affecteds saying most often that it was wrong and the self-defined affecteds agreeing least often (see Table 4.3). There was also some noteworthy variation when one considers the combination of these two measures. Since such a large proportion of the affecteds saw taking off work for a rest as wrong, almost all of those affecteds who had a high inclination to adopt the sick role felt that way. Only 5 out of 39 high inclination affecteds said there was nothing wrong with such a practice. In very striking contrast, almost as many high inclination self-defined affecteds saw this as acceptable as saw it as objectionable (five versus seven). The controls fell between these two extremes. Thus, although all three categories of women seemed to define rather minor symptoms as medically relevant, they differed considerably in their willingness to cope with discomfort and fatigue without recourse to medical authorities.

It is as if there were alternative ways of dealing with the experience of symptoms. One can define them as an "official illness" and seek medical attention, or one can attempt to cope with them oneself. Although the great majority of the women said that they would seek medical attention if they had symptoms which are defined in medically acceptable terms (having a temperature or not feeling well), they differed in their ability to cope with the more everyday problems such as fatigue. Some of them evidently were unable to cope with such difficulties unless they defined them as "official illnesses," whereas others were better able to deal with them by themselves. If we view those with a high inclination to adopt the sick role as women who became disturbed by minor symptoms, it is clear that there were some who could handle such problems better than others. The affecteds had the highest proportion who were sensitive to minor symptoms but who seemed incapable of coping with them on their own, while the self-defined affecteds had the smallest proportion of such women and the highest proportion of those who were sensitive to minor symptoms but seemed quite capable of coping with them.

It is also true that a larger proportion of the self-defined affecteds with a low inclination to adopt the sick role seemed to be capable of dealing with such problems.

This pattern, of course, corresponds to the behavior of the affecteds and self-defined affecteds during the epidemic. The former, when faced with an upsetting experience, were either overwhelmed with the experience and fainted or sought medical attention. The latter, faced with what they said was a similar experience, managed to cope with it by themselves. It may very well be, therefore, that a major difference between these two categories of women was the ability of the self-defined affecteds to handle their own problems without defining them as medically relevant and without any socially conspicuous behavior.

HEALTH EXPERIENCE

In describing their own health experiences, the respondents in the three categories present a picture which is generally consistent with their attitudes toward health as discussed in the previous section. On practically all questions, the controls indicated the least experience with health problems, and in general the affecteds indicated the greatest experience (see Table 5.2). In response to the question: Have you been sick during the past several years? less than one-fourth of the controls answered "yes," compared with almost two-fifths of the affecteds. Similarly, the affecteds were more likely to say that they had had to stay home from work during the past year because they had been sick,[1] and they were more likely to acknowledge that they were taking medicine of some kind at the time of the interview. In most cases, the self-defined affecteds were more similiar to the affecteds than the controls. There is the possibility, of course, that the self-defined affecteds were really organically weaker. Look-

---

[1] It is rather striking, however, that in all three categories there are many more women who admit they had stayed home from work during the past year because of illness than admit they had been sick during the past several years. Evidently there is a general tendency to view some illnesses as sufficient to warrant staying home but not serious enough to refer to as a sickness. This presumably would be the case with menstrual difficulties, but it might also be the case with other ailments. We will return to this peculiar pattern later in the chapter.

TABLE 5.2

Health Experience and Assessment of Affecteds, Self-Defined Affecteds, and Controls

Characteristic	Affecteds (N = 56) %	Self-Defined Affecteds (N = 17) %	Controls (N = 71) %
Had been sick during the past several years	39.3	29.4	21.1
Had had to stay home because of sickness during the past year	64.3	70.6	52.1
Had had to stay home because of organic sickness only during the past year	28.6	35.3	28.4
Had been taking medicine or pills recently	41.1	47.1	28.2
Described own health as "excellent"	16.1	5.9	25.4

ing at the description of the illnesses which made them stay home, we can isolate the strictly organic cases from those due to such things as nausea, alcohol, or nervousness. If we look only at staying at home for these organic reasons, the self-defined affecteds are the highest, while the other two groups are almost identical. The self-defined affecteds are also more likely to take medication. We may infer that they are dealing realistically with health problems just as they were dealing realistically with environmental strain.

When one considers that the interview took place only two months after an epidemic which had led all of the affecteds and self-defined affecteds to feel sick and many of them to stay home and/or to take medicines, the order of these findings is not particularly surprising. In fact, the surprising thing is that so *few* of the affecteds said they had been sick. When we look at the content of the interviews, it becomes apparent that only eight of the affecteds mentioned anything about the epidemic when discussing the reasons they had had to stay home. Given the recent experience during the epidemic, it was surprising both that there were not more affecteds who said they had been sick and that there was not a greater difference between the affecteds and the self-defined affecteds. After all, the former were *known* to have been sick and had even received medical treatment, some of them in the hospital, while the latter had not been as sick during the epidemic but were about as likely to admit to a recent illness.

The findings reported in the previous section suggest that the affecteds were very likely to define minor symptoms as a legitimate reason to seek medical treatment, but they now appear to be less willing than we might have expected to admit that they actually had been sick. It may be, of course, that they defined the epidemic as something wholly outside the category of "sickness," and thus did not see it as relevant to the question we asked, but this pattern of responses suggests that there may be something unusual involved here. This is also suggested when we notice that a larger proportion of the affecteds defined their state of health as "excellent" than did the self-defined affecteds. As we would have expected, the controls were most likely to give that response.

THE OCCURRENCE OF SYMPTOMS

One set of questions which was included in the interview was taken from the Cornell Index (Weider et al., 1948). The full Index includes sets of questions about possible somatic symptoms and some additional questions directed toward more psychosomatic symptoms. For this study, a set of the psychosomatic items and a set of somatic symptoms which might be considered relevant to the experiences in the epidemic were chosen. We had expected that the affecteds would be more likely to experience such symptoms. There were 30 items in the set. The items were divided into three factors on an a priori basis independently by the two authors, each one defining his own criteria for which items belonged together. We were impressed by the degree of similarity in our sets of items, and we thus used those which we had both quite independently grouped together. In this way, 23 of the 30 items were put in three clusters. For the moment, the other seven were set aside, and we factor analyzed the three clusters. All but one of the items had factor loadings of .200 or better in the set to which we had assigned it, and all but three of them had loadings of .300 or better in the assigned set. Because of the consistency of classification and the high loadings, we decided to keep all 23 items in their respective sets.

The three factors selected in this way were seen as measuring (1) a general feeling of tension and anxiety, (2) a feeling of exhaustion, and (3) the experience of psychosomatic symptoms. The tension index consisted of nine items including such questions as "Do you often cry?" "Are you constantly keyed up and jittery?" "Do you go to pieces if you don't constantly control yourself?" The nervous exhaustion factor consisted of five items including such questions as "Does every little thing get on your nerves and wear you out?" "Must you do things very slowly in order to do them without mistakes?" "Do you often get spells of complete exhaustion or fatigue?" The third factor included nine items which asked about psychosomatic symptoms such as "When you catch a cold do you always have to go to bed?" "Do you suffer from frequent cramps in your legs?" "Are you constantly made miserable by poor health?"

There was a general tendency on the part of all women to reject the items, thus giving a very skewed distribution on all scales. More women admitted to tension and anxiety than to other kinds of symptoms, yet almost two-fifths of the women denied having any of the nine symptoms in the scale. Because of the skewed distributions, we looked at both the average scores of our three categories and the tendency of the women in each category to admit to *any* of the symptoms. Whichever we did, the same pattern emerged in all three scales, and it was quite different from what we had expected (see Table 5.3). The affecteds consistently received the lowest scores, and more of them than the others denied having any of the symptoms included in each of the scales. The greatest difference, however, was between the affecteds and the self-defined affecteds. The latter acknowledged all kinds of symptoms more readily than either the affecteds or the controls. Thus, whatever basis of comparison is used, the affecteds had the lowest scores and the self-defined affecteds had the highest scores.

This tendency to deny symptoms was so strong, both within the total sample and particularly among the affecteds, that we returned to the original set of 30 items and raised the basic question of the extent of this denial pattern using the total set. We again find the

TABLE 5.3
*Admission of Any of the Symptoms on Three Scales from the Cornell
Medical Inventory Among Affecteds, Self-Defined Affecteds, and Controls*

Scale	Affecteds (N = 56) %	Self-Defined Affecteds (N = 17) %	Controls (N = 71) %
Tension and anxiety (9 items)	55.4	88.2	60.6
Nervous exhaustion (5 items)	17.9	29.4	28.2
Psychosomatic symptoms (9 items)	39.3	64.7	47.9

most striking difference between the affecteds and the self-defined
affecteds rather than between the affecteds and the controls. Thirty-
one percent of the affecteds and 21 percent of the controls denied all
30 symptoms, but none of the self-defined affecteds did so. There is
thus a continuing pattern: the affecteds were least capable of coping
with minor symptoms, they had been sick rather often (even more
often than they admitted) but described their state of health rather
favorably, and they denied having a whole series of symptoms more
often than the other women. The self-defined affecteds, in contrast,
were best able to cope with minor symptoms, they had been sick
about as often but admitted that their state of health was less than
excellent, and they readily acknowledged symptoms. There is a strong
suggestion here that many of the affecteds were what could be
called "false lows" in that their low symptom scores were probably
due to their unwillingness to admit to health problems. In contrast,
the self-defined affecteds did not seem to mind such an admission at
all. It is possible, therefore, that these findings indicate a more general tendency on the part of the affecteds to deny problems and for
the self-defined affecteds to be willing to admit to them. We will return to this theme later in the chapter.

ANXIETY AND REPRESSION

Closely related to some of the items in the symptom scales was an
index taken from the Minnesota Multiphasic Inventory. Ten items
were selected from the "A and R" scale devised by Welsh to measure

anxiety and repression (Welsh & Dahlstrom, 1956). The index was again subjected to factor analysis, and factor loadings were all .297 or higher. Some of the items used were "I find it hard to keep my mind on a task or job"; "I am easily embarrassed"; "People often disappoint me." We had originally expected the affecteds to score higher than either of the other categories on this scale. But again the same pattern occurred. The affecteds were most likely to reject all items, but about two-fifths of both the affecteds (41.1 percent) *and* the controls (39.4 percent) rejected all 10 items while only 1 of the 17 self-defined affecteds (5.9 percent) did so. Thus, again the affecteds tended to deny difficulties while the self-defined affecteds were most willing to admit to them. Before discussing this persistent pattern, we will present the findings from our final measure of personal characteristics.

ACQUIESCENCE

We had included a simple measure of acquiescence in the interview schedule because we had assumed that social influence had played an important part in the epidemic and it seemed likely that if the women varied in acquiescence, the more acquiescent would be most susceptible to social influence. The measure was not very adequate for the purposes for which it was intended, but it proved to be more useful than we had expected. It consisted of four pairs of attitude items, each pair including two items which were very similar in wording but opposite in meaning; for instance: All in all, it would have been better if so many factories had not come into this area, and All in all, it is good for our area that so much new industry has been built here. The logic of the measure was that agreement with both statements of a pair indicated acquiescence or suggestibility. Although there were four pairs, no one agreed with all eight items, and only a fourth of the women agreed with two or three of the four pairs.[2]

[2] It is fortunate that so few women gave acquiescent responses. If this had been a common tendency, there would have been reason to doubt the validity of the whole interview, or at least those aspects which asked for opinions. Even as it is, the degree of presumed distortion of the answers of some of the women, especially the affecteds, presents serious problems of interpretation. If there had been even more suggestion of distortion, the problems would have been impossible to cope with.

The affecteds were most likely to agree with one or more such pairs of items. Seventy-one percent of them did so, compared with 47 percent of the self-defined affecteds and 57 percent of the controls. The fact that the affecteds were most acquiescent fits into the original expectation, using this measure as an index of some general characteristic of suggestibility.

However, it is perhaps even more important to notice that the stronger tendency toward agreement with the items on the part of the affecteds is in direct contrast to their tendency to say "no" to the symptom questions. Also, the self-defined affecteds, who were most likely to say "yes" to the symptom questions, were least likely to do so in response to these questions. We have some greater confidence, therefore, that the denial of symptoms by the affecteds was not simply a function of a general tendency to respond negatively to our questions, nor was the self-defined affecteds' acceptance of symptoms simply a function of a tendency to respond positively. Again, we reach the thin dividing line between disregarding the manifest content of responses and distrust of the reliability of the whole interviewing technique. In the last chapter we discussed the direct and indirect expression of confidence in management; in this chapter we interpret answers as "denial" and "acquiescence." We realize that a respondent in an interview, especially a worker interviewed in a factory, may adapt her answers to the appropriateness of the conditions. However, the differences which we are investigating between the groups remain the same whether we interpret them as conscious distortion or not. Thus the affecteds are women who claim not to have had any symptoms and who accept plausible statements even if they are contradictory. Whether they are women who convince themselves to believe in these attitudes or whether they feel they have to act this way in the mildly threatening situation which the interview may have represented, actually makes little difference. In contrast to the other women the affecteds are likely to present this pattern of responses, and in turn, this pattern makes sense if we consider their behavior in the epidemic. The same reasoning applies to the answers of the other groups. We therefore must return to the pattern of responses on health-related issues and attempt to understand it.

EVIDENCE OF DENIAL

In many respects, our findings with regard to the personal character-istics of the women we interviewed conflicted with the expectations we had. Although we did find that the affecteds appeared to be less capable of coping with minor health problems, when they were asked about specific symptoms, they were more likely than any of the women to deny all of the symptoms listed. They also refused to agree with the MMPI items designed to measure anxiety and repression. This raises a very basic question: Should we accept the symptom measure as it was originally intended and thus conclude that the affecteds experienced fewer symptoms than the others, or should we reject the manifest content of our finding and thus emphasize the *denial* rather than the lack of symptoms? We have chosen to do the latter, but we need to defend this decision.

The impression of the affecteds which we derive from this set of findings is one of women who tend to resist admitting to physical problems which require attention but who are likely to define such problems as quite serious and as requiring expert attention once they admit to them. In contrast, the self-defined affecteds appear to be women who readily admit to the experience of physical problems but who are generally capable of dealing with them. It does not seem possible to determine from these data whether the one or the other category of women "actually" had experienced more symptoms. The interpretation we suggest would assume that all of the women prob-ably experienced some of the symptoms listed, but that the important differences were the ease and the manner in which such symptoms were acknowledged and dealt with. Let us see how the data lend themselves to this interpretation.

The measure of the inclination to adopt the sick role indicates the willingness of the women to seek medical treatment *if* particular symptoms are recognized, and we find that there is little variation among the three categories of women on this measure. It does not, of course, measure the frequency with which the women actually did have such symptoms, but only their readiness to get medical attention if they should have them. The average scores on this measure suggest that the three categories of women were about equally likely to seek medical aid. It will be recalled, however, that the total score was made up of three parts. On the two questions which asked if the woman would go to the doctor if she had a temperature, there were very small differences among the responses given by the three categories of women. In neither case was there more than an 8 percent variation in the percentages of the women in the three categories who said they "certainly" or "probably" would go to the doctor. In striking contrast, when asked if they would go to the doctor if they had been "feeling poorly for a few days," 57.1 percent of the affecteds, 41.2 percent of the self-defined affecteds, and 32.4 percent of the controls gave one of these two replies. Thus, the less tangible and less easily diagnosed the symptom, the more likely the affecteds were to deviate in the direction of seeking medical treatment.

This is consistent with the affecteds' unwillingness to feign illness as a means of coping with fatigue on the job. Whether because of a more rigid morality or because of a special orientation toward health and sickness, they seemed to require that they be "really" sick before leaving work, and they seemed also to require that their sickness be officially recognized and dealt with by a doctor. There thus seemed to be a greater tendency for the affecteds to seek medical assistance for relatively limited and vague symptoms once they acknowledged their presence.

It is an interesting general finding, reported in Table 5.2, that all three categories of women were more likely to say they had stayed home during the past year for sickness than they were to admit they had been sick during the last several years. Evidently there are kinds of illnesses which women are willing to define as sufficiently serious to warrant staying home but are not sufficiently serious to call sickness in the more general sense. This seems reasonable, particularly among women, since minor problems associated with the menstrual cycle often require them to miss work. It may be of greater importance, however, to note that the difference in response to these two questions was smallest among the affecteds and greatest among the self-defined affecteds. Although more affecteds than self-defined affecteds said they had been sick, more self-defined affecteds said they had stayed home. (The controls were lowest on both measures.) This relationship becomes more pointed if we eliminate staying home because of possible functional reasons and concentrate on the absentee-ism for illnesses which the respondents described as purely organic. Fewer of the affected women reported having stayed home for these reasons than said they had felt sick. The other two groups are almost identical and report slightly more absenteeism for these reasons than they report being ill. This lower absenteeism among the affecteds indicates again their inability to cope with illness, as with other stresses. The self-defined affecteds, by the same token, cope as well as the controls, although they seem objectively to have had more health problems.

Most importantly, of course, the affecteds were most likely to deny having any of the 30 symptoms suggested to them in the inter-view. This pattern of denial also carried over to the 10 items from the MMPI, all of which are in the form of statements to the effect that "something is wrong with me." There is thus an indication that many of these women wished to deny that anything was wrong with them. And, as we have noted, the exact opposite was true of the self-defined affecteds. None of them denied all of the symptoms, and only one rejected all of the MMPI items.

We have also seen that these two types of women responded very differently to the items in our acquiescence measure. The af-fecteds were more likely than any of the others to say "yes" to two contradictory items, and the self-defined affecteds were least likely to do so. The affecteds thus not only did not seem to have a general tendency to say "no," they seemed to be rather consistent in giving "agreeable" or "socially desirable" responses.

Again we must stress that we cannot say the affecteds "really" did have as many of the symptoms as the self-defined affecteds. We can only suggest that it is unlikely that many women could honestly say they had none of these symptoms and that complete denial of them probably tells us something about the personal characteristics of the woman beyond her physical state of health. This same kind of logic is used, for instance, in defining a "denial" measure on the MMPI, and it has been used by others in discussions of "social de-sirability" kinds of response patterns (Welsh & Dahlstrom, 1956; Edwards, 1967; Crowne & Marlowe, 1964). Also, we found much less denial when we used the same symptom list in a similar factory in the same area (see the Appendix).

Finally, the interpretation of the denial of symptoms as indicative of a self-protective tendency on the part of the affecteds is also strengthened by the fact that all four of the affecteds who told us in the interview that they had not "really" been affected cases denied all 30 of the symptoms. Certainly for these four women at least there seems to be good reason to say that their responses involved denial.

The overall weight of the data, therefore, seems to point to a modal tendency on the part of the affecteds to define even vague and minor symptoms as evidence of sickness but to resist the admission of symptoms. There is also a modal tendency for the self-defined affecteds to acknowledge the experience of symptoms but to be willing (and presumably able) to cope with minor difficulties without requiring medical assistance. The controls were in many respects more like the affecteds, although they usually fall between the other two categories on the relevant measures. Given this pattern of findings, one can appreciate why it might have been possible for the affecteds and the self-defined affecteds both to have experienced symptoms during the epidemic with only the affecteds coming to the attention of the doctor. These data are less useful in distinguishing between these two categories and the controls. This is another way of saying that these data help us to understand differences in response to the experience of symptoms, but they do not help us very much to understand why some women experienced symptoms and others did not. As we have seen in the last chapter, this depends partly on the distribution of sources of strain. However, even more important is the network of social relations, to be discussed in Chapter 6.

6

THE SOCIAL CONTEXT
OF CONTAGION

Thus far in our analysis we have only examined the relevance of the characteristics of the women as individuals. No attempt has been made to investigate the importance of the fact that this epidemic occurred in a work situation which permitted the workers to interact with each other to a considerable extent. The earlier analysis has indicated that knowledge of the women as individuals aids our understanding of the epidemic in that there is evidence that those who were in some sense "more susceptible" were in fact more likely to be affected by the "bug." However, if we are to use the word "contagion" in this context, we must face the problem of how the phenomenon in question "contaged" or spread among the women. What was the medium of transmission? What pattern of dissemination can be discerned?

Our basic assumption in carrying out the present analysis was that the social relations among the women were probably relevant to their response during the epidemic. However, as we noted in Chapter 2, we were less than certain about the nature of this relevance. There seemed to be bases for different kinds of expectations. Thus, we approached the analysis with a question rather than a clearly derived hypothesis. Our central question was: What relevance does a woman's position in a network of social relations have for predicting whether she will or will not exhibit the hysterical symptoms which spread through a population?

THREE CONCEPTUALIZATIONS

There seemed to be some basis for three very different specific expectations: those who were linked together in a network of social relations should be more likely to be affected; those who were outside the network of social relations should be more likely to be affected; and the pattern of social relations should be irrelevant to the spread of the hysterical symptoms. We will refer to these under the following headings: "group influence," "social isolation," and "crowd response." The basis for each of these expectations will be considered first, after which we will examine the data in light of these three expectations.[1]

GROUP INFLUENCE

There is a considerable body of literature which can be used to generate the prediction that the contagion should follow channels of interpersonal ties. The many studies of the adoption of innovations, especially those of farming innovations, indicate that social relations among adopters are often found, and that once informal leaders adopt a new practice, it is likely to be adopted by others (Lionberger, 1953; Barnett, 1953). Even more closely analogous to the present case is the study by Coleman, Katz, and Menzel (1957) of the diffusion of the use of a new drug among physicians. In that study it was found that the adoption of the drug followed sociometric channels, and that members of social cliques were likely to adopt the drug at about the same time. There is a body of experimental literature which might also lead to the expectation that sociometric channels would facilitate diffusion. The classical experiments of Sherif

[1] Some of this material was published earlier (Kerckhoff, Back, & Miller, 1965). The analysis to be presented here goes beyond that earlier publication in a number of ways, but the theoretical underpinning as well as the general outcome of the analysis in relation to the theory is the same. We are grateful to the editor of *Sociometry* for permission to use those portions of this material which were previously published.

(1935) and Asch (1956), and the numerous experimental variations and theoretical interpretations of them (Festinger, 1950), all
indicate that both perception and behavior can be made to conform
to group definitions when the other members of the group define
the situation consistently.

There is thus considerable basis for expecting that interpersonal
relations will be highly relevant to dissemination of a new pattern
of behavior in a population. However, one may well question whether
the literature just cited is, in fact, germane to our interests. The
studies of the adoption of innovations deal with the spread of a behavior pattern which is positively related to a central value in the
population studied. Farmers certainly value abundant crops and high
quality produce, and the studies of innovation in farming deal with
adoption of practices which are supposed to serve these ends. The
doctors studied by Coleman and his associates value effective drugs
as aids in their professional duties; and the drug whose adoption was
studied was, in fact, an effective drug. On the other hand, it could
hardly be argued that the behavior pattern whose spread we are
studying was valuable in the same sense. However it is viewed, one
must acknowledge that it was dysfunctional in the specific situation
in which it was observed. Not only did the hysteria disrupt the operations of the plant and thus lead to losses for the company, it also
led to lost work time for the affected persons and thus reduced their
income for the period in question, not to mention the emotional costs
involved. It is possible that the dissemination of *any* behavior pattern within a population follows the same channels, but the differences in the kinds of behavior studied in the earlier investigations
and the behavior found in the present situation makes such an assumption at least questionable.

The experimental studies noted above, although they often deal
with bizarre and dysfunctional behavior (such as misperceiving the
relative length of two lines), also provide some reason to doubt the
"group influence" expectation in the present situation. These experiments indicate that *if* there is consistent behavior on the part of the
members of the group, the naive subject will tend to adopt that behavior as his own, even though it might ordinarily be rejected by
him. They also indicate that if there is *not* consistent behavior by
the group members, the naive subject is much less likely to adopt
the unusual behavior. In the plant we studied the majority of the

workers never exhibited the hysterical symptoms. Thus, there were always social reference points for those who might have tended to resist the contagion. Also, since the behavior in question was not only dysfunctional but also rather bizarre, it seems unlikely that we could assume that any social grouping had developed a facilitative "norm" regarding such behavior in advance of the initiation of the contagion. It is much more likely that most people in the plant would have defined the behavior as at least "unusual" and "undesirable." If a facilitative norm functioned at all, it must have evolved during the period of the contagion, and this would certainly take time and would probably have had to occur in the face of some social resistance. Finally, and perhaps most importantly, the relevance of this body of experimental literature may be questioned because it is based on *ad hoc* groups in which prior social relations had not been formed, whereas the central focus of our inquiry is the importance of such previously established social relations.

SOCIAL ISOLATION

Given the fact that only a minority exhibited the hysterical symptoms, it seems likely that the average worker in the factory would have some significant social contacts with persons who did not exhibit hysterical symptoms and who rejected the seriousness of the threat. This would not be true, however, for the person who was a social isolate. The isolate would not have access to such social reference points; at least they would not be as significant to him. Although isolates might vary in the degree to which they would be personally susceptible to the effects of contagion, as a category they would seem to be more likely to be susceptible than would those who are socially integrated.

The converse of this can also be argued. At least since the work of McDougall (1920, pp. 68–70), it has been noted that the structure of groups tends to inhibit the spread of contagion among its members. If this is so, socially integrated women would be *less* likely to be susceptible. The same expectation would be reasonable if we interpret the hysterical behavior as an attention-getting device, isolates being seen as more in need of such social response than those with prior social ties. Finally, it has been noted by many students of collective behavior that the outcast, the person with little investment in the social system, is more likely to take part in all forms of collective behavior. This kind of person has been defined either in terms of his social position or his personal degree of "social adequacy," but in both cases the point is made that a lack of full integration into the network of social relations increases the tendency for a person to become a participant in collective behavior (Turner & Killian, 1957; Lang & Lang, 1961). For all these reasons, then, we might expect isolates to exhibit the hysterical symptoms more frequently than those who are socially integrated.

CROWD RESPONSE

A third expectation is also possible from the literature on collective behavior, namely, that social relationships would have no relevance to the spread of the contagion. There is a common belief with respect to crowd behavior, substantiated by participants' reports, that contagion is often effective for persons who are not at all related to others in the crowd and who are not particularly concerned with the issue central to the crowd action (Turner & Killian, 1957, pp. 106–110). The "magic" of contagion has been described and analyzed by many, but our knowledge remains less than adequate. Yet, it is very easy to find references to the unstructured nature of contagion, especially hysterical contagion, within a population. Perhaps this passage from Lang and Lang (1961, p. 227) says it as well as any:

The kind of identification that occurs in hysteria, Freud maintains, "may arise with every new perception of a common quality shared with some other person who is not an object of the sexual instinct. The more important this common quality is, the more successful may this partial identification become, and it may thus represent the beginning of a new tie." *The identification does not presuppose any prior emotional or sympathetic relationship; it results directly from the definition of the situation of those exhibiting the behavior as analogous to one's own.*

If this is the case, we might expect that the simple fact that all of those affected by the hysteria in the plant were fellow workers, and the great majority of them women, would be enough basis for the kind of identification just referred to. There would thus be no reason to expect that previously established social relations would be at all relevant to the spread of the symptoms.

We thus have three theoretical positions, each based on literature that is presumably relevant, and each calling for a different
kind of relationship between sociometric position and the probability
of being affected by the spread of hysterical contagion. Each is
plausible in its own way, but clearly all three cannot be correct in
any simple fashion. We believe that all three *are* correct to some
extent, but the data must be examined with some care before such
a statement can be justified.

A FIRST APPROXIMATION

In keeping with the usual definition of "social relationship" used in
sociometric literature, we asked the women who their three best
friends were within the plant. Our original analysis focused on this
type of relationship. However, we also questioned the women about
other relationships they had with their fellow workers. We asked
them if they came to work with others, usually in car pools, and
if they usually took their lunch breaks with particular workers. We
asked them whom they would turn to for help if they had a personal
problem in the plant, and who they thought might turn to them
under such circumstances. We asked who they thought was the best
worker in their section. Finally, we asked them to name the people
with whom they routinely came in contact during their working
hours—their supervisor, their steward, the person who gave them their
work, the one who picked it up, and so on. We thus had not only
the usual picture of a network of friendship relationships to work
with but also a picture of practically the whole network of social
relations these women had with others in the plant.

We approached these data in stages. Our first analysis was of the
friendship data only. We then added to these the names given as
ones they might turn to or who might turn to them for help on a
personal problem. (We called these confidantes.) Then we added
the names of lunch associates, car pool members, best workers and
work associates, in that order. At each point, we computed a number
of indexes to give us some idea of the relative merits of the three
theoretical positions just discussed.

It was possible, of course, for a woman to name the same person
in all of these categories. To avoid giving undue weight to such in-

dividuals in the indexes of social relations, we counted such a relationship only once, the first time the name appeared in the analysis. Thus, as we moved from the more intimate friendship relationships to the less intimate work relationships, we added only those names which had not appeared earlier. We expected any tendency for these social relations to be related to participation in the epidemic, therefore, to become less pronounced as we added what were presumably progressively less significant names to our lists. We have recorded here only the two end points of the analysis: the summary data using friendship choices only and the summary data using all of the different kinds of choices.[2]

The summary data in Table 6.1 provide us with a basis for evaluating the three theoretical perspectives. If we simply ask which of the three predictions comes closest to the mark, and if we base our evaluation on the overall differences among the three categories of women, the prediction based on the "group influence" argument seems to be the best. First, there are fewer isolates among the affected women than among either of the other two categories when friendship choices are used as the basis for measurement. This is also related to the fact that the affecteds are chosen as friends more often on the average than are the other women: 1.39 times each (i.e., 56 affecteds received 78 choices) versus 1.07 for controls and .95 for self-defined affecteds. Even when all bases for choice are considered, the affected women are chosen somewhat more frequently than the controls (2.71 versus 2.44 times each), and they are chosen much more frequently than the self-defined affecteds (1.71 times each on the average). Thus, there is certainly no general tendency for the

2 We should also note that, although it was at least theoretically possible for our subjects to choose *any* of the women in the sample (as well as those outside the sample), the choices were so heavily concentrated within the categories we had defined, it is not necessary to present all of the data on all of the categories at this time. Both the Negroes within the dressmaking area of the plant and the subjects who worked outside this area tended to choose and be chosen by only each other rather than choosing and being chosen by those women in the more critical portion of our sample. A very limited number of contacts were reported with the Negroes and with those outside the big room which housed the dressmaking departments, but these were proportionally so insignificant as to make it possible to leave them out of the present discussion completely. This fact, of course, increased our confidence in the original decision to concentrate on the three categories of women within the big room.

TABLE 6.1
Sociometric Status of Affecteds, Self-Defined Affecteds, and Controls

Characteristic	Friendship Choices Only			All Choices		
	Affecteds	Self-Defined Affecteds	Controls	Affecteds	Self-Defined Affecteds	Controls
Percentage who are isolates	28.6(56)	35.3(17)	32.4(71)	12.5(56)	11.8(17)	12.7(71)
Percentage of those chosen who are in the sample	50.9(193)	39.6(53)	34.0(203)	41.8(373)	36.4(132)	30.3(495)
Percentage of within-sample choices directed toward affecteds	55.4(83)	42.9(21)	29.0(69)	50.6(156)	43.8(48)	32.0(147)
Percentage of within-sample choices directed toward self-defined affecteds	8.4(83)	28.6(21)	4.3(69)	7.7(156)	18.8(48)	5.4(147)
Percentage of within-sample choices directed toward controls	33.7(83)	28.6(21)	62.3(69)	39.7(156)	37.5(48)	57.1(147)
Percentage of choices received from affecteds	59.0(78)	43.7(16)	34.6(78)	51.3(152)	37.9(29)	34.7(176)
Percentage of choices received from self-defined affecteds	11.5(78)	37.5(16)	7.7(78)	13.8(152)	31.0(29)	10.2(176)
Percentage of choices received from controls	26.9(78)	18.8(16)	57.7(78)	31.6(152)	27.6(29)	49.4(176)
Percentage chosen by affecteds only	32.1(56)	23.5(17)	14.1(71)	28.6(56)	23.5(17)	15.5(71)
Percentage chosen by controls only	7.1(56)	5.9(17)	1.4(71)	5.4(56)	11.8(17)	2.8(71)
Percentage chosen by self-defined affecteds only	7.1(56)	17.6(17)	35.2(71)	5.4(56)	17.6(17)	22.5(71)
Percentage of mutual choices with affecteds	60.5(43)	50.0(10)	33.3(33)	63.0(81)	35.0(20)	23.9(73)
Percentage of mutual choices with self-defined affecteds	11.6(43)	20.0(10)	9.1(33)	9.9(81)	30.0(20)	9.9(73)
Percentage of mutual choices with controls	25.6(43)	30.0(10)	57.6(33)	25.9(81)	35.0(20)	60.6(73)

NOTE: The frequency on which each percentage is based is noted in parentheses. To the extent that the percentages of any given kind do not total 100.00 percent, the remaining contacts were with Negroes or those outside the dressmaking departments. Such outside contacts never exceeded 8.0 percent of the total, and in only two cases did they exceed 5.0 percent of the total. Only three contacts between Negroes and whites were recorded. All three were nonfriendship choices of whites by Negroes, two of controls and one of a self-defined affected.

affected women to be socially ostracized, and there may even be a limited positive relationship between sociometric position and being affected.

More important, we find that the links between affected women and *other* affected women are more common than between affected women and either of the other categories. The affecteds direct a higher proportion of their choices to other affecteds than do the other two groups of women.[3] They also receive a greater proportion of their choices from other affecteds than do the women in the other two groups. Affecteds are much more likely than the other women to be chosen solely by other affecteds. Finally, a greater proportion of the mutual choices participated in by the affecteds are with other affecteds.[4] There is thus considerable evidence that the affected women are more closely linked to each other than they are to the other women.

We were somewhat surprised to discover that the same kind of network of relationships is noticeable for both of the other categories as well. By the process of exclusion, if a choice within the sample is not directed toward an affected woman, it must be directed toward a self-defined affected woman or a control. The distribution of choices between these two categories is hardly random, however. Two char-

[3] In our original publication of these data, we reported the proportions of the *total* number of friendship choices which were directed to affected and nonaffected women (Kerckhoff, Back, & Miller, 1965, p. 10). We have chosen to report the proportion of choices within the sample here, however, because the affected women tended, on the average, to direct a somewhat higher proportion of their choices to other women in the sample. As reported in Table 6.1, half of their friendship choices were of women in the sample in contrast to less than two-fifths of the choices of the women in the other two categories. We feared, therefore, that presenting the proportions of the total choices which were directed to the various groups of women in our sample might give an exaggerated view of the differences involved. As a comparison of the original report and the tables in this chapter will indicate, however, the pattern of results is very similar whichever statistic is used.

[4] We also computed other indexes of social linkages, all of which led to the same picture as those reported in the table. For instance, we asked if the affected women were more likely than the others to have *some* relationship with affecteds. The proportion of affecteds who chose or were chosen by at least one other affected was about twice the proportion of controls who chose or were chosen by an affected. Thus, whether we ask about the overall proportion of *choices* which involve affecteds with each other or the proportion of affected *women* who are linked together, the result is the same: the affecteds are more closely tied together than they are with the other women.

acteristics of the pattern of choices are noteworthy. First, both the
self-defined affecteds and the controls direct a greater than chance
proportion of their choices within their own category. The self-
defined affecteds direct as many of their friendship choices within
their own category as they direct toward controls, and they receive
twice as many friendship choices from other members of their category as they receive from controls. The ratios for controls are fourteen
to one and seven to one. If choices by these two categories of women
were directed randomly, one would expect about four times as many
choices in both categories to be directed toward or received from
controls as directed toward or received from self-defined affecteds
because the categories are so different in size. Therefore, the actual
pattern deviates in both cases in the direction of a much greater
proportion of within-category choices than would be expected. There
is thus a tendency for *all three categories* of women to choose within
their own category more frequently than they choose women in the
other categories. All three categories have some of the characteristics
of a *group,* therefore, even though clear-cut group boundaries are certainly not evident.

A second fact regarding the self-defined affecteds is also worth
noting: they are much more clearly linked with the affecteds than
with the controls. Again, using a random model for comparison, we
would expect them to have somewhat fewer contacts with affecteds
than with controls since there are more of the latter than the former
with whom they have a potential for a relationship. Whatever measure is used, however, the self-defined affecteds clearly deviate from
this model in the direction of being more closely linked to affecteds
than to controls. This is especially evident in the data on friendship
choices. Thus, the self-defined affecteds exhibit both an internal
structure of relationships with each other and a pattern of greater
linkage with the affecteds than with the controls.

In sum, all of the discussion thus far leads to the conclusion
that, of the three theoretical positions, the "group influence" position
is the most promising. This is clearly true when the friendship choices
are used as a basis for evaluation. It is even true when *all* known
social relations are considered, even those which are presumably of
a rather low level of personal significance. It must be noted, however, that as we move from friendship to work relations, the pattern

becomes less obvious. All the proportions presented in the right-hand portion of Table 6.1 still deviate from a random pattern in the direction of within-category cohesion, but the deviation is not as extreme as in the left-hand portion of the table. Each successive, and less intimate, form of relationship reduced the deviation to some extent, but this was particularly true when work associates (the least intimate category) were included. This would lead us to conclude that the *kind* of relationship is of considerable importance in understanding such an epidemic. As we will see later in the chapter, however, if we were to limit ourselves completely to friendship choices, there would be a number of gaps in our understanding, gaps which may be filled, at least in part, by consideration of the other kinds of relationship.

A SEQUENTIAL PERSPECTIVE

It is fortunately possible to go beyond this initial view of within-category choice tendencies. From the records of the epidemic it was possible not only to determine who had come to the attention of the medical authorities but also approximately when they had done so. It will be remembered that the vast majority of the cases were reported on two successive days. Six of our 56 first-shift affected white women came to the attention of the medical authorities before these two big days, however, and 4 did so after the two big days. All but 1 of the 6 early cases were seen on the day before the first big day. The 4 last cases were distributed over three days following the two big days of the epidemic. Our initial analysis, then, simply differentiated among the affected women according to whether they had been seen "Before" the two big days, on "Day One," "Day Two," or "After" the two big days.[5]

[5] In the earlier publication using these data we classified the women according to when they were supposed to have been affected rather than when they came to the attention of the authorities. Since further analysis indicated the importance of the self-defined affected category, we considered the possibility that a distinction should be made between "being affected" and "acknowledging being affected." Going to the doctor was an admission that something was wrong; the initial sense that something was wrong (in most cases, as a result of being "bitten") might have occurred earlier, but its importance was not clearly acknowledged to others until the time of the medical visit. In terms of social influence, both phenomena might be significant, at least if the feel-

Table 6.2 presents the same measures as presented in Table 6.1 but only for the 56 affected cases classified according to when they came to the attention of the medical authorities. Although the numbers of cases in the "Before" and the "After" categories are quite small and the data must thus be assessed with considerable caution, these two categories of affected cases are rather clearly different from those affected on the two big days of the epidemic. The most striking difference is that 5 of the 6 women in the "Before" period are social isolates when friendship choices are used as the basis of analysis. Only 1 of the 6 is mentioned as a friend by *anyone* in our sample. This is made even more striking when we note that these 6 women are mentioned with considerable frequency when other bases for choice are used. In fact, they are chosen more frequently on a "nonfriendship" basis than are the women in any of the other categories. The average number of times chosen on all bases is 2.17, 3.54, 2.00, and 2.54 for the four categories. Thus, they are not completely isolated in the plant; they just aren't very well liked.

Both of the two big days show great evidence of choosing within the affected category. The pattern noted in Table 6.1 is accentuated during either or both of these two days on all of the measures, and this is most striking when friendship choices are the basis for analysis.[6]

---

ing were reported to one's fellow workers before the medical visit was made. Particularly in the early stages, some women permitted a time lag between "being affected" and "acknowledging being affected." Evidently the significance of "being affected" increased as others reported symptoms. Because of the lag in these early cases, therefore, we have chosen here to emphasize the importance of "acknowledging being affected" as the socially significant phenomenon in the spread of the epidemic. As a comparison between the data in the original report and those presented in Table 6.2 of this chapter will indicate, there is a greater difference between those who acknowledged being affected in the early stages of the epidemic (in the "Before" period) and those who did so later than there is between those who were affected in the early stages and those who were affected later.

[6] Our original impression was that the pattern of internal choices increased from "Before" to "Day One" to "Day Two" (Kerckhoff, Back, & Miller, 1965, p. 12). However, this original pattern seems to have been a function of the fact that we had included in the "Before" period people who actually saw the doctor on "Day One." They claimed to have been affected on the day before, but did not get to the doctor until "Day One." The change in definition of time affected, then, led to an accentuation of the isolated position of the "Before" period women and an increase in the social links of the "Day One" women with other affecteds.

TABLE 6.2
Sociometric Status of Affected Cases by Time Affected

Characteristic	Friendship Choices Only				All Choices			
	Before	Day One	Day Two	After	Before	Day One	Day Two	After
Percentage of isolates	83.3(6)	20.8(24)	22.7(22)	25.0(4)	16.7(6)	12.5(24)	13.6(22)	00.0(4)
Percentage of choices within sample	57.9(19)	58.6(70)	41.3(63)	27.3(11)	43.6(39)	49.7(149)	37.0(146)	28.2(39)
Percentage of choices of affecteds	45.5(11)	61.0(41)	53.6(28)	33.3(3)	47.1(17)	55.4(74)	50.0(54)	27.3(11)
Percentage of choices of self-defined affecteds	9.1(11)	7.3(41)	10.7(28)	00.0(3)	5.9(17)	5.4(74)	9.3(54)	18.2(11)
Percentage of choices of controls	45.5(11)	31.7(41)	28.6(28)	66.7(3)	47.1(17)	37.8(74)	37.0(54)	54.5(11)
Percentage of choices from affecteds	00.0(2)	61.0(41)	66.7(30)	20.0(5)	69.2(13)	47.1(85)	56.8(44)	30.0(10)
Percentage of choices from self-defined affecteds	50.0(2)	12.2(41)	10.0(30)	00.0(5)	15.4(13)	11.8(85)	13.6(44)	30.0(10)
Percentage of choices from controls	50.0(2)	26.7(41)	16.7(30)	80.0(5)	15.4(13)	37.6(85)	25.0(44)	40.0(10)
Percentage chosen by self-defined affecteds only	00.0(6)	8.3(24)	9.1(22)	00.0(4)	00.0(6)	4.2(24)	9.1(22)	00.0(4)
Percentage chosen by controls only	00.0(6)	4.2(24)	4.5(22)	50.0(4)	00.0(6)	4.2(24)	4.5(22)	25.0(4)
Percentage of mutuals with affecteds	00.0(2)	72.7(22)	58.8(17)	00.0(2)	70.0(10)	65.7(35)	61.3(31)	40.0(5)
Percentage of mutuals with self-defined affecteds	50.0(2)	9.1(22)	11.8(17)	00.0(2)	10.0(10)	8.6(35)	9.7(31)	20.0(5)
Percentage of mutuals with controls	50.0(2)	18.2(22)	23.5(17)	100.0(2)	20.0(10)	25.7(35)	25.8(31)	40.0(5)

NOTE: The frequency on which each percentage is based is noted in parentheses. To the extent the percentages of any given kind do not total 100.00 percent, the remaining contacts were with Negroes or those outside the dressmaking departments. Such outside contacts never exceeded 8.0 percent of the total, and in only two cases did they exceed 5.0 percent of the total. Only three contacts between Negroes and whites were recorded. All three were nonfriendship choices of whites by Negroes, two of controls and one of a self-defined affected.

The women affected during these two big days, therefore, are even more clearly related to each other than are the affected women as a total category.

Since the number of women in the "After" category is so very small, one can comment on a pattern of choices only with considerable hesitation. However, the social position of these four women seems to be so different from those affected during the two big days as to warrant some cautious comment. Only 1 of their 3 friendship choices and only 3 of their 11 choices of any kind directed toward women in the sample are directed toward other affected women. Only 1 of the 5 friendship choices and only 3 of the 10 choices of any kind which they receive come from affected women. None of them is linked only with other affected women, and none of them has a mutual friendship choice with an affected woman. Similarly, whatever measure is used, these women are much more frequently linked with the controls than are the other affected women. Perhaps equally noteworthy is the fact that a larger proportion of their choices is directed to persons not even in the sample than is true of the other affecteds. In all these respects, they resemble the controls more than they do the affecteds. Thus, even though they are very few in number, these four women seem to fit into the social system of the plant in a rather different way than do the other affected women.

This sequential analysis has illustrated some striking contrasts between the women affected during the height of the epidemic and those affected before and after this peak period. Although the core of the epidemic follows the "group influence" pattern, both the early and late phases deviate from this pattern. Each deviates in a different way, and the two patterns they exhibit fit more nearly the other two conceptualizations than they do the "group influence" conceptualization.

During the "Before" period we have found that social isolates predominate. All but one of the early cases are isolates. Although they have work and other kinds of relations with others in our sample, they are not chosen as friends. It is these social isolates who get the epidemic started. They are the ones who exhibit the rather bizarre behavior originally, and it is only later that the contagion enters into the intricate network of interpersonal relations among the affected women. These early cases, therefore, seem to be the kind of cases one would expect from the "social isolation" conceptualization.

The four women in the "After" phase are also rather different from the women affected at the height of the epidemic. They are not isolates like the "Before" women, but they have much more limited contact with the other affected women. Their social relations seem to be outside the affected category for the most part. If we assume that this is a meaningful rather than chance ordering of a very small number of cases, two interpretations are possible. First, we might argue that the contagion is simply entering another sociometric network, and that since the spread is curtailed by the end of the entire epidemic, there are not enough cases to demonstrate what is occurring. On the other hand, it might be argued that a more random distribution of cases is taking place, that the spread of the epidemic has moved out of sociometric channels and is becoming more general. This would be another way of saying that it has become a "crowd response." We are inclined toward the latter interpretation and will present other evidence below which suggests that this was the case.

This analysis may indicate, therefore, that the epidemic begins as a few unusual and socially insignificant women exhibit a form of behavior which, though rather bizarre, is meaningful in the work setting. Not much excitement is generated until the behavior pattern (and a "reasonable" explanation of it) spreads among those who are socially more central, and then the contagion is rather rapid and follows sociometric channels. Finally, as larger and larger numbers of persons exhibit the behavior, the sheer size of the affected category makes the credibility of the phenomenon greater. Ultimately almost everyone believes in "the bug," and cases begin to occur throughout the population. At that point, the pattern becomes a kind of "crowd response." Although the validity of this conceptualization cannot be determined in the present context, the data do seem to fit a pattern of this kind.

THE PATH OF CONTAGION

The discussion in the previous section leads to the temptation to reconstruct the spread of the contagion through the population. There are a number of alternative means of doing so, no one of which is clearly superior to the others. As in the previous section, a basic problem which faced us was to decide what constituted a "link" between two women. We might have considered only a friendship choice as a link because this was the most intimate type of relationship on which we had information, and it was reasonable to assume that the degree of interpersonal influence would vary with the degree of significance of the relationship to the person being influenced. On the other hand, it was not at all clear that only this most intimate link would operate in the way most relevant to our interests. Such a consideration suggested that we include any type of relationship on which we had information as one that would possibly be relevant to our concerns.

We have attempted to encompass both of these extremes in our final view of the contagion. In Figure 6.1 we have represented *all* of the known links among the affected and self-defined affected cases. These are presented according to their degree of intimacy. In so doing, we felt that we would be able to suggest more clearly the total pattern of relationship while yet giving greater emphasis to those presumably more significant relationships.

Before discussing Figure 6.1, however, we must digress a bit to clarify one of the features of that figure which is not anticipated in the earlier part of this chapter. In Chapter 3 we indicated that we asked the women not only if they themselves were affected by the epidemic but also whether they knew anyone who was so affected. Our specific question, which followed their description of the events of the epidemic, was: Did this happen to anyone (else) in the plant whom you know well? If they answered in the affirmative, we obtained the names of those they said they knew and whom they defined as having been affected. As would be expected from the other data reported in this chapter, the affecteds named many more such persons than did the self-defined affecteds or controls (an average of 1.36, .88, and .65 names, respectively).[7] Since the women named in

7 Other results from this question are also worthy of note and are consistent with our earlier findings: (1) None of the controls was named as having been affected compared with 24 percent of the self-defined affecteds and 79 percent of the affecteds. (2) Exactly half of the controls said they knew no one who was affected compared with only 18 percent of the self-defined affecteds and 9 percent of the affecteds. (3) There were 19 people named as having been affected who were not even in our sample, 5 of them outside the dressmaking departments.

FIGURE 6.1. *Social Relations Among Affected and Self-Defined Affected Cases*

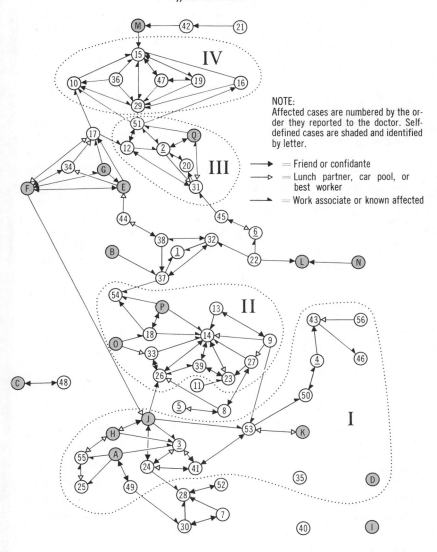

NOTE:
Affected cases are numbered by the order they reported to the doctor. Self-defined cases are shaded and identified by letter.

⟶ = Friend or confidante

⇢ = Lunch partner, car pool, or best worker

➤ = Work associate or known affected

response to this question were necessarily known to the respondents, at least to the extent of being able to give their full names, the data so derived are evidently relevant to our present interests. However, since we had no basis for assuming that the respondent's relationship with a woman named *only* in response to this question was a particularly close one, we included these choices in the least intimate category.

Returning to Figure 6.1, therefore, we combined those links which were based on either the work-contact question or this question to form the least intimate category, represented by the half-headed arrows. The open-headed arrows represent relationships of a medium range of intimacy—eating lunch together, riding in the same car pool, viewing someone as the best worker in one's section. Finally, the solid-headed arrows represent the most intimate relationships—being a friend or being one to whom the respondent would turn with a personal problem or whom she would expect to turn to her with a personal problem (a confidante). As in the tables presented earlier, if a woman was named under more than one of these categories, the relationship is represented as on the most intimate level at which she was named.

This figure is, of course, a very oversimplified view of the context of the contagion since none of the relations these women have with the controls or with women outside the sample is represented here. Such a complete figure becomes impossible to analyze, however, if the choices of all 181 women or even the choices of the 144 women we have studied in the dressmaking departments are included. Thus, we have chosen to present rather full information about the smaller number of women in these two categories. As it is, there are 73 women and 149 choices represented in the figure.

We have included the self-defined affecteds since there seems good reason to believe that they were active in the spread of the epidemic even though they did not report to the doctor for assistance. This is borne out, in part, by the fact that four of them were named by others as having been affected. If we assume that interpersonal relations played a major role in the spread, such women could act as "carriers" even though they never became known to the medical authorities. By the same logic, of course, any number of other women may have acted in this same capacity. This is suggested by the fact that others who were not in our sample were named as having been affected. Not only were there those who were defined by others as having been affected, but there were undoubtedly many others whom we did not interview who would have defined themselves as having been affected. And, of course, even some of those who would not fit either of these categories might have acted in ways which increased the probability that some of the other women would become affected. But such agents in the epidemic must remain unknown, and we must be content with the limited data at hand. We thus include the self-defined affecteds in our chart because they can more easily than any other nonaffecteds in our sample be assumed to have played some role in the spread of the epidemic.

The most striking impression gained from a first glance at this figure is that there is a remarkable number of links among these women. Although more than one-third (37 percent) of these links are of the least intimate type (half-headed arrows), there are still almost 100 links of the two more intimate varieties, 68 of them being of the most intimate type. Only two affected and two self-defined affected cases have *no* known relationship to any of the other women in these categories. Besides them, there is only one dyad which is unconnected with the others. The fact that the figure requires only one very long arrow (from case F to case J of the self-defined affecteds) also indicates that the relationships noted here are not just random among the women. Instead, the figure suggests a set of nucleated groupings of women. Forty-three of the 73 women belong to four work groups as reflected in the dotted outlines in the figure. Group I consists of inspectors, groups II and III, sewers, and group IV, menders. Other clusters also seem to be based largely on work-group relations, though not so clearly as those outlined in the figure. Work groups are not the *only* basis of choice even in these four groups, however. This is indicated by the fact that numbers 42 and 21, at the top of the figure, are in work groups I and II, respectively. Some women serve as links between groupings. This is most obvious in such cases as 44, in the upper center section, but it is also true of others like 53 in the lower right portion of the figure.

If we focus on the numbered sequence of the affected cases, we find some very interesting paths that may be traced through this network of relations. Since the numbers 1 through 6 were those cases affected before the first big day of the epidemic, locating them in the figure permits us to see "where it all began." (We have under-scored these six numbers to make them easier to locate.) We find that these six women vary considerably in the positions they occupy in the network. As we have seen earlier, they were not chosen as friends very often. Only case 2 (upper center) receives a friendship choice, and she is the *only* early case to receive a friendship choice from *anyone* we interviewed. Numbers 2 and 3 (lower center) are named frequently, however, in the two less intimate categories. By the usual sociometric standards, they are "stars," only four other cases being chosen more frequently than number 2 and only three others being chosen more frequently than number 3.

Perhaps of greater note than the simple sociometric status of these women, however, is the way in which they tie in with the various chains of relationships. Both 2 and 3 are linked with women who were later affected on Day One, the day after they themselves were affected. The same is true of 5 and 6. The affecteds with whom 4 and 1 are linked, however, were not affected until relatively late in the epidemic.[8] Some interesting paths may be discerned in the clusters which include numbers 2, 6, 5, and 3 and are worthy of closer examination.

The most closely knit cluster in the figure is the one in the lower center portion, which forms around number 14. Here we find that number 5 is the first affected case. She directs a friendship choice toward number 8 who only acknowledges that they ride in the same car pool.[9] This tie between 5 and 8 seems to be the "lead-in" to the whole cluster. Number 8 was stricken almost immediately upon arrival at work on Day One, the record showing that she reported to the doctor at 8:05 A.M. Presumably she rode to work that morning and/or returned home from work the night before with number 5

[8] The situation with number 1 is rather ambiguous. Although she was the first recorded case in the period covered by our survey of the medical records, she was also affected again on the morning of Day Two. This was at about the same time as numbers 32 and 37 were affected. Thus, whether she should be seen as having influenced them or they as having influenced her, or both, is difficult to say.

[9] This pattern is repeated elsewhere in the network of choices: the early cases direct friendship choices toward women who either ignore their presence in their own responses or who direct choices of a lower level of intimacy in return.

since they both say they are in the same car pool. Number 5 reported to the doctor at 4:20 that previous afternoon. Within an hour of the time the doctor saw number 8, number 9 became nauseous and reported to the doctor. She evidently had come to work that morning with number 27 who is a friend of number 8 (and who became ill that afternoon). At 11:00 that morning number 13 (a friend of number 9) was stricken with nausea, and 15 minutes later number 14 almost passed out. Number 14 is such a star of the cluster, it is not surprising that numbers 18, 23, 26, and 27 were all stricken that same afternoon. Not only is number 14 a star in the sociometric sense of this term, she is also a union steward who represents most of these women. Thus, both her formal position and her place in the network of informal ties make her a very significant reference point for many of the workers around her. This one small cluster, then, contributes one-third of the Day One cases.

At this same time, in the cluster at the bottom of the figure another pattern was developing. Number 3 had gotten sick and passed out the afternoon of the previous day. The first thing the next morning (Day One) number 7 passed out and was sent to the hospital when she said she had been bitten the previous day and was still sick. That noon number 3 presumably had lunch with 24, who is her sister, and 41 whom she defined as a friend. At 2:00 that afternoon number 24 passed out and was sent to the hospital. At about the same time, number 3 was again bitten and again passed out. By the time the plant was closed that afternoon, numbers 28 and 30, whom number 7 defined as friends, were also affected, 28 being sent to the hospital. In fact, number 30 claimed she was bitten several days earlier (even before number 7) but had not sought medical aid until Day One.

During this same period the cluster which includes number 2 (top center) was also active. Number 2 had reported to the doctor in the middle of the previous day. Her importance is undoubtedly increased by the fact that she was the union steward for the other five women in the work group III cluster. By the middle of Day One, her two work associates, numbers 12 and 20, were stricken. Four others (10, 15, 16, and 19) in the related cluster of menders (above them in the figure) were also stricken at about this same time, and a fifth (number 29) almost passed out at about the time the plant was closing that afternoon. Again, number 29 is a union steward serving all six of the other women in cluster IV. Although there are ties between these clusters, particularly through number 51, the only known link between these two sets of Day One cases is number 17. This link may be more significant than it first appears to be since 17 said she had been bitten earlier, even before number 10.

There were other scattered cases on Day One also, of course. Number 22 has a work relationship with number 6 (right center). Number 21 (at the top of the figure) has only very indirect connections with anyone who was affected before her (although she is a member of work group II). Number 11 (lower center cluster) and number 25 (bottom cluster) are also very marginal to the majority of the Day One cases (although number 25 is a member of work group I). The great majority of the Day One cases, however, are linked with other cases who were affected at about the same time.

It is difficult to have much confidence in the order of cases beginning the next morning, the morning of Day Two. Eleven cases were recorded between 8:15 and 8:30 that morning, and an additional seven cases were logged in by 10:00. By the middle of the afternoon four more cases had been reported, and the plant management made the decision to close down again. The first flurry of cases included numbers 32, 37, and 38 who are clustered around number 1 in our figure. Number 1 again reported to the doctor that morning. Also included in that early rush were cases 33 and 39 who are part of the cluster around number 14. This completes that cluster, all cases except number 5 being affected within 24 hours of each other. Also affected early that morning were 34, whose lunch partner (number 17) got sick the previous noon and who claimed that she (34) too had been bitten the previous day; 41, whose lunch partners (3 and 24) had both been stricken the day before; 31, whose friends (12 and 20) were bitten the previous day; and 36, whose friend (number 10) was still in the hospital with symptoms developed the previous day. There were two other cases in that early flurry (numbers 35 and 40) who had no known connection with other affecteds, though 35 was a member of work group I.

Connections with earlier affected cases are apparent for some of the cases affected later that day (Day Two). For instance, number 47 in the top cluster and number 51 just below her in the figure have close relations with one earlier case and less intimate connections with others. In both cases, their union steward had gotten sick earlier. Number 44 (left center) and number 52 (bottom cluster) chose as friends women who were affected that morning and the previous afternoon, respectively, although they have no other known connections with affected women. The links between the others affected during this period and earlier affected cases, however, are either very weak or nonexistent. Number 42 (top), numbers 46 and 43 (right center), and number 48 (lower left) do not name an earlier affected woman in any of our categories, although they have some ties that might have been of some significance in their having been affected. Numbers 45 (center right), 49 (lower left), and 50 (lower right) all name earlier affected cases in some category, but the ties are either rather weak or the connection (as with number 45) is with someone affected much earlier in the epidemic. The pattern of contagion is thus much less clear in these cases than in those affected during Day One and early on Day Two.

The impression gained from this analysis of the late Day Two cases is similar to the one noted in our discussion of the cases affected during the After period. They do not seem to be as well integrated into the network of relations among the affected women. The general conceptualization we have suggested in this chapter called for a number of isolates being affected early, a move into sociometric networks, and a final dispersion of cases throughout the population in a way less clearly relevant to social relations. This pattern is different from the type Coleman, Katz, and Menzel (1957) have called the "snowball effect." In a snowball pattern, which would be expected if social relations were the principal means of transmission of the contagion, there is an increasing tendency for a participant in the contagion to be linked with a person who has already been a participant. If such were the pattern, we would, of course, expect persons affected early to have no links with persons previously affected, but we would expect that as we move through the period of the contagion such links would be increasingly common. We would *not* expect that the later cases would be *less* frequently linked with early cases, which is what has been suggested in this analysis.

We had been somewhat hesitant to emphasize this deviation from the snowball pattern solely on the basis of our data from the four cases in the After period. There is now indication, however, that this deviation may be seen even during Day Two. To make the matter more explicit, it may be worthwhile to add here a systematic summary of the relationships we found.

If we divide the cases reported on Day One and Day Two into early and late cases for those two days, we have 12 early and 12 late cases on Day One and 11 early and 11 late cases on Day Two. If the snowball effect is the dominant effect in this part of the epidemic, we would expect an increasing proportion of the cases to be linked to earlier cases as we move from the early Day One cases to the late Day Two cases.[10] This pattern is actually found through *early* Day Two. Only 1 of the 12 early Day One cases chooses an earlier affected woman as a friend, but 6 of the late Day One women do so. Six of the early Day Two cases make such a choice, but only 4 of the late Day Two women choose an earlier case as a friend. The proportions of cases in the four periods having such a friendship choice are .08, .50, .55, and .36. The same pattern is found whatever definition of a link we use. For instance, if we consider all links as represented in Figure 6.1 instead of just friendship links, the proportions are .50, .75, .82, and .64. Rather than an increasing tendency to "snowball" throughout the period of the epidemic, therefore, there is a decided decline of the snowball pattern toward the end. Evidently after about the middle of Day Two the epidemic more clearly leaves its original sociometric channels and begins to become more of a "crowd response" type of phenomenon. This, of course, is in keeping with our earlier conceptualization and gives us greater faith in it.

THE INFLUENCE PROCESS

The analysis in the previous section made the implicit assumption that in order for a social link to be seen as a source of influence the influencer had to become affected before the woman she supposedly

[10] Here, as in all similar subsequent analyses, we will consider that individual A has a tie with individual B if A *chooses* B in one of the relevant categories but not if A is *chosen* by B. This is done because we would argue that a person whom one chooses is a more salient reference point and thus more likely to influence the chooser than is a person who chooses one but is not chosen in return.

influenced. This is the usual assumption in studies of a spread of a phenomenon in a collectivity. In studies of the adoption of an innovation in farming or medicine there is little grounds for quarrel with such an assumption. In our particular case, however, such an assumption may be more questionable. At least it is doubtful if going to the doctor is the most significant act involved.

Throughout this report we have had to emphasize the difference between "experiencing symptoms" and "going to the doctor," but our criterion of being affected has been the act of going to the doctor. It seems quite possible that not only did the self-defined affecteds experience symptoms without seeking medical assistance, but also that many of the affecteds experienced symptoms and reported them to their friends and associates long before they went to the doctor. They may have "adopted the innovation" well before the medical authorities became aware of it. We have found, in fact, that many of the early cases told the doctor they had actually been bitten several hours or even days before they went to see him. This became less true as the epidemic progressed, but it certainly seems to have occurred in the early stages. It may well be, therefore, that the kind of interpersonal influence which is suggested by our data took place between cases which were related to each other in a way not reflected in any simple temporal sequence of reporting to the doctor. This kind of logic has led us to pay close attention to the self-defined affected cases. Even though they did not go to the doctor, they evidently experienced symptoms, and this fact may have been known by (and thus tended to influence) some of their friends and associates. The influence process presumably acts largely to increase the credibility of the threat of the mysterious insect. If a friend has been stricken, one is more likely to develop symptoms or to define current symptoms as being associated with the insect. If she develops symptoms, she may go to the doctor, but whether she does or not, knowledge of her condition is likely to influence those associated with her.

Such reasoning leads to further questions which we must investigate. For instance: Do we still find a decrease in social ties among late affecteds if we consider a woman's ties with *any* other affected case? In fact, we should probably consider not only affected cases as possible sources of influence but also self-defined affecteds. Does the pattern hold if they are included? Also, if a woman's ties with any affected or self-defined affected woman might have been significant, it becomes possible to differentiate cases according to *how many* such ties they had. Is it true, as we should expect, that the more such ties a woman has the more likely she is to become affected?

Tables 6.1 and 6.2 provide evidence that, in general, those with social relations with affecteds and self-defined affecteds are themselves more likely to be affected or self-defined affected. Is it also true that the more such ties a woman has the more likely she is to become affected? The answer is clearly "yes." Of those 41 women with one affected friend, 20 (or 48.8 percent) were themselves affected. Of those 16 women with two affected friends, 12 (or 75.0 percent) were affected. If we use all of the more intimate kinds of ties as our definition of a social relationship (the open-headed and solid arrows in Figure 6.1), the same thing is found. Fifty women had one such tie, and 46.0 percent of them were affected; 18 women had two such ties, and 61.1 percent of them were affected. All 5 women who had two such ties were themselves affected. The same pattern repeats itself when we use ties with both affected and self-defined affected women and when we use being either an affected or self-defined affected case as the criterion. For instance, there were 51 women who had an intimate tie with one affected or self-defined affected; of these, 58.8 percent were themselves either affected or self-defined affected. There were 27 who had two intimate ties with affecteds or self-defined affecteds, and 85.2 percent of them were either affected or self-defined affected. Again, all 5 who had three such ties were affected cases. Thus, whether we are attempting to predict a woman's being an affected or a self-defined affected case, and whether we are using ties with affecteds alone or with them and self-defined affecteds as a basis for prediction, the same result occurs: the more such ties a woman has, the more likely she is to become "affected," however that term is defined.

This is the first time that we have found such a close resemblance between the affecteds and the self-defined affecteds. With respect to both personality characteristics and situational strains they were often more dissimilar from each other than either was from the controls. That dissimilarity, together with the present similarity, makes their different positions in the epidemic more understandable.

Evidently the self-defined affecteds were themselves members of the same network of relations as the affecteds. But they had less original strain to contend with, and they were better able to cope with the problems they faced. Their social position, therefore, suggests the reason they felt affected by ("caught up" in) the epidemic, but their personal and situational characteristics suggest the reason why they did not fully succumb to the point of requiring or seeking medical assistance.

We may now turn to our other question: Is there still evidence of an increasing tendency for the epidemic to break out of the sociometric network? Clearly there is. Using the same four periods (early and late on Days One and Two), we computed the proportion having significant ties in four different ways: using friendship ties with affecteds, using friendship ties with affecteds or self-defined affecteds, using intimate ties with affecteds, and using intimate ties with affecteds or self-defined affecteds. In all four cases, there is an increase between early and late Day One. The increase ranged from 8.3 to 25.0 percentage points. In all four cases also, there was a sharp drop from early Day Two to late Day Two. The decrease ranged from 18.2 to 36.3 percentage points. It is also interesting to note that in all cases there was at least a slight drop between late Day One and early Day Two. It may well be, therefore, that the decrease in the significance of intimate social ties in the spread of the epidemic began even earlier than we had at first thought. In any event, there is little doubt that sometime on Day Two and continuing until the end of the epidemic new cases were more likely to occur outside the original sociometric networks. We are also again impressed with the similarity of the findings whether we use ties with affecteds or with self-defined affecteds.

FURTHER COMPLEXITIES

We have offered three different theoretical bases for predicting the relevance of sociometric ties to the spread of the epidemic, and we have suggested that our data support all three of them to a limited degree. What we have called the "social isolation" theory seems to fit the early stages of the epidemic best, the "group response" theory seems to fit the major portion of the epidemic best, and the "crowd

response" theory is evidently most appropriate for the late stages of
the epidemic. The data analysis we have offered is generally in keeping, then, with a multiple-process view of such a contagious spread.

It is well to emphasize, however, that although we have some
confidence in the pattern of processes suggested, each being dominant at a different period in the epidemic, no such conceptualization
is fully in accord with all the data from the case. We must assume that all three processes are going on at the same time throughout
the period studied. There are, after all, isolates who are affected late
in the epidemic, and even the last cases affected show *some* evidence of social ties with earlier affected cases. We would also expect
that the more unstructured "crowd response" begins to develop early
in the contagion and tends to increase in importance. We have found
some suggestion that it became noteworthy as early as the morning
of Day Two. It is necessary to keep in mind too that isolates should
be affected at least as much by the crowd effect as those with social
ties, perhaps more so. Thus, it would presumably be impossible to
distinguish the "social isolation" and "crowd response" effects once
the epidemic has gotten well under way. By the same token, we cannot with any confidence claim that all of those affected during the
height of the contagion who had social ties with other affected cases
were influenced by these ties more so than by a "crowd response"
type of influence.

Not only are the three theories evidently all applicable to the
situation to some extent at all times, but we must assume that other
factors not clearly included in these theories were also operating.
After all, we found notable differences among our three categories of
women with respect to both personal characteristics and the degree
of strain they were experiencing. There is no reason to believe that
there is a neat correlation among these several kinds of forces in the
situation, and we must thus face the problem of attempting to put
these various pieces together. We will turn to that problem in the
next chapter.

This chapter, however, has contributed to the solution not only
by pointing up the importance of social relations in the transmission
of the contagion, and thus helping to understand why some women
became affected cases, but also by helping to clarify the position of
the self-defined affecteds. The earlier analysis of the self-defined

affecteds has been puzzling since it seemed to show little reason for these women to have been affected at all. The data on personal characteristics suggested that perhaps they simply liked to talk about their symptoms and thus wanted to be included in any unusual experiences like the epidemic. The data on the strains experienced by the women gave a more sanguine picture, however. They showed them to be rather "sensible" women who were realistic about their situations, were subject to some strain, and had more adequate means of coping with strain than did the affected women. The present analysis, however, shows that they were intimately implicated with the affected women in a network of social relations. These ties presumably tended to increase the strain they experienced during the epidemic and made it more likely that they would develop symptoms. We might thus speculate that it was their more realistic outlook and better coping mechanisms that saved them from becoming some of the doctor's patients.

7

PERSON, POSITION, AND PATTERN

In this chapter we will pursue several earlier ideas in an attempt to develop a more holistic view of the epidemic. In each of the previous three chapters we have approached our data with a particular theoretical interest, and we have, for the purposes of each of these chapters, generally ignored other perspectives. In each case, we have noted significant relationships in keeping with the theoretical position central to that chapter. However, in each case we have also noted some puzzling and sometimes contradictory findings. The burden of this chapter will be to examine these data in the context of a more comprehensive perspective.

It may well be that some kinds of personality are particularly prone to react in an hysterical fashion, and that interpersonal influence often hastens the process. On the other hand, it is also undoubtedly true that a given type of personality faced with one type of strain or social process will respond differently from another type of personality faced with the same strain or social process. In fact, we might postulate that all of these factors function in different ways depending on how they are combined. Our chief interest in this chapter, then, will be to examine the significance of several combinations which are suggested by the previous findings.

We have noted that there were various responses to the epidemic experience. We began with the rather simplistic notion that there were just two types—the affecteds and the controls—but found that at least a third category—the self-defined affecteds—needed to be viewed separately. In Chapter 3 we also discussed the various symptoms exhibited by the affected women, and we reported that all three categories of women varied in their postepidemic assessments of the causes of the epidemic. Are there systematic differences in the personal characteristics of these women? Do those affecteds who responded to the epidemic in one way (e.g., by fainting) have different personal characteristics from those who responded in another fashion?

In Chapter 4 it was suggested that some of our measures of strain might also be indices of factors which would deter a woman from becoming involved in the epidemic. Since the data in Chapter 6 indicated differences in social position between the women affected early and late in the epidemic, is it also true that these early and late affecteds differed in their response to these "two-edged" or complex sources of strain? Do personal characteristics enter the picture here also? More generally, are the people who were affected early different kinds of people from those affected later, both with respect to their personal qualities and their exposure to sources of strain? Also, do the early and late cases tend to respond differently when they do become affected?

The central theme in Chapter 6 was the importance of social relations in the dissemination of the epidemic. Do those people who seemingly respond to social influence differ on personal or situational dimensions from those who do not? Are there differences in the way they respond to the epidemic if they do become affected? Is there a pattern of interaction among personal characteristics, sources of strain, and social position which is related to if, when, and how a person is affected?

Although we attempted to investigate all of these questions, part of our analysis was so inconclusive as to make it difficult to give a satisfactory answer to some of them. We were most successful in determining the correlates of different kinds of responses of those women who were affected; that is, which ones fainted, almost fainted, or did neither. We were also able to combine the three kinds of variables (personal characteristics, levels of strain, and social relations) into an overall prediction profile. Discussion of these two kinds of analysis will constitute the bulk of the chapter. Before presenting those data, however, we will discuss briefly a few other issues which our data helped to illuminate.

KINDS OF STRAIN AND THE SEQUENCE OF AFFECTED CASES

In Chapter 4 we noted some difficulties involved in the interpretation of our indexes of strain. One of these was the fact that on some of our measures the self-defined affecteds exhibited as high (and sometimes a higher) incidence of the strain as did the affecteds. We suggested that the kinds of indexes which produced this result were very largely those involving a "two-edged" effect. That is, they not only indicated a situation likely to put the woman under a greater strain, but they also indicated a reason why she would be motivated to resist giving expression to the strain she was experiencing. For instance, the self-defined affecteds were more likely than the affecteds or the controls to have been laid off, to be the sole wage earners in the family, and to be widowed, divorced, or separated. Although each of these conditions presumably adds a strain to the situation in which the woman finds herself, it also suggests that such a woman would be more concerned about her job and maintaining the income which it produces. We have thus suggested that women who bore such burdens might be more likely to be extremely conscientious workers and less likely to give way to the expression of tension experienced on the job. If this were true, it would help explain why some of the self-defined affecteds who experienced this kind of strain did not actually seek or require medical attention.

But if this interpretation is to be accepted, it should also imply some difference between the affected women who experienced such forms of strain and those who did not. Other things equal, the former should have been affected later in the epidemic than those who did not bear this kind of burden. We thus divided the affected women into those who had been affected on or before Day One and those who had been affected after Day One and examined the distribution of such strains. On all three measures just noted, more of the late affected cases had experienced the strain. They were more likely to have been laid off, more likely to be the sole family wage earner, and more likely to be widowed, divorced, or separated. Only on the second factor, however, was the percentage difference very great. Thirty-one percent of the late cases were the sole family wage earners compared with only 13 percent of the early cases.

THE DISTRIBUTION OF SOCIAL LINKS

In Chapter 6 we have suggested that social relations with affected cases tend to facilitate a woman's becoming affected herself. However, we have also noted in that chapter that many of the self-defined affecteds and some of the controls also had social ties with affecteds. If such relations are facilitative in the manner we have proposed, why weren't these other women affected?

In order to study this issue, we repeated the comparisons which had proved of interest in the earlier chapters using only those cases who had links with affected women.[1] The resulting data are presented in Table 7.1. The findings are generally similar to those using all of the cases, but there are some notable differences. With respect to the measures of strain, working overtime most clearly differentiates the affecteds from the others, and seeing variation in output in the section does so most poorly. Although this was generally true for the total sample, the second of these two measures was more effective with the total sample than it is here. We again find that supplying half or more of the family income characterizes both the affecteds and self-defined affecteds more clearly than the controls. The summary measure of strain again discriminates as before. The differences with respect to the measure of ability to cope with strain (willingness to take time off for a rest) are even greater than with the total sample.

The differences previously noted in the distribution of the measures of denial are again found here. Denial is even more fully concentrated in the affected category than it was with the total sample. Finally, the striking differences in degree of acquiescence

[1] As before, we defined a link in terms of the two more intimate types of social relations. These are the relations represented by the solid and two-headed arrows in Figure 6.1. Also as before, A is defined as linked with B if she *chooses* B but not if she is *chosen* by B. We also re-ran data using ties with both affecteds and self-defined affecteds as our criterion as well as using only ties with earlier affected cases. Although the patterns varied somewhat with these other definitions, the general conclusion we reach is justified in all cases.

TABLE 7.1
Characteristics of Affected, Self-Defined Affected, and Control Cases
Who Have Links With Other Affected Cases

Characteristic	Linked Affecteds (N = 40) %	Linked Self-Defined Affecteds (N = 11) %	Linked Controls (N = 23) %
Worked overtime at least two or three times a week	62.5	36.4	34.8
Do not mention supervisor as one to go to with a complaint	45.0	18.2	47.8
Provide half or more of family income	47.5	45.5	26.1
The section varies in output	37.5	45.5	34.8
Have two or more of these sources of strain	67.5	45.5	39.1
It is wrong to stay home when not sick	80.0	45.5	65.2
Deny all symptoms	37.5	00.0	17.4
Deny importance of role conflict	25.0	00.0	8.7
Acquiescence (double "yes" responses)	70.0	45.5	52.2

suggest that the affecteds, more than either of the other categories, might be more responsive to cues received from those around them.

Thus, although the pattern is not as striking as one might have expected on the various individual measures of strain, the total picture gained from an examination of this table is one of the affected women being under greater strain, less likely to be able to cope with strain, and more likely to accept influence from others. There is thus little reason here to discard our interpretation of the significance of social relations as a means of influence in the epidemic. When we ask why the linked controls and self-defined affecteds were not affected, the best answer still seems to be that they experienced fewer *other* forces operating to lead them in that direction.

THE PATTERN OF LASTING BELIEF

We referred in Chapter 3 to the fact that a number of characteristics might have been viewed as the major dependent attribute

in this study. We stressed the importance of three kinds of indexes of response to the epidemic: a belief, an emotional response,
and an action which came to the attention of the medical authorities.
However, since our measure of belief was not only made after the
epidemic had ended but also after it had been branded as "only
hysteria," we were hesitant to emphasize this measure. On the other
hand, if we view the women's beliefs as the *result* of the experience in the epidemic rather than as the *cause* of their behavior during the epidemic, it is possible to gain further understanding of the
subjects.

Several questions in the interview might be seen as related to
this issue, but we will report on only the most directly relevant item.
After we had asked a number of open-ended questions about the
epidemic, the women were asked: "What do you think caused this
to happen?" The responses naturally varied greatly, but they could
be classified into four major types. Some of the women made very
definite statements to the effect that an insect was the cause. Others
made less clear-cut statements which either indicated that an insect
was "probably the cause" or that the epidemic was "mostly" caused
by an insect. Some, of course, stated that they simply did not know
what brought the whole thing about. And, finally, a few said it was
not an insect and specified some other cause (hysteria, poisonous
dyes in the fabric, and so on).

We examined the same kinds of classifications of subjects as
discussed earlier using these four types of responses as our dependent
measure. The findings that proved of interest are reported in Table
7.2.[2] There is no mention there of the measures of strain because
they were not clearly related to the beliefs the women reported. Their
responses were, however, related to the women's role in the epidemic,
their personal characteristics, and the pattern of social relations with
affected cases.

As we have already pointed out in Chapter 3, the affected women
were much more likely to express an unequivocal belief in the bug,
and the controls were least likely to be so certain about the matter.
It is a bit surprising that three of the affected cases said the epidemic

[2] Table 7.2 is organized in the opposite manner from our previous tables
by having the dependent attribute in the column headings. This is done simply
for ease of presentation and does not imply a different view of the nature of
these relationships.

TABLE 7.2
Distribution of Explanations of the Cause of the Epidemic, Within Affected, Self-Defined Affected, and Control Categories

Category	Definitely an Insect %	Mostly or Probably an Insect %	Don't Know %	Not an Insect %
Affecteds (N = 56)	62.5	23.2	8.9	5.4
Self-Defined Affecteds (N = 17)	41.2	23.5	29.4	5.9
Controls (N = 71)	26.8	40.8	23.9	8.5
Affecteds who fainted (N = 21)	76.2	19.0	00.0	4.8
Affecteds who almost fainted (N = 15)	60.0	6.7	26.7	6.7
Affecteds who did neither (N = 20)	50.0	35.0	10.0	5.0
Affecteds who are symptom deniers (N = 17)	58.8	17.6	11.8	11.8
Controls who are symptom deniers (N = 14)*	00.0	42.9	50.0	7.1
Affecteds who are role-conflict deniers (N = 16)	62.5	25.0	6.3	6.3
Controls and Self-Defined Affecteds who are role-conflict deniers (N = 8)*	12.5	62.5	00.0	25.0
Affecteds with high symptom scores and no role-conflict denial (N = 13)	61.5	23.1	7.7	7.7

136

Self-Defined Affecteds with high symptom scores and no role-conflict denial (N = 10)	60.0	10.0	30.0	00.0
Controls with high symptom scores and no role-conflict denial (N = 22)	45.5	40.9	9.1	4.5
Early linked Affecteds (N = 23)	78.3	17.4	4.3	00.0
Early not linked Affecteds (N = 7)	57.1	42.9	00.0	00.0
Late linked Affecteds (N = 17)	52.9	11.8	23.5	11.8
Late not linked Affecteds (N = 9)	44.4	44.4	00.0	11.1
Linked Self-Defined Affecteds (N = 11)	54.5	9.1	36.4	00.0
Not linked Self-Defined Affecteds (N = 6)	16.7	50.0	33.3	00.0
Linked Controls (N = 23)	43.5	34.8	17.4	4.3
Not linked Controls (N = 48)	18.8	43.8	27.1	10.4
Affecteds who were not acquiescent (N = 16)	43.8	37.5	12.5	6.3
Affecteds who were acquiescent (N = 29)	70.0	17.5	7.5	5.0
Self-Defined Affecteds who were not acquiescent (N = 9)	55.6	22.2	22.2	00.0
Self-Defined Affecteds who were acquiescent (N = 8)	25.0	25.0	37.5	12.5
Controls who were not acquiescent (N = 29)	37.9	27.6	24.1	10.3
Controls who were acquiescent (N = 42)	19.0	50.0	23.8	7.1

* There were no self-defined affecteds who were symptom deniers and only one who was a role-conflict denier. The latter is combined with the control role-conflict deniers. She said that the epidemic was "probably caused" by an insect.

definitely was *not* caused by an insect. One of them even said she thought it was caused mostly by excitement and hysteria. The majority of those who clearly rejected the insect cause, however, were controls (six out of nine). Since those who fainted during the epidemic had made the most clear-cut behavioral commitment to the proposition that something very toxic was among them, it is also not surprising that more fainters expressed complete belief in the bug than any other type of affected case, and none of them expressed serious doubt about the cause. We again are faced, however, with the fact that one of those who fainted said she thought an insect was not the cause. She thought it was due to poisonous dyes.[3]

Among the nonaffecteds, the greatest doubt about the causal importance of an insect was expressed by those who were either symptom deniers or role-conflict deniers. Most impressive about this portion of Table 7.2 is that, among the affecteds, deniers are just as likely to accept the insect theory as the nondeniers. Evidently it was necessary for a denier to have the personal experience and make a public commitment before she would accept the validity of the threat of the bug.[4] The pattern is clearly different with those who are not deniers by either definition and who readily admit to symptoms. All three categories of women with these characteristics are very likely to acknowledge the importance of the insect as a causal factor in the epidemic. The controls with these characteristics are very different from the controls who are deniers by either definition.

A similar relationship holds if we consider acquiescence. It may be thought that acquiescence is a measure of suggestibility and therefore related to bizarre beliefs. However, Table 7.2 shows that there is no direct relationship between acquiescence and belief in the insect,

[3] This woman was a denier by both of our definitions. One of the other affecteds who rejected the insect as a cause was a symptom denier; the other was not a denier by either definition.

[4] It is also worth noting, however, that the two kinds of affected deniers were somewhat different in this respect. If those deniers who fainted (and thus were most irrevocably committed to the validity of the threat) are set aside, the two types of affected deniers are quite different. Of the 8 role-conflict deniers who did not faint, only 2 expressed complete belief in the bug. Of the 12 symptom deniers who did not faint, 7 believed fully in the bug. It would seem that the very fact of their public acknowledgment of their symptoms necessitated a clear "external" explanation for the symptom deniers, but not for the role-conflict deniers.

but that the relationship depends on the experience in the epidemic. Among the affecteds acquiescence does relate to lasting belief, while in the control group there is an inverse relationship. Among the self-defined affecteds there is also an inverse relationship. The total picture is similar to that of deniers. Those who gave acquiescent responses were more likely to believe in the insect if they had been conspicuous during the epidemic and less likely if they had not been conspicuous.

In addition, we find that those who were affected early in the epidemic have greater faith in the full causal significance of the bug than do those affected later. It is also true that those with social relations with other affected cases were more likely to believe than were those without such relations. It is not surprising that this is so among the controls (or even among the self-defined affecteds), but it is striking that it is also true among the affecteds.

These data indicate that belief in the causal significance of an insect is related to one's part in the epidemic and to one's personal and social characteristics. We find evidence of the importance of denial and acquiescence on the one hand and social relations on the other. They operate in different ways in this case. Social relations with affected cases facilitates both becoming affected and belief in the potency of the insect. Denial facilitates becoming affected but reduces the woman's tendency to believe in the insect *unless* she herself was affected during the epidemic. With but one exception, the *only* deniers of either type who fully believe in the insect are those whose own behavior during the epidemic could only be justified through such a belief. And the more extreme the affected denier's response to the epidemic, the more firmly she believed: only one of the 13 deniers who fainted had any doubt at all that an insect was the cause. This is in striking contrast to 4 of the 8 nondenier fainters who expressed some doubt.[5]

The same kind of relation is true with acquiescence. Respondents who showed tendencies toward reacting to the interview situation itself (as contrasted to the content of the questions) were most

[5] Respondents can be said to play two "games" in an interview, information-giving and ingratiation (Back & Gergen, 1963). Tendency to play the latter game gives information about the respondent and we are interpreting here the relationship between denial, acquiescence, and consistency of action and belief in this way.

likely to show consistency between belief and action. We might say that they subordinated their belief to justifying their actions, looking not at the facts to which the question was directed, but at the way in which they presented themselves.

In summary, strongly persistent belief is a function of going to the doctor during the epidemic, especially going early or of having friends who did so. It is also a function of a need for self-presentation which we have also seen to be related to being affected at all. Self-presentation, as shown by stereotyped responses in the interview (denial or acquiescence) leads to efforts to be consistent, showing more belief among affecteds and less belief among controls.

PERSONAL CHARACTERISTICS, SOCIAL RELATIONS, AND MODE OF RESPONSE

Several of the earlier findings have suggested that *how* an affected woman responded during the epidemic was an important variable, and we had several cues to factors associated with different modes of response. We differentiated among the affected women according to whether they fainted, almost fainted, or did neither. We reasoned that the woman who fainted was evidently overcome with fear and tension before she could get medical assistance, whereas the others evidently got to the doctor before experiencing such overwhelming emotions. We were thus alerted to look for factors which would encourage a woman to seek help when her difficulties were relatively minor and for factors which would deter a woman from seeking aid until it was too late. Our original conceptualization and some of the early findings suggested several possibilities. Those who were deniers presumably would tend to delay acknowledging a problem and should be more likely to faint, whereas those who easily acknowledge symptoms should be unlikely to do so. Those who had friends who were also affected might be expected to be alerted to the reality of the danger and be more likely to seek aid before they were overwhelmed. Those who had a generally high inclination to adopt the sick role would presumably seek assistance under conditions of less distress than those who normally had a low inclination to seek medical aid. We examined each of these possibilities. The findings are presented in Table 7.3.

TABLE 7.3
Mode of Response of Affected Women by Personal and Social
Characteristics

Characteristic	Fainted %	Almost Fainted %	Did Neither %
Role-conflict denial (N = 16)	56.3	12.5	31.3
Deny all symptoms (N = 17)	35.3	17.6	47.1
High symptom scorers (N = 16)	25.0	56.3	18.8
High inclination to adopt sick role (N = 39)	35.9	23.1	41.0
Describe health as "excellent" (N = 9)	66.7	22.2	11.1
Linked with other affecteds (N = 40)	32.5	30.0	37.5
Linked with *earlier* affecteds (N = 25)	20.0	32.0	48.0
Total Affecteds (N = 56)	37.5	26.8	35.7

As expected, those affecteds who were role-conflict deniers were much more likely than the other affected women to faint. The pattern with respect to symptom denial and admission, however, is not quite what we expected. Although those who easily acknowledged symptoms very seldom fainted, those who denied symptoms did not faint any more frequently than the other affecteds.[6] We also find that those with a high inclination to adopt the sick role fainted as frequently as the other affected women, although we had expected them to do so less often.

Our first examination of the relationship between social ties with other affecteds and response during the epidemic also appeared

---

[6] It is also worth noting that the women who easily acknowledged symptoms were also the most likely (and the deniers are least likely) to be listed as having "almost fainted." When we consider that such a listing in the doctor's records could only have come from the woman's self-report of her response during the epidemic, this pattern is also consistent with our interpretation of the relationship between personal characteristics and kinds of response. Those who easily acknowledged symptoms during the interview were also most likely to acknowledge to the doctor that they had had a very serious upset during the epidemic, even when they had not actually fainted.

to contradict our expectations. If we consider links with any other affected woman, there is no difference between linked women and the others. But if we use as our criterion the presence of social ties with affecteds who reported to the doctor before the case in question, the expected tendency is quite strong, women with such ties tending to faint only about half as often as affecteds in general. This suggests that, although the sequence of affected cases was not an important factor in the interpersonal influence which led a woman to become affected, sequence was important in determining whether or not a woman would seek medical aid before she was overwhelmed by her tension and fainted. Having a close associate who was already affected and had been to the doctor evidently made it easier to seek help before it was too late.

In this analysis, then, the two factors which stand out are role-conflict denial (which evidently delayed a woman's admitting the need for help and thus increased the probability that she would faint) and social ties to earlier affected cases (which seems to have accelerated the tendency to seek aid and thus lowered the probability of fainting). We were surprised to find that symptom denial and inclination to adopt the sick role were not related to the type of response the women exhibited. We knew from an earlier analysis, however, that both of these variables were related to having ties with earlier affected cases. Those with ties to earlier cases tended to be symptom deniers more often and to have a lower inclination to adopt the sick role. It thus seemed possible that there was some kind of interaction effect between having social relations with earlier affecteds and some of our measures of personal characteristics. To test this possibility, we computed the proportion who fainted for each of the major personal characteristic categories, holding social relations constant. The findings are reported in Table 7.4.

Although the patterns are somewhat different, in all three cases we find that when the woman had both social relations with earlier affecteds and the particular personal characteristic, she was least likely to faint. The combination of being a nondenier and having a tie with an earlier case or having a high inclination to adopt the sick role and having such a tie produced the fewest fainters. The interaction effect between social relations and the personal characteristic is most apparent, however, for the two measures of denial. There is

TABLE 7.4

Distribution of Cases of Fainting According to Symptom Denial, Role-Conflict Denial, and Inclination to Adopt the Sick Role, Controlling for the Presence of Social Ties with Earlier Cases

| | Affecteds | |
| | Linked | Not Linked |
Characteristic	%	%
Denial of all symptoms	36.4 (11)*	33.3 (6)
Acknowledge some symptoms	7.1 (14)	56.0 (25)
Role-conflict denial	57.1 (7)	55.6 (9)
No role-conflict denial	5.6 (18)	54.5 (22)
Low inclination to adopt sick role	20.0 (10)	71.4 (7)
High inclination to adopt sick role	13.3 (15)	50.0 (24)

* The number in parentheses following each percentage is the number of affected cases in that category. For instance, there are 11 affecteds who are symptom deniers and who have links with earlier affected cases. Of these, 36.4 percent fainted.

a much greater difference between deniers and nondeniers who have links with earlier cases than there is between those with high and low inclination to adopt the sick role who have such links. One is also tempted to interpret the differences in the "not linked" column, but the numbers of cases are so small that this would be quite hazardous. The general pattern, however, is for particular combinations of social and personal characteristics to be associated with varying probabilities of fainting during the epidemic.

An even more fundamental point to be made on the basis of this analysis is that the role of social ties with affected cases is different depending on whether we are trying to understand *how a woman gets sick* or *how she comes to the attention of the medical authorities.* Having ties with any other affected case, whatever the order of reporting to the doctor, tends to be associated with getting sick. But having ties to a case that has already had medical attention tends to be associated with seeking such attention before fainting. We saw in Chapter 6 that the sequence of affected cases did not seem relevant to the interpersonal influence process. In the present analysis we find a very different pattern. Here what we are interested in, though, is not whether a woman developed symptoms but whether she was able to get medical assistance before her symptoms overwhelmed her. And here the order of reporting to the doctor is quite significant. We find, for instance, that of the 25 affecteds who had ties to earlier cases, only 5 (20.0 percent) fainted. In contrast, of those 15 who had ties only to later cases, 8 (or 53.3 percent) fainted. This is almost exactly the proportion (50.0 percent) who fainted among the 16 who had no ties to any other affecteds. Thus, again we find that the difference between using one or the other of the possible dependent attributes discussed in Chapter 3 is considerable. If we use the emotional experience as our dependent attribute, the order of affected cases is not important, but if we use the behavior which follows from that experience (fainting or going to the doctor) the order affected is quite important.

A MULTIDIMENSIONAL MODEL

Throughout our analysis it has been apparent that no one of our variables is a completely successful predictor of a woman's becoming affected, even though the three different types of predictors (strain, personal characteristics, and social relations) have all proved to be effective. In several instances we have seen that combinations of these variables have proved more effective than the individual measures. The implication throughout has been that different kinds of people, under different kinds of strain, and with different patterns of social relations, respond differently. We should thus expect that some kind of multidimensional model would be most effective in organizing our findings.

If we are to attempt an overall statement of the contribution our analysis makes to an understanding of the dynamics of the epidemic, however, we must again recognize that we have to this point been dealing with only a part of the population of plant workers who were exposed to the experience of the epidemic. Although there seems to be good reason to leave the Negroes and those outside the dressmaking departments out of our analysis, it is also true that thus far we have not even dealt with all of those white women in the dressmaking departments. The fact that we have a sample of those who did not report to the doctor plus the total population of those who received medical aid complicates the situation. This is particularly true since the self-defined affecteds have played such an important part in our analysis. Ideally, a summary statement should reflect the process occurring throughout the relevant population (i.e., white women in the dressmaking department). We must therefore make some assumptions about those women in the population whom we did not interview. The most reasonable assumption appears to be that our sample of nonaffected cases (controls plus self-defined affecteds) is representative of the population of nonaffected cases, and that the distribution of all characteristics within that sample is the same as the distribution within the population. We must also assume that we actually achieved a one-fourth sample of those nonaffected cases. Thus, whenever we examine the distribution of a particular characteristic, we need to multiply the data we have on the nonaffected cases by four and then add it to the data we have on the affected cases. This should then allow us to make the best estimate of the distribution of these characteristics within the total white female population in the dressmaking departments. Given such assumptions, we can analyze the distribution of the important characteristics within what can most legitimately be called the "population at risk."

In order to present in summary fashion the effect of the kinds of factors we have discussed earlier within the total population at risk, we selected the three most important measures from the earlier analysis and combined them. First there was the summary measure of strain which we viewed as an index of the situations in which our subjects found themselves. It will be recalled that this consists of four measures of strain: working a great deal of overtime, failing to mention the supervisor as one to go to with a complaint, seeing variation in output among the members of one's section, and providing half or more of the family income. This was then combined with the measure of the woman's position in the interpersonal influence process during the epidemic. Since we were going to use as our dependent measure the fact that a woman was or was not an affected case, we counted intimate ties with *any* other affected woman as an indication of a woman's social position. Such ties ranged in number from zero to three. Finally, within the categories defined by these situational and sociometric measures, we differentiated between two kinds of persons, those who were and were not deniers by one or both of our measures. Since there were 5 possible levels of strain, 4 degrees of social linkage with affecteds, and 2 types of persons, this led to 40 possible combinations. Since some of the combinations did not appear and others were very infrequent, we reduced the number of categories by collapsing the strain and social position measures into 3 levels each. This provided the basis for an 18-cell table.

The data are reported in Table 7.5. The first number in each cell is the number of affecteds of that type, the second is the num-

TABLE 7.5

Distribution of the Population at Risk Classified by Level of Strain, Ties with Affected Cases, and Denial

| | | Level of Strain | | |
		0–1	2	3–4
No Affected Intimates	No Denial	4-16-96	2-4-36	2-0-0**
	Denial	3-0-56	2-4-4*	3-0-0**
One Affected Intimate	No Denial	4-20-52	2-8-12*	4-0-4**
	Denial	3-0-4*	7-0-4**	4-0-4**
Two or More Affected Intimates	No Denial	3-4-0*	3-4-8*	2-8-0**
	Denial	3-0-0**	2-0-4**	3-0-0**

NOTE: The first number in each cell is the number of affecteds, the second is the number of self-defined affecteds, and the third is the number of controls. An "intimate" is a friend, one to whom one would go for advice or would expect to come to her for advice, a carpool or lunch partner, or one defined as the best worker in the section. "Denial" includes both the denial of symptoms and role-conflict denial. Cells with double asterisks designate those categories in which more affected cases are found. Those with single asterisks, together with those with double asterisks, designate those categories in which more affected and/or self-defined affected cases are found (see text).

ber of self-defined affecteds, and the third is the number of controls. Both of these latter two numbers were arrived at by multiplying the number of self-defined affecteds and controls of each type in our sample by four, thereby providing an estimate of the number of such women within the population at risk. The total number of cases in the table is 408.[7]

If we wish to "predict" which cases were affected, using the three factors of strain, social influence, and denial, we might pick out cells containing 56 cases in such a way as to maximize the accuracy of prediction.[8] The cells with the double asterisks contain a total of 54 cases. To fill out the required number we might draw randomly 2 more cases from some adjacent cell. Since no such cell has half or more affecteds, we may assume that both cases so drawn would be nonaffecteds. How well does such a table order the cases? Perhaps most important is the fact that there is a simple pattern to be seen. First, there is a general tendency for the proportion of affecteds in the cells to increase as we move from upper left to lower right. All but one of the cells with double asterisks are in the last column or last row of the table. Second, either an extreme level of strain or close association with two or more other affecteds tends to lead a woman to be affected, irrespective of the other factors. Third, denial, when added to either social influence or strain, greatly increases the probability of being affected.

Also, it is striking that so many of the 56 cases we have just singled out are affecteds. Not only are 30 (or 53.6 percent) of them

[7] This number is much smaller than the 490 women in these departments listed in Table 1.1. Although some of the difference may be due to errors in sampling, most of it is due to three other facts: (1) the Negroes in the dressmaking departments are excluded in this analysis; (2) all supervisory personnel were excluded before the sample was taken; and (3) some of the women who were at the plant at the time of the epidemic were not there when the interviews were carried out (and their replacements were excluded from our analysis).

[8] This is not, of course, an actual case of prediction. In effect we are asking the following question: Given the fact that we know that 56 out of an estimated total of 408 women were affecteds, which combination of our three predictors permits us most accurately to identify the affected cases? To answer the question, we must find those cells (cells defined in terms of the predictors) which contain 56 cases and which include the maximum possible proportion of the affecteds. We are thus using the predictors to pick out 56 cases which have the highest probability of being affecteds.

affecteds, but of the remaining 352 cases, 326 (or 92.6 percent) are *not* affecteds. There is thus an overall accuracy of designation of 87.3 percent. This level of accuracy, of course, is far greater than could be accomplished using any of the three kinds of measures individually. Although it is clear that the strain and social relations measures predict well in the more extreme cases, the *combination* of variables is clearly important at the less extreme levels.

We may also ask whether such a table helps to single out the self-defined affecteds as well. Since there were 17 such cases in our sample, we can assume that there were 68 in the population at risk. These, plus the 56 affecteds, would give a total of 124 women who experienced symptoms during the epidemic. The cells with the single and double asterisks contain 115 cases. To fill out the required number, we could draw 9 cases randomly from the cell in the first row and second column, and we could assume that 1 of these 9 cases would be either affected or self-defined affected. Of these 124 cases, 72 (or 58.1 percent) are either affecteds or self-defined affecteds, and of the remaining 284 cases 232 (or 81.7 percent) are controls. There is thus an overall accuracy of designation of 74.5 percent.

The important part of these results, however, is the high proportion of affected (or self-defined affected) cases in the critical cells, since only a very small percentage of the total of 408 were either affected (13.8 percent) or self-defined affected (16.7 percent). Perhaps the best way to illustrate the effectiveness of the three independent attributes is to note that the cells in Table 7.5 which are marked with asterisks represent less than three-tenths (28.1 percent) of the population at risk, but they contain more than three-fourths (76.8 percent) of those who received medical treatment and more than half (57.3 percent) of all those who experienced symptoms. The three independent measures are thus much more effective in discriminating between those who did and did not go to the doctor than they are in discriminating between those who did and did not experience symptoms, although they do both to a significant extent. We will return to this matter in the next section.[9]

---

[9] The apparent effectiveness of our independent attributes makes it tempting to compute some kind of summary statistic to measure their effectiveness. We have not presented such a statistic because none appeared appropriate for our data. Multiple correlation assumes that the same equation applies (with

THE PREDICTABLES AND THE DEVIANTS

Although the degree of accuracy of discrimination achieved is very striking, it is still true that a number of cases we might have expected to be affected were not, and other cases that were affected are found in cells that are not generally predictive of being affected. The most easily predicted affected cases (those who got medical treatment) are the deniers with at least one affected close associate. Of the 38 such cases in Table 7.5, 22 (57.9 percent) were affected. Those with high levels of strain (irrespective of other characteristics) are also very likely to have been affected: 18 of 34 such cases (52.9 percent) had been seen by the doctor.

When we turn to the misplaced cases we find, not surprisingly, that those nonaffected cases which are included in the cells having a high proportion of affecteds (those cells with the asterisks) are very likely to be self-defined affecteds. There are 72 nonaffected cases in the cells with the asterisks, and 28 of these are self-defined affecteds, the rest being controls. This represents 41.2 percent of the self-defined affecteds and only 19.7 percent of the controls. It is also important to see, however, that the rest of the self-defined affecteds are in the cells without asterisks. Also all but 4 of the 68 self-defined affecteds appear in the "no denial" rows. In fact, we have reported in Chapter 5 that none of the 17 self-defined affecteds in our sample was a symptom denier, and 10 of them were in the high symptom category. Because of the small number of such cases in our sample, we have until now tended to de-emphasize this fact. Now that we are examining the total population at risk, however, it assumes

---

minor deviations) to all cases, whereas we have found that different contributions are made by the critical characteristics under different conditions. Of the other possible techniques, those suggested by Coleman (1964, Ch. 6) appeared most promising. However, the cell frequencies in Table 7.5 are sometimes so small that some kind of reduction would be necessary. Whatever reduction is made tends to combine cells of the nondeniers which are quite different in their proportions affected, and this leads to a summary measure which suggests that only deniers contributed significantly to the epidemic. The fact that nondeniers tend to become affected only when strain and/or social influence is great (and also the cell frequencies are small) thus means that the various summary statistics we have tested seem to distort the results too much to be very useful.

greater importance. It gives further meaning to the pattern of deviant cases.

Since in our sample there were 17 affecteds, 15 controls, and no self-defined affecteds who denied all symptoms, we may assume that there were 17 out of a total of 77 symptom deniers in the total population at risk who experienced symptoms. In the high symptom category (those who exceeded the sample mean of one or more of the symptom scales by at least one standard deviation) there were 16 affecteds, 10 self-defined affecteds, and 26 controls in our sample. On the assumption that both affecteds and self-defined affecteds experienced symptoms, we may also assume that there were thus 56 out of 160 high scoring women who had symptoms during the epidemic. If this was actually the case, then a greater proportion of those with high symptom scores (35.0 percent) experienced symptoms than did those who were deniers (22.1 percent). Evidently, therefore, those with high symptom scores were more likely to "feel affected," but they were less likely to need or seek assistance, while deniers were less likely to experience symptoms but were more likely to require or seek medical aid if they did.[10]

This suggests with respect to Table 7.5 that many of the self-defined affecteds who are found in the cells without asterisks should be women who were in the high symptom category. This is actually

[10] The problems of interpretation here are considerable, however. Since the two definitions of being affected are so different, they bring into play to very different degrees the same characteristics we are attempting to interpret. Those who deny symptoms, for instance, presumably would be less likely to acknowledge during the interview that they were affected by the epidemic. In fact, four women who were known to the medical authorities as having been affected denied their involvement in the epidemic during the interview, and three of these are in our category of symptom deniers. We cannot say with any real confidence, therefore, that more of those with high scores *actually* felt affected during the epidemic. However, it seems highly likely that many more women than we know "felt affected," and presumably many more than those we have called affecteds actually "acted affected." This suggestion is further supported by the women's responses to the question: Did this happen to anyone (else) in the plant whom you know well? Although none of our controls was named in response to this question, 4 of the self-defined affecteds were named as well as 14 women in the dressmaking departments who were not in our sample. Since only 79 percent of the affected women were named, it seems likely that this represents a less than full accounting of those who in some way "acted affected," but it strongly suggests that others besides the affecteds were actively involved in the development and spread of the epidemic.

the case. Of the 40 self-defined affecteds in these cells, 32 had high symptom scores (on the assumption that the population at risk had the same proportions of such scores as the sample). It may well be, therefore, that the self-defined affected category is a mixed one, being composed in part of women with few predictive characteristics but a readiness to admit to symptoms and in part of women who had the predictive characteristics but who also had means of coping with the strain they experienced.

When we turn to the affecteds who seem to be deviants, we find 13 of them in the cells with no asterisks. In 9 of these cases the woman has one of the predictive attributes. Four have one affected intimate, 2 have two of the four sources of strain, and 3 are deniers. There are 4 cases, however, who were affected in spite of having none of the predictive characteristics. Although these must be viewed as evidence of the limitations of our predictors, it may be well worth mentioning that 3 of the 4 cases were affected quite late in the epidemic. They are cases numbered 40, 43, and 54. If we accept the notion that some kind of "crowd effect" was involved in the epidemic, it would certainly have been stronger if more cases had been already affected. We find, in fact, that of the 13 affected cases in these four cells, 7 were numbered 40 or higher. Seven of the last 17 and 4 of the last 11 cases are found in these cells.

The cases which seem to deviate from the pattern predicted by our three independent attributes, therefore, tend to be largely of three types. Those which are incorrectly predicted as affected cases are more frequently self-defined affecteds than one would expect if this were just random error. Those which are predicted as nonaffected but are self-defined affected more frequently have high symptom scores than one would expect if this were just random error. And those which are predicted as nonaffected but are actually affected are more frequently affected late in the epidemic than would be expected if this were random error. We may thus at least speculate that factors which are not included in the construction of Table 7.5 are involved here. For those cases which were predicted to be affected but were not, it may be that the self-defined affecteds' greater facilities for coping with strain are at least partly involved. For those cases which were predicted to be nonaffected but were self-defined affecteds, it may be that their readiness to acknowledge symptoms was involved. And for those which were predicted to be nonaffected but were actually affected, it may be that a crowd effect late in the epidemic was operating. Although this can be nothing more than speculation, such an explanation fits well with both our other data and the conceptualization we have evolved of the process of hysterical contagion.

A GENERAL OVERVIEW

In this chapter we have followed several of the cues suggested in the earlier analysis, in each case attempting to bring together some of the parts of that earlier analysis into a more comprehensive and cohesive view of the epidemic. We have examined a number of connections among the findings and the presumed processes involved in the analysis of the earlier chapters.

Evidence of the distribution of the "two-edged" measures of strain among the affecteds tends to support the idea that such sources of strain both added to the woman's burden and deterred her from giving expression to the tension she experienced. Affecteds who experienced such sources of strain were more likely to be affected late in the epidemic. The effects of social ties with affecteds have been presumed to be in the direction of impelling a woman to believe in the threat of the insect and thus increasing the probability that she will also be affected. If we ask why self-defined affecteds and controls who had such social ties were not affected, the best answer offered by the data seems to be that these women generally had fewer sources of strain, were better able to cope with strain, and were less sensitive to interpersonal influence. Although the pattern of belief in the threat of the mysterious insect which our data provides cannot be used in our explanation of the epidemic, the data suggest that one's role in the epidemic is an important determinant of such beliefs afterwards. Those who became affected or were closely associated with someone who did were most likely to express complete belief in the bug. Those who were deniers (by either definition) were most likely to doubt the significance of the bug, unless they had themselves been affected. Among the affecteds, the most complete belief in the bug was expressed by those who fainted.

All of these findings add to the picture gained from the earlier analysis. But the most fruitful parts of the investigations reported here were those which examined the combined effects of two or more of the independent attributes on the probability that a woman would become affected or that, if affected, she would exhibit the most extreme form of response by fainting. With regard to the latter issue, we found that having social ties to others who were affected earlier decreased the probability that a woman would faint. Even more striking was the tendency for women with such ties not to faint if they were either nondeniers or had a high inclination to adopt the sick role.

When we attempt to identify the affected cases through the use of the several independent attributes, we are able to do so with a considerable degree of accuracy. Using three levels of strain, three levels of social relations with other affecteds, and the difference between deniers and nondeniers, it is possible to identify categories representing less than three-tenths of the total population at risk but which contain more than three-fourths of the cases treated by the doctor and well over half of those who experienced symptoms during the epidemic. Those cases which are misclassified in this procedure are largely self-defined affecteds who had the predictive attributes and affecteds who were affected late in the epidemic who did not have the predictive attributes. Also, those self-defined affecteds who did not have the predictive attributes tended to be women who very readily admitted to having symptoms. All of this analysis adds force to the argument that multiple factors must be considered if we are to account for the women's behavior during the epidemic and that different combinations of the same factors lead to very different outcomes.

Even though our data fail to provide a completely adequate explanation of the facts of the epidemic, the analysis presented in this and the previous chapters has indicated that there is more order in this seemingly chaotic situation than one might at first have expected. Before turning to the matter of a general conceptualization of hysterical contagion, therefore, it may be well to state in a more succinct summary form what we believe this analysis has done to clarify the order in the chaos. We will do this through a set of statements, each of which will be followed by a brief review of the relevant data. (In reporting the data, all frequencies and percentages are based on our estimate of the assumed population at risk.)

Most affecteds were exposed to a great deal of strain, or were deniers or both. Although we have suggested that various combinations of these factors, plus social relations with other affecteds, are predictive of an affected status, this is the simplest general statement that can be made about the affecteds. Almost two-thirds (66 percent) of the affected cases have these characteristics. In contrast, only slightly more than one-fourth (27 percent) of the nonaffecteds have the same characteristics. Only 18 percent of the self-defined affecteds had these characteristics, compared with 30 percent of the controls. Thus, those qualities which most clearly distinguish the affecteds from the nonaffecteds are particularly successful in distinguishing them from the self-defined affecteds. When social relations with affecteds are used as a predictive attribute, greater distinction is seen between the controls and the affecteds, but the line between affecteds and self-defined affecteds becomes less clear.

The difference between affecteds and self-defined affecteds was largely due to differences in personal qualities and in sources of strain. In general, the affecteds acknowledged symptoms much less readily and more frequently denied the importance of role conflict. The self-defined affecteds also were exposed to less strain than the affecteds, and the strain they did experience was more likely to be of the "two-edged" type which generally tended to delay the woman's becoming affected.

The difference between self-defined affecteds and controls was largely a difference in social relations and personal qualities. The self-defined affecteds were more likely to have close social ties with affecteds, but they much more easily acknowledged symptoms. The controls were more like the affecteds in their denial of symptoms, but they less frequently were socially linked with affecteds. If we view social ties, strain, and denial as forces leading a woman to become affected, it is apparent that the self-defined affecteds had more of the first, the controls had more of the last, and neither of them had a great deal of the second.

If the strain experienced was sufficiently great, it alone was likely to lead a woman to become affected during the epidemic. Not only were several of our measures of strain (such as working a great deal of overtime) clearly related to the tendency to be affected, but our summary index using four such measures showed that more than one-half of those in the population at risk who were under heavy strain became affected compared with less than one-tenth of those under little or no strain. There is a general pattern of increasing probability of being affected as the level of strain increases.

If social influence was strong enough, it alone was likely to lead a woman to become affected. There were 44 women who had two or more social ties with affecteds and 16 (36 percent) of them were affected cases. In contrast, only 7 percent of the 232 women who had no ties with affecteds became affected. More generally, the more ties a woman had with affecteds the more likely she was to become affected herself.

Among those affecteds with social ties with other affecteds, the ones who became affected first exhibited the most extreme symptoms. Although social ties with any other affected increased the probability that a woman would become affected, if she became affected before her associate, she was much more likely to faint. Of linked pairs of affecteds, over one-half of the earlier affected members of the dyads fainted, but only one-fifth of the later affected members fainted.

The combination of denial and a moderate level of strain or social influence greatly increased the tendency to become affected. Those who were deniers but experienced low levels of strain and no social influence were not very likely to become affected—only 5 percent did so. But deniers who had two sources of strain and/or one affected associate were very likely to become affected themselves— 43 percent did so. This is in contrast to those nondeniers who had two sources of strain and/or one affected associate, only 5 percent of whom were affected. There is thus a kind of interactive effect of social or situational influence with the personal characteristic of denial to produce a high probability of becoming affected.

Personal and social characteristics interact to affect the tendency to exhibit the most extreme symptoms. Those affecteds who were nondeniers and who had ties with someone affected before them, were very unlikely to faint, less than one-tenth doing so. In contrast, over one-half of nondeniers without such ties fainted. Among deniers, the presence of ties with earlier affecteds did not influence the tendency to faint.

There were many persons who played an important part in the development and spread of the contagion who were not known by the authorities to have been affected. It is difficult to demonstrate this statement as convincingly as the others, but it seems very likely that within the population of women in the dressmaking departments there were at least four times the number of women as in our sample who would have been self-defined affecteds if we had been able to interview them. If so, there would have been more of them (68) than affecteds (56). Since they were likely to acknowledge symptoms rather easily, it seems almost certain that they were influential in convincing many other women that there was a reason to be fearful, and thus they contributed significantly to the epidemic.

8

THEME AND VARIATIONS

In this chapter we will return to a more abstract level of theoretical statement in an effort to present in general terms those propositions which our analysis seems to justify. In doing this, we will attempt both to remain consistent with the data from this single study and to conceptualize this case in sufficiently general terms to make our discussion potentially applicable beyond the limits of the single case. Since the data we have are limited to a single case, and since all such cases are certain to have their own idiosyncrasies, some of our data are judged to be less relevant to the more general discussion, and some of that discussion will necessarily go beyond the available data.

THE GENERAL PERSPECTIVE

In Chapter 2 we discussed a number of earlier conceptualizations of hysterical contagion and closely related types of collective behavior. We approached this particular case with a number of general expectations. The epidemic was viewed as an expression of frustration and a reflection of the inadequate structural characteristics of the work situation. It was argued that in such a situation as existed

in Montana Mills prior to the epidemic there were a number of
people subjected to many sources of strain which they found frustrating and from which there was no simple, socially legitimized means
of escape. In such situations, individuals become tense and, presumably, they tend to reinforce each other's sense of frustration and
tension.

There is undoubtedly a wide range of possible outcomes from
such tension-filled collective situations. In some cases, there might
simply be a selective elimination from the situation of those who are
least able to cope with the tension. This could be on a permanent
basis through resignation or being fired or on a temporary basis
through absenteeism and "illness." In other cases, the source(s) of
the strain might be temporarily limited and, after a period of extreme
tension, a period of relaxation of strain might occur which would
permit a reduction of the tension. In still others, the individuals in
the situation might band together in some way to combat the strain
and/or to release the resulting tension in socially approved or socially
disapproved ways. Thus, the outcome will depend on a number of
things including the structure of the situation within which the strain
is experienced, the kinds of individuals experiencing the strain, the
potential for collective as opposed to individual reactions, and the
possible occurrence of a number of random events.

In order for the kind of epidemic we have studied to occur,
there must be provided, from some origin, a suggestion that the situation possesses a threatening element whose potency is high and whose
"behavior" is mysterious and unpredictable. That is, the threat must
be seen as one which is genuinely frightening (to the extent it is believed), and the means of avoiding the threat must be seen as very
limited and/or undefinable. If the threat is not seen as very serious,
the added tension due to its presence will not be appreciable; and if
there are easy ways of avoiding the threat, it thereby becomes much
less threatening.

The particular kind of threat which will meet these criteria in
any given situation can undoubtedly be highly variable. The most
effective kind, however, will be one which is easily accepted as
genuine. Although almost *any* kind of threat *might* have provided
the basis for such an epidemic of symptoms (e.g., a vengeful spirit

whose "home" was disturbed by the building of the plant), the credibility of some kinds of threat will be greater than others. This credibility will be a function of general cultural norms and the specifics of the situation in which the collectivity is located. In our case, the threat of a poisonous insect was rather easily accepted since such insects are known in the area (e.g., the black widow spider). Also, the foreign origin of some of the machinery and materials used in the plant made it possible that some similar but unfamiliar insect might have been shipped in (like the tarantula spider in the bananas) and thus might pose a threat which was located only in the plant. We cannot say that belief in a threat of this kind *had* to develop, of course, but only that it was easier for it than for other possible beliefs to develop in this situation.

It may well be that the threat is originally completely "invented" by one or more persons in the situation as a need-fulfilling element. That is, there may be no manifest evidence of the threatening element at all from the point of view of the outside observer. It may simply be a need-fulfilling hallucination. On the other hand, the element may be manifestly present, even though its potency may be less than fully evident. That was apparently the case with the Montana Mills epidemic. Certainly there were insects in the plant. Even after several sprayings some were found, and there must have been more before the sprayings. The significant "invention" here was the effect of the insect, its potency. In such a case, it is much easier to evolve a belief in the threat since it is both common in form and possible in its effect. Belief in this threat seemed reasonable not only to the women who worked in the plant but also to management and a number of outside specialists who found it sufficiently credible to warrant serious investigation. This type of response on the part of outsiders tends to reinforce the belief and to make the threat appear even more genuine.

However, a connection between the stressful situation and the newly invented external source of potent threat is required. Smelser (1963) suggests that the *function* of belief in such a threat is to give substance to the feeling of frustration and anxiety. Instead of simply having a feeling that something is awry, the belief in a tangible threat makes it possible to *explain* and *justify* one's sense of discom-

fort—instead of anxiety, one experiences fear, and it is then possible
to act in some meaningful way with respect to this tangible threat
rather than just feeling frustrated and anxious. The belief in the
threat, then, solves the problem of objectifying the source of the discomfort.

The crucial point here, however, is that, for some reason the
actual source of discomfort is not (or cannot be) clearly recognized
by at least some of those in the situation. In our case, the principal
presumed source of the frustration and tension was the strain on the
job and the conflict between home and job responsibilities. The
women were tired and torn between conflicting demands. But, why
did they not simply face their problems and cope with them directly? What possible connection could there be between working
overtime and being bitten by a poisonous insect? Basically, this is a
question of identifying the alternative modes of behavior in the situation. Given the stress, what could the women do about it which
would have constituted coping directly with the problem? They
might have simply stayed home and rested up. They might have
refused to work overtime. They might have complained to their
supervisor and asked her to relieve them of this burden. They might
have used the union as a basis for bargaining with management for a
better work load. We have found that, for at least some of the women,
each of these various modes of direct coping posed serious difficulties.
They were either ineffectual or they were unavailable to some of the
women for various reasons.

In the face of such difficulties, the original strain remained, and
the fact of impotence in coping with it provided an additional source
of stress. Also, the difficulties involved in coping create one or more
additional sources of strain. If the supervisor is not trusted, the most
"rational" thing to do is to treat her as if she is not trustworthy.
Yet a worker would find such a reaction very threatening, and the
necessity of controlling one's distrustful tendencies becomes an additional burden. Likewise, if having a small child makes the life of a
working woman more stressful, it might be seen as "natural" or "reasonable" to reject either the job or the child. But if both of these
are important to the woman, the very thought of either type of rejection is threatening. One dare not even *think* about being unhappy

with the job or the child. In this way, each of the sources of strain and each of the barriers to coping with the strain places the woman in a position of compounded stress.

But, why does getting bitten by a poisonous insect enter the picture at all? At the most simple level of functional analysis, we have said that it objectifies the source of discomfort and helps solve the problem by providing the woman with a legitimate and credible reason for leaving the situation. For some women, the simple existence of this threat provided an acceptable reason for "clocking out of there." For others, it was necessary to get sick before leaving could be justified, but once they got sick even management condoned their leaving, and the insect made it "easier" to get sick. Not only did the insect provide a legitimate reason for leaving the plant and getting the needed rest, it also provided a means of "striking back" at management. From this point of view, the epidemic could be seen as a kind of "psychological strike." It is not likely, of course, that it was consciously viewed in this way by any of the women, but the insect did legitimize leaving the plant, and it did cause management a great deal of difficulty.

This functional view of the epidemic is only one side of the picture. It is equally important to see the close relationship between the symptoms one might expect to develop under the frustrating conditions and those symptoms which were attributed to the toxic insect. As stated by Engel, when a person is faced with psychological stress with which he cannot adequately cope, he develops both a cognitive sense of distress and "the awareness of physiological changes such as palpitation, sweating, flushing, muscle tension or 'butterflies in the stomach'" (Engel, 1962a, p. 384). Such symptoms are general emotional responses, and it is but one small step from the experience of such symptoms to the definition of them as due to a much-discussed toxic insect. In fact, it is reasonable to postulate a need to identify and label (to understand) such symptoms, and we know that similar physiological experiences are capable of very different interpretations. This is where the "generalized belief" becomes significant. It is at this point that those who, for whatever reason, do not accurately attribute their symptoms to the stress they are experiencing accept the newly evolved explanation. In our particular case, the newly evolved explanation was ideal in that such an insect could easily be accepted as the cause of the kinds of symptoms the women experienced.

Our general view of such cases as we have investigated here, therefore, may be summarized briefly as follows: there are a number of people exposed to common sources of strain from which there are available but not easily acceptable avenues of escape. The combination of the original strain and the added stress experienced because of available but forbidden solutions brings about a general state of tension whose intensity is probably increased by interstimulation among the people so situated. The state of unresolved tension leads to the experience of physiological symptoms. These symptoms become associated in the minds of the distressed people with some credible (but factually incorrect) "cause" in the situation, the connection deriving from what are probably random events that become interpreted in the context of the experienced discomfort. This external cause both objectifies the source of the discomfort and adds a further source of strain to the situation—fear of a threatening force. Given this evolved credible explanation of symptoms, various means of coping with the (newly found) threatening force become legitimate, and those who were unable to cope with the original sources of strain are provided with acceptable forms of response not originally available to them (e.g., staying away from the plant). Another acceptable form of response, under the new definition of the situation, may be to acknowledge one's inability to handle the problem and to seek assistance from outside experts (usually, as in our case, medical experts) who are capable of dealing with the symptoms. Whatever means of coping are deemed legitimate (and legitimacy is undoubtedly a function of both the participants' and outsiders' definitions) will become socially facilitated, and the probability of any given participant's use of these means will tend to increase as the epidemic runs its course. The manifest phenomena of the epidemic are thus the reports of the external threat, the physiological symptoms (which purport to be the result of the external threat), and the coping behaviors of the participants (and various relevant outsiders).

The central problem faced in this study, however, goes beyond this general conceptualization. In fact, it actually takes this conceptualization for granted and asks the further question: Given such a development, *which* persons in the situation will be most active in the epidemic? We have operationally put this question in the following form: Which persons will seek the aid or behave in such a way as to come to the attention of outside (medical) experts? To deal with this question, we have had to go beyond the general conceptualization just presented, but we have also had to remain within that general framework. We have consequently raised more refined questions about variations in the experiences and character-istics of the persons found in the stressful situation. The basic logic involved has been that, if a particular combination of circumstances is likely to lead to a case of hysterical contagion, those who become involved in such a collective behavioral expression should be more likely to exhibit this combination of circumstances than should those who are not affected. We have defined the conditions which are likely to form the basis of hysterical contagion as being the collective experience of strain which cannot be adequately coped with oc-curring in a situation where interpersonal influence is possible. We have thus sought evidence of variations in strain, variations in per-sonal qualities associated with effective coping with strain, and varia-tions in social position.

VARIATIONS IN SITUATIONAL STRAIN

Many discussions of collective behavior approach the subject as if all of the participants (or potential participants) were responding to the same situational factors. There is considerable gain in such an assumption from the point of view of conceptual parsimony. In most cases, it is possible to point up salient features of the action setting which are presumably relevant to the behavior of all persons in the situation and which are related to the kind of collective phenomenon being studied. Such general factors were undoubtedly important in the development of the case we studied. But, being general factors, they cannot be used to explain why some people were affected by the epidemic and others were not.

When one looks for situational factors which might differentiate between those affected and those not affected, several possibilities come to mind. One of these, and the most obvious one in our particular case, is the fact that all of the potential participants were not and could not be physically located in exactly the same place. Studies of crowd behavior have made a point of differentiating between those in the center and those on the periphery of the crowd and have noted that the experience of the situation is quite different depending on such differences of placement. In a more structured situation, such as the one we studied, there are other structural bases of differentiation, such as the departmental organization of the plant and the fact that the dressmaking departments were in a separate area marked off by walls. This factor was so clearly relevant that we did not even include in this analysis (except in the Appendix) any of those persons located outside the dressmaking departments. The fact that working conditions, and thus the level of strain, were so different in these departments made such exclusion very appropriate.

In addition to this kind of spatial and organizational differentiation, prior knowledge of the distribution of cases and of cultural factors made further limitation of our analysis possible. We knew that very few men were involved in the epidemic. Both the absolute number of male affected cases (three) and the percentage of the male work force affected (1.0 percent) were so small, we immediately ruled out their inclusion in the study.

The other categorical difference we have used in this report represents a type that is not easily generalized to other similar situations. This is the elimination in the present discussion of the Negro women in the dressmaking departments. These women were in the same big room with the majority of the affected cases, and two of them in fact were affected. We have separated them from the others in those departments in this report as a matter of analytic convenience as well as for conceptual reasons. However, the data support the view that they were sufficiently different and so clearly socially segregated from the others that, although they were spatially involved in the activity of the epidemic, they were much less socially involved. To the extent that social relations and processes of identification are significant in the dissemination of hysterical symptoms, such people are much less "in the situation" than are others in the same room.

Whatever the justification of the separation in this case, however, the more general point is that cultural factors may differentiate between kinds of persons all of whom are physically in the same situation. To the extent that this is true, some structural features of the situation which are stressful for some persons may not be for others. Although there may be good reason to expect such cultural differences in the significance of situational strain, however, our ability to predict their significance in any given situation is probably so limited that it is safer to make the analytic differentiation only after the data are in hand. This, of course, is what we did with respect to the Negro women in the dressmaking departments.

Such categorical bases of differentiation are important in understanding the reasons for different levels of participation in such events, but we also know that other, more individual, factors are similarly relevant. Not only are the situational sources of strain unevenly distributed among those in the situation, but each of the actors finds himself in a total action context, only one part of which is represented by the situation in which the collective behavior occurs. The situational context of collective behavior is therefore a point of intersection of the total behavioral contexts of all of the actors. It is thus only one part of the total relevant context for any given actor. Because of the immediacy of that setting, the force of the collectively evolved definition of the situation, and the pressure of the feared threat, it is an immensely important part of the total context, but all of these characteristics of the immediate situation will be responded to in light of the total situation of the actor. And, both as a function of these different bases of response and as a result of varying locations in the action setting, each actor's perspective is likely to be somewhat unique.

It is not possible in such a study as this to take into account all of the potential sources of variation resulting from these kinds of differences. What we have done here rather crudely is to focus on two sources of variation in levels of strain. One of these was variation in sources of strain on the job, the other was variation in sources of strain off the job that might have carry-over relevance to the work situation. More generally, this would call for an examination of variation in sources of strain in the immediate action situation and variation in sources of strain outside that situation which would presumably be relevant to the individual's behavior in that situation. Since the latter kinds of sources of strain are theoretically unlimited, we have chosen to focus on those which are both structurally common in the population of actors and known to have direct significance in the action setting (i.e., family relations and role-conflict problems). Of course, the sources of strain in the action situation are also potentially very numerous. We have distinguished among those sources which are interpersonal (relations with peers and with superiors), those which are personal (ability to do the work tasks), and those which are structural (requirement to work overtime). However, we have done a better job of dealing with the first and third than with the second of these.

The general point to be made in this section, then, is that even those persons who are in the same action situation are differentially subject to sources of strain. The variations involved come both from their varying positions (spatially and socially) in the action setting and from their varying involvements in other action settings outside the immediate one. The general hypothesis relevant to these variations, and one which proved fruitful in the present study, is that those who face a greater number and more intense sources of strain have a greater probability of being affected by the hysterical contagion. This is to be expected because the greater the strain, the greater the probability that the individual will be unable to cope satisfactorily with it, and thus the greater the probability that physiological symptoms will occur which may be interpreted in terms of the belief in an external source of attack. Even though our catalogue of sources of strain was certainly far from complete, one of the clearest patterns to emerge from the analysis was the increasing probability of becoming affected by the epidemic as the number of sources and the intensity of strain increased.

THE PERSON AND COPING MECHANISMS

If the general conceptualization we have followed is to be accepted, it is obvious that there should be other factors involved in determining the distribution of affected cases besides the level of strain experienced by the actors. One of these factors should be the characteristics of the actor and the resources he has to cope with the strain he experiences. Situational strain is not as likely to bring about psychological stress and the disturbed affective states and somatic symptoms associated with such stress if the problem posed by the strain is adequately dealt with by the actor. Thus, the characteristics of the actor and the coping mechanisms he has at his disposal are certainly important in determining the ultimate psychological (and physiological) effect of any given level of strain he experiences.

For the women at Montana Mills, most of the kinds of strain experienced on the job were such that direct "rational" coping was limited to a few mechanisms. The women could leave work and pretend to be sick, they could complain to their supervisor, they could refuse to work overtime, and so on. In general, these mechanisms were either morally unacceptable to many of the women (if we are to believe their verbal reports) or they were threatening to them because of the importance of the job and the fear of losing it. Those who were most clearly affected by the epidemic were more likely to reject such direct coping mechanisms. They were thus not only left with the original strain but they presumably had the added strain of knowing that these mechanisms could be (and probably were) used by others.

Although such norms and attitudes are certainly qualities of the individual actors, they are more specific to the situation than others which we have considered to be relevant. We assumed that the women would vary in personality structure and that such variation would be significant in understanding the distribution of affected cases. Our original expectation was that those women who were generally more anxious and more concerned about physiological disturbances would be more likely to be affected (particularly since "being affected" meant going to the doctor), and we expected this concern to be reflected in their admission that they experienced a number of physical symptoms. We found, on the contrary, that those who were affected were much more likely to *deny* having any of the symptoms we asked them about than they were to admit to a large number of symptoms. In fact, there were so many affected women who denied having *any* of these symptoms that this extreme denial was viewed as potentially significant in the dynamics of the epidemic.

We interpreted the fact that symptom deniers were likely to be affected as being due to the greater significance for such women of symptoms experienced during the epidemic. That is, it seems reasonable, with the wisdom of hindsight, that if a woman takes some pride in not being subject to physical disturbances (or is for some reason threatened by a conscious admission of such disturbances), she will respond in a more exaggerated manner to an undeniable experience of physical symptoms (e.g., by fainting) than will a woman who easily accepts such symptoms as part of her normal life. Also, one who denies the reality of symptoms is not likely to cope with them very effectively. By the same token, we would expect that such women, who normally deny symptoms, would more easily accept some external explanation for these symptoms.

Here again we must keep in mind that our original definition of "being affected" was based on a woman's being known to the medical authorities. Given that definition, it is true that those who normally denied symptoms were more likely to be affected than were those who readily admitted to such symptoms. However, if we base our definition of "being affected" on a woman's admission in the interview that she had been affected by the epidemic ("Did anything like this happen to you?"), we get a picture much more like our original expectation. Many more women admitted being affected than ever became known to the medical authorities, and most of those who said they were affected but who were not known to the medical authorities also readily admitted to having symptoms. Thus, it is not unreasonable to assume that actually there were more who experienced symptoms during the epidemic among the high symptom women than among the symptom deniers. It also seems very reasonable to assume that they played a very important part in the development and spread of the epidemic.

Relevant here also is the contrast between what some of the affected women actually experienced and what they said about their experience. In some cases there seemed to be evidence of denial of the significance of external sources of strain. We followed this lead most systematically with respect to the denial of the significance of role conflict, and again such denial was associated with becoming an affected case. In fact, such role-conflict deniers were more likely than any others to faint during the epidemic. In some respects, this kind of denial may be viewed as the opposite of symptom denial. In the one case the respondent denies the significance of external forces; in the other she denies the existence of internal experiences.[1]

Although our measure of role-conflict denial is far from a convincing measure of a "tendency to deny the significance of external forces," the data from our study do support this view. Those who denied the significance of role conflict were very likely to become affected, and they were also very likely to faint if they did become affected. At the same time, both symptom deniers and role-conflict deniers who were not affected were more likely than any others to question the exclusive role of an insect in causing the epidemic. This corresponds to our interpretation of these women as resistant to admitting that they had problems and thus as being incapable of coping with them.

Our analysis of the personal characteristics of the subjects suggests, then, that such characteristics will "make a difference" in the probability of a person's becoming an active participant in such an epidemic, but that the characteristics which will increase the probability will depend upon the nature of the epidemic and what "part" in it we study. Since all epidemics of hysterical contagion involve the experience of physiological symptoms which are interpreted as being the result of an external threat, both symptom deniers and "external force deniers" should have a high probability of becoming active participants and of being seriously affected by the epidemic. Those

---

[1] In both cases, of course, we have had to *assume* that these factors were "really" more important than the women were willing to admit. We might therefore expect that a woman who denies the significance of external forces would find it difficult to accept the explanation that the physiological symptoms which developed during the epidemic were caused by an insect or any other external source. Thus, when she experienced such symptoms, she would be more likely than the other women to feel internally threatened, to think that something was drastically wrong with *her* rather than with her environment. Or she would at least be forced to admit that there really was something wrong with her environment. In either event, the experience would undoubtedly be a very upsetting one. Another interpretation of the role-conflict deniers is also possible. It may be that these women actually *did* prefer to avoid their responsibilities at home, that they welcomed the chance to escape their children and other familial obligations. If this were the case, one would expect that their real problem lay in the strain between their personal preferences and cultural expectations of devoted motherhood. It is not possible, of course, with the data in hand to determine the validity of either of these interpretations. We can only point out that the verbal responses and the actual situation of the role-conflict deniers are inconsistent in the context of our culture's role definitions.

who easily acknowledge symptoms, on the other hand, should be readily affected, but they should not be so seriously upset by the experience. To the extent that the accessibility of coping mechanisms (such as being willing to leave the scene of the threat) is a function of personal characteristics, such characteristics of the individuals should also influence who becomes affected. Thus, both the ability to recognize a problem and the ability to cope with it enter the picture. Finally, since such events are examples of *collective* behavior, the sensitivity of the person to suggestion from others should contribute to the probability of his being affected by the contagion.

SOCIAL RELATIONS AND CONTAGION

The term "contagion" clearly implies that the hysteria moves from one individual to another, and all discussions of this phenomenon emphasize the importance of interpersonal influence and communication. Our investigation indicates that the role of social relations in such epidemics is much more complex than the previous literature would seem to suggest. We have found that in the initial stages of the epidemic social isolates were most active and seemed to supply the basic new idea that an external threat was causing physiological symptoms. Only after the impetus was supplied by these isolates did the role of social relations and interpersonal influence become manifest. During the major portion of the epidemic, the period in which the symptoms spread most rapidly, intimate relations among the participants appeared to play an important role. Finally, there is the suggestion that if such an epidemic continues long enough interpersonal ties are no longer as significant, presumably because the reality of the threat is validated by such a large number of cases and the method(s) of responding to the threat becomes legitimized through widespread use.

In our case, we found that five out of six of the earliest victims were social isolates. Several of them had a history of "nervousness" and fainting. They were generally dissatisfied with their jobs and their role as workers. By comparison, those affected during the major portion of the epidemic were both socially and personally more secure. The epidemic spread through networks of friends and close associates, the networks in many cases consisting of women in the same work groups. Beginning sometime during the second big day of the epidemic, however, and continuing through the rest of the period, such social ties appear to be much less significant. There are fewer who have ties with other affected cases during this period in spite of the fact that after so many cases had appeared there was a higher probability that any case would be linked with another one.

We also found that when we were considering whether a woman became affected or not the order of the cases made little difference. Being linked with *any* affected case was as predictive of becoming affected as being linked with an *earlier* case. We interpreted this to mean that the process of becoming affected was not identical with the process of reporting to the doctor. Evidently two or more women could influence each other in the direction of believing in the insect threat and interpreting symptoms as due to the insect without necessarily becoming "stricken" at the same time. Influence of this kind did not necessarily depend on one of the women's going to the doctor. However, we did find that the seriousness of the symptoms exhibited varied with the order of the cases. If a woman were the first one of a network of close associates to become stricken, she was more likely to faint, whereas later cases in the network reported to the doctor before fainting. Evidently the experience of the first case in the network was enough to convince the women that the threat was really serious and that medical aid was necessary.

We have interpreted our findings as indicating that the social context of contagion is significant in at least two different ways. First, it operates as the medium of influence with respect to establishing the veridicality of the external threat. Those who know someone who has gotten sick (or even who believes in the bug) are likely to believe that a real threat exists. Second, it acts as the basis for defining the appropriate response for those who feel the influence of the symptoms. It also seems true, although it is more difficult to demonstrate, that these contributions of the social context occur in two parallel ways. They occur as a result of direct interpersonal influence, and they occur as a result of the force of a more general social validation. In the first case, it is the fact that one or more of a woman's close associates is affected that leads her to believe in the reality of the threat and to interpret her symptoms accordingly. In the second case, it is the fact that so many others have been affected that leads to this effect. The distinction here is thus between intensity and extensity of social influence. This is not an either/or distinction, of course, but it helps to emphasize the fact that both dimensions seem to be significant.

The effect of social influence on the response made by the individual who experiences symptoms in this setting can presumably be one of many different kinds. We have emphasized the effect in terms of increasing the probability of the woman's feeling sufficiently upset to faint or to seek medical attention, which has been our basic definition of being affected. Affecteds with ties to earlier cases were much less likely to faint, for instance. Their ties with other affecteds presumably both increased their chances of becoming affected and increased their tendency to seek help before it was too late. However, it is equally likely that social influence operated in the opposite manner in many cases. If one were almost wholly in contact with those who had *not* become sick and those who did *not* believe in the validity of the external threat, presumably this association would reduce the probability of one's becoming sick. Also, if one's associates had evolved a different definition of the proper response to the experience of symptoms (such as to "clock out of there"), even if a woman got sick she would be less likely to seek medical help or to stay in the situation until she fainted. It seems likely that this was the case with many of the self-defined affecteds. Although our focus of attention has been on processes leading to a medical report, clearly there were other processes leading to other outcomes also occurring at the same time.

Perhaps the most important generalization to suggest on the basis of this analysis is that social relations supply the medium through which the processual aspects of such an epidemic operate. Social relations act not only as channels of communication and interpersonal influence but also as mechanisms of collective definition and decision making. It is, of course, this dynamic aspect of the epidemic which is most difficult to illuminate directly. We cannot unequivocally demonstrate that the social relations actually functioned in the way we have suggested, but it is impressive that so much of the evidence points in this direction. Not only is the *fact* of being affected related to the pattern of social ties, but the *response* to this fact (fainting or not) and the *interpretation* of the experience (belief in the causal significance of the insect) are also related to this pattern. The orderliness of this pattern of findings is probably the most significant part of the study.

PROBLEMS AND PROSPECTS

Some of the limitations of the present study result from the fact that it occurred so long after the event in question. The delay was in part a function of the peculiar characteristics of the situation we were investigating. Since we had to carry out our interviews in the plant for the most part, we needed the cooperation of management, and this cooperation was granted with the proviso that a time lag occur. However, some of this delay would have been necessary in any case. We had to prepare a research instrument and get it printed; we had to draw a sample and set up interviewing procedures; we had to obtain trained interviewers. Even without management's restriction, therefore, some lag would have occurred.

We may assume, therefore, that no matter how well-equipped or well-financed we might have been there would have been a sizeable time lag between the time the epidemic came to our attention and the completion of our data collection. The alternative would have been to send in a limited number of investigators immediately without a uniform interview schedule or a well-defined sample so that they could gain some general impressions. Even then, the process *during* the epidemic could have been viewed only in retrospect. It may well be, though, that a combination of these two approaches would have been the best arrangement if it had been possible.[2]

When one considers these alternatives, or the combination of both approaches, however, another factor must be taken into account: the effect that the data collection itself has on the situation being investigated. We were required by management to limit our

[2] It is our impression that the alternatives noted here are the only ones available and that, of the two, the one we chose is to be preferred if only one can be used. One of the basic inadequacies of the considerable work that has been done in the area of disaster research is the necessarily hurried and non-systematic way in which the data have been collected. It has led to some interesting insights into human behavior during such disruptive events, but it has not contributed very much systematic information upon which generalizations may be based.

questions about the epidemic to an absolute minimum, and we even presented these questions as if they were an aside rather than a central concern of the interview. Though we had to do this under the circumstances, it is likely that we would have done something similar to this in any event. One of the problems faced by anyone investigating such an event is the fact that it is a highly significant event in the lives of the participants. They are very much involved with the experience and its aftermath. Any suggestion that the interview was intended to find out why some became affected and others did not would have been threatening to many of the women.

We cannot be sure, of course, that we did not give this impression, but there was little evidence that we did. In fact, most of the evidence points the other way. There were only 4 women who had reported sick during the epidemic who did not acknowledge this fact in the interview. Of the remainder, two-thirds acknowledged their own participation when they were asked for only a general description of the incident, and the remainder acknowledged after a simple probe. On the other hand, 17 women, about whom we had no record, mentioned their connection (the self-defined affecteds), about one-third of them without even being asked directly. This would indicate, if anything, an attempt in the interview of trying to be included but not of being defensive.

We had one other check on the accuracy of the reports. We asked the respondents whether they knew of anybody else who had been affected. Within the population at risk, all persons who were so identified, and who fell into our sample, mentioned themselves as affected.

Thus, our evidence would show that the women did not feel ashamed of their participation in the epidemic, but perhaps acknowledged it too freely. We can learn from our experience that it is possible to overcome resentment and suspicions but also that one should not assume how labeling an epidemic as hysteria might affect answers. Leaving a time lapse after the event and imbedding the questions in a general context helped to dissipate suspicion; further, it was important that we had some cross-checks to evaluate their answers. It was not obvious, however, how defensiveness would affect the answers. Respondents could deny the event, but this did not seem to have happened. They could also insist on the reality of the epidemic in spite of the labeling of the epidemic as "hysterical" by the mass media. There is a possibility of this having happened as indicated by the self-defined affecteds and the pattern of lasting belief. However, both these phenomena assume relevance in relation to other data. The epidemic seen from a vantage point of two months later, even with possible attending distortions, can be explained within the framework which we have studied.

We would conclude that events of this kind can be studied in a retrospective survey technique, with proper cautions in organization of the study and interviewing as well as in providing possibilities of cross-checks and care in data analysis.

Closely related to these issues is the effect of the experience during the epidemic on the measures made. To what extent does the fact of that experience change the conditions which the analysis assumes to be the "independent attributes"? For instance, is it more reasonable to say that women who were socially related to each other were more likely to become affected, or that women who were affected *became* socially related to each other? Short of omniscience, there seems no way to collect the relevant data before the occurrence of the hysterical contagion, and thus this problem appears to be inherent in such research. One can only attempt to insure against obtaining measures that are contaminated in this way. The most vulnerable of our major independent attributes were probably the sociometric and personal attribute measures. The latter are probably necessarily vulnerable if we assume that such an experience can appreciably alter the personalities of the victims. We rather doubt that this would be a common outcome, however, and would suggest that measures which deal with the more stable continuing qualities of the person should be subject to little criticism. Undoubtedly our own measures could have been improved in this regard. With respect to sociometric measures, the crucial question is whether the relationships existed before the incident. Although we did not have such a safeguard, it would be possible to include questions about how long one had had such a relationship with persons named. Such safeguards would increase one's faith in the findings, but it is important to acknowledge that this temporal problem is a necessary part of such studies.

There were other aspects of the research which we recognize as less than ideal and which could be done more effectively in future studies. Basically, these aspects are all a function of the fact that we collected our data in the manner of the survey researcher. Both the strengths and the weaknesses of this approach are reflected in our results.

The fact that we have comparable data from all of our subjects, that we can speak of the distribution of responses and the position of any individual or subgroup of our sample with respect to this distribution, is a strength which we value highly. The fact that the vast majority of our questions had precoded responses and did not permit any great degree of internal analysis is a weakness which we would hope could be counteracted in the future. The major difficulties we have experienced because of this structured approach have come with respect to the characteristics of the individuals, in part because of the inadequacy of our prior conceptualization. The several scales from the Cornell and MMPI inventories were originally included to help us tap such dimensions as anxiety, tension, and so on. We found, however, that the subjects' responses seemed to reflect another dimension which we had not originally considered but which appears to be highly relevant: the dimension of denial. Similarly, some of our straightforward attitude questions were answered in such a way as to indicate some denial of the significance of external forces. In both cases we have interpreted the findings to our own satisfaction as relevant to the dimension of denial, but we would feel more secure in this interpretation if we had a greater diversity of sources of insight into this dimension.

The solution to this problem is not to negate the strengths of the survey approach, of course, but to combine these with the strengths of more intensive, less structured methods. To argue on the basis of our experience that this would be desirable in future studies of this kind, however, is to assume that the kinds of effects of personal characteristics which we have noted would be expected in other studies. We think that this is a reasonable assumption. In such cases as the one we have investigated, one of the salient characteristics is the combination of a level of strain and difficulty in coping with it by direct means. Since there will evidently always be something blocking effective coping, we would expect that various psychological defense mechanisms would often be involved, and one important mechanism which should be expected to appear is denial.[3]

In any event, whether or not denial as a specific defense mechanism is to be found universally in such cases, we should expect to find some kinds of defense mechanisms playing an important role in the responses made by the individuals involved. This would suggest that the investigator should be sensitive to *some* kind of latent content in the subjects' responses, and it would be well for him to have included in his research instruments a method of investigating this possibility.

One other factor which is related to our survey research approach is the question of sampling. There are two issues to be noted here. First, the fact that we originally drew a sample and then added all of the remaining affected cases is in many respects one of the strengths of the study. It presented some problems of analysis, however. We found ourselves faced with a population (the affected cases) and a not very easily defined sample (the original sample with the sampled affected cases removed). We now think that it would have been better to take all of the affected cases out of the population before sampling and then draw a sample of the population of nonaffected cases. This would have strengthened our discussion of the characteristics of "the population at risk." We do not think that this has been a serious flaw in the current study, but it is an issue worth considering in future investigations of this kind.

Second, we found that in the analysis of the sociometric data we were hampered by the fact that we had only a sample of the population rather than the entire population. We thus found a sizeable number of our subjects' choices were individuals not in our sample, and therefore, we could not make statements about either the personal characteristics or the choice patterns of such individuals. Again, the fact that we had a sample of nonaffected cases and the

---

[3] Miller and Swanson (1960) have discussed defense mechanisms as falling into two "families," and they say (p. 200) of the first of these: "Members of the first family share the characteristics of simplicity, maximal distortion, generality, and the creation of social difficulties. Denial is representative of such mechanisms. Almost anything can be denied, be it observable fact or motivational state, since the mechanism results in a blotting out or reinterpreting of the event." (See also, Swanson, 1961.) It is also interesting that they suggest that this family of defenses should be more frequently found in lower class people in our society, people such as our subjects.

population of affected cases raised problems. Although we feel that
our statements about the relative tendencies to choose within or between any of our three major subject categories are reasonably well-
founded, the kind of sample we had made it impossible to be very
confident with respect to statements about the absolute numbers of
choices received by any of our subjects. We cannot say with any
certainty, for instance, that those whom we have called "isolates" did
not actually have many good friends in the plant. We only know
that we did not find any and that it is probable that more absolute
isolates are among those who received no choices than are among
those who received some choices from our subjects. There would be
real advantages, therefore, in having information about the total
population at risk if this were possible.

Given the difficulties of research in this kind of situation, is
there good reason to persist in attempting to investigate such epidemics? We think there is, because we view such situations as prime
examples of dynamic human events. We have referred to such epidemics earlier as "pure behavioral events" because we believe that
in these situations one can observe social and psychological forces at
work under conditions in which other kinds of factors play as limited a role as possible. The discomfort that is experienced is a function of situational factors that have little or no direct physical or
biological relevance, and the definition of the meaning of this discomfort as well as the process through which one decides what to do
about it are almost purely social and psychological in nature.

However, the fact remains that the experience is a physical one;
actual physiological disturbance does occur. Of course, we have
simply assumed this for our purposes and moved on from there. And
yet this is a big assumption, and at best it is a crude one. There is
good reason to view such epidemics as *both* medically and behav-
iorally relevant even if we are correct in assuming that the physiological upset is "only" a manifestation of situational pressures and
psychological characteristics related to one's ability to cope with stress.
There seems to be little doubt that the physical characteristics of the
individuals involved are important components of the ultimate action
taken, just as the cultural context is an important factor in determining what kinds of definitions of their experiences will be seen as
credible.

We did not have any data on the psychophysiological character-istics of the women, but it seems reasonable to assume that indi-viduals vary both in their abilities to keep stress "psychologically compensated" and in the kinds of physiological responses they ex-hibit when they fail to do so. Differences of this kind may be highly related to such factors as the use of certain kinds of psychological defense mechanisms such as denial, but it seems just as likely that different defenses could be used by persons with similar levels of ability in psychological coping.[4] Important aspects of this kind of collective event, therefore, which we have been unable to deal with at all, are the processes through which situational strain is trans-formed into psychological stress and then into physiological arousal. Such processes are also highly significant ones and should receive careful study.

All of this discussion would indicate that we need more and better investigations of the type we have carried out, and we hope that the success of the present study has been sufficient to motivate others to move in that direction. However, it is equally clear that further clarification at the conceptual level is a necessary part of such future work. In the next chapter we add as a kind of postscript a discussion of one type of clarification we think desirable. The con-cepts of epidemic, contagion, and diffusion are all somehow related to each other, but the relationship is not very clear. It is toward a clarification of that relationship that our last chapter is directed.

---

[4] Such studies as that of Funkenstein, King, and Drolette (1957) have made a contribution here. They make an interesting distinction between the immediate reaction to the initial experience of stress and the ability to "master" the stressful experience over time. They found these two characteristics to be almost completely independent of each other.

9

DIFFUSION, CONTAGION, AND EPIDEMICS

Throughout this report we have referred to the event we were study-ing as an epidemic. This term is generally used in medical settings and usually refers to the spread of a disease. As a result, the term may be seen as not really applicable to our case since no evidence of a toxic element in the environment could be found. Although such a conclusion does not seem justified to us, it can be defended. In fact, those experts whose business it was to deal with epidemics ultimately defined this event as outside their realm of expertise. We have also emphasized throughout this volume that this was close to a "pure behavioral event," and we have called it a case of hysterical con-tagion. The term "epidemic" is not usually used by the behavioral scientist to refer to events within his area of inquiry; he is likely to use the term "contagion." But evidently the contagion normally dealt with by the medical epidemiologist is different from the contagion of the behavioral scientist. We also know that the behavioral scien-tist uses another term, "diffusion," which is evidently closely related to contagion. We have suggested elsewhere (Kerckhoff, Back, & Mil-ler, 1965) that these two terms may refer to phenomena which are quite similar, but we have not yet attempted to describe the similarities and differences. The purpose of this chapter will thus be to clarify the distinction between diffusion and contagion and to locate hysterical contagion and epidemic in this conceptualization.[1]

The term "contagion," as used by the behavioral scientist, generally suggests a more rapid dissemination of the pattern than does the term "diffusion." There is also often the suggestion that diffusion is a process which occurs through the free choice of the participants, whereas contagion occurs against the participants' wishes. Both of these characteristics of contagion are reflections of its traditional use by the medical profession in reference to the spread of communicable diseases. We will begin, therefore, with an examination of a set of postulates which reflect the usual meaning of contagion in the medical setting and contrast them with the characteristics of diffusion as viewed by the behavioral scientist. We will then turn to a consideration of the distinction between contagion and diffusion in behavioral science, and, finally, we will discuss the difference between hysterical contagion and other forms of contagion and diffusion and relate these terms to the concept of epidemic.

MEDICAL CONTAGION AND BEHAVIORAL DIFFUSION

Most discussions of medical epidemics in which the toxic element is known to be involved postulate either or both of two sources of dissemination of the malady in question. These may be referred to as the "constant source" and the "interpersonal" postulates. The former would be likely if some single source of pollution (e.g., a garbage dump) were viewed as the source of the spreading sickness in a community. The second would be the approach taken in studies of communicable diseases. It is possible, of course, for both of these processes to operate simultaneously. But whatever process is postulated, the logic calls for some form of contact between the source (the garbage dump or an infected person) and a new victim.

Such contact between source and new victim may be postulated

[1] The discussion in this chapter has profited from a number of earlier considerations of some of the issues involved. Of particular importance are those of Wheeler (1966) and Katz, Levin, and Hamilton (1963).

to occur in one of two general ways. It may occur wholly at random, in which case each uninfected person in a population has an equal chance of making such a contact, or there may be some assumed structure which increases the probability that some persons will make contact. This structure may be a spatial one (who lives closer to the garbage dump) or a social one (who is likely to interact with an infected case).

These several postulates appear to be applicable in differing degrees to cases of the spread of some behavior within a population (e.g., using a technological innovation, adopting a new fad, reporting an unusual experience, etc.). For instance, an innovation that is being advertised widely by a manufacturer may be viewed as emanating from a constant source, whereas the dissemination of a new fad that begins in a college dormitory and spreads over a campus may be viewed as largely a function of interpersonal channels. In some cases the random exposure postulate may seem appropriate for both of these examples, for others a more structured postulate may seem appropriate.

Although we could undoubtedly construct examples in which any combination of these postulates is applicable, it seems safe to say that in most examples that are of interest to the behavioral scientist it would be unwise to assume that only a constant source is involved,[2] and it would be equally questionable to assume that all persons have an equal opportunity to be exposed to the sources of influence. In general, we must assume that diffusion occurs in structured contexts in which preestablished social and spatial patterns are highly relevant to the rate and pattern of dissemination.[3]

Several other characteristics of the kinds of diffusion which interest the behavioral scientist must be considered and contrasted with the traditional view of the contagion of disease. In the pure case of a medical epidemic, the important aspect in the spread of a disease

[2] The media of mass communications represent the most likely "constant source" in the social setting, but there is considerable evidence that even these media function through a network of interpersonal relations. See Katz and Lazarsfeld (1955).

[3] For a thoughtful discussion of the implications of such structured situations for the development of mathematical models of diffusion, see Coleman (1964, Ch. 17). Coleman acknowledges the complexities involved by referring to such situations as "incomplete social structures."

is the contact between the infectious element (e.g., a germ) and the victim. Although there are complications introduced by the fact that all sorts of things may transport such an element (the air, food, another person), the crucial "cause" of a new infection is the contact between that element and the victim, and this is a physical contact between a person and a physical element. The behavioral scientist is also concerned with the contact between an element and a potential new case, but both the element and the form of the contact are different. In these cases the most important element is an idea, a belief, or an attitude; it is basically a cognitive rather than a physical element. The contact in question is likely to be a visual or an auditory one which may occur over a widely varying set of spatial relationships; it does not require physical contact or even a close spatial association between the "carrier" and the "victim."

With good reason, most behavioral scientists expect that there will be more contacts, and more potential influence per contact, between friends, relatives, or others who have a continuing relationship involving positive affect. A more subtle and perplexing issue is involved here, however. It is quite possible for transmission of a behavioral innovation to occur between persons who normally do not interact at all. The most obvious example of this is one in which a very prestigious person adopts an innovation and a less prestigious person observes this and models his behavior after the first. This is still not a case of random contact in the population, but it involves a different kind of relationship than that implied by the examples of friend or relative. Discussions of reference group behavior illustrate the importance of such relationships, but, unfortunately, the situation is still more complex. Since the core element being transmitted is a cognitive one, it is quite possible for someone to "receive" that element from a person with whom he normally has no relationship at all, simply by observing such a person's behavior. This is an underlying assumption in much of the literature on crowd behavior.

This is not to say that spatial or social relationships are irrelevant, but it does mean that different kinds and degrees of relationship will be important in different cases. In order to suggest the conditions under which they will be more or less relevant, we must discuss two other differences between the process of spread of a physically transmitted disease and the process of dissemination of a behavioral pattern. First, there is the difference between what constitutes "susceptibility" in the two cases. Second, there is the nature of the link between the "causal" element and the manifest behavior (or symptoms) in the two cases.

It is commonly recognized that some people are more susceptible to certain diseases than others, and the concept of immunity suggests that some persons may be fully exposed to the infectious element without becoming infected. Our discussion thus far has been limited to factors influencing the probability of exposure, but it is equally obvious that susceptibility is an important factor in the spread of disease. The same is true with respect to the spread of a behavior pattern. We would suggest that there are at least two kinds of determinants of a person's susceptibility to behavioral innovation: the qualities of the person and the characteristics of the situation he is in. There seems little doubt that any given innovation may have special appeal to those with particular personal characteristics because it meets some need (to be expressive, successful, popular, different, and so on). But it is equally obvious that being in a given situation may enhance particular kinds of needs in any person and thus increase the attractiveness of an innovation. Though it is not always possible to keep these "internal" and "external" sources of needs fully distinct, they are both important. And as the need increases, it is likely that less significant sources of social influence which offer a means of serving that need will become effective. Closely associated with the need element in the individual is the nature of the innovation—the degree to which it is acceptable in terms of personal and cultural values.

Turning to the second point, we note that in the pure case of a medical epidemic it is not the overt symptoms which are directly transmitted, but some infectious element. One gets sick (exhibits symptoms) because he is infected by a germ. At the risk of seeming to overintellectualize the process, we would argue that a similar process is involved in the diffusion of behavioral innovations. Behind each such innovation lies an idea or belief which gives meaning to the behavior. It is not the behavior as such that is disseminated, but the idea or belief. Just as the sick person exhibits symptoms because he is infected with the germ, the adopter of an innovation is likely to behave as he does because he has accepted the idea. However, whereas there is a rather direct link between the germ and the sickness, there is another step involved between the idea and the behavior. According to the traditional view of epidemics, if a person is infected, he gets sick; but if a person accepts the idea, he may or may not behave in the innovative manner. The new idea may "make a difference" in his behavior, but that "difference" may be something other than a direct adoption of the innovation. One may believe that a new type of fertilizer will grow better plants but actively urge its rejection because its use violates community norms. One may believe that the theater is on fire but stay in his seat to avoid being trampled. We shall suggest later that there may be a similar relationship between the physical cause and the disease.[4]

It seems likely that many of the same factors which determine whether a person will accept a new idea or belief also determine whether he will take the kind of action, based on that belief, which forms the manifest evidence of dissemination. The nature of the actions taken by those around him, his own needs, and the cultural definition of the act should be equally relevant here. But, as we have suggested, in the case of the spread of a behavioral innovation there are actually two processes occurring at the same time. One is the process of dissemination of a belief, the other is the process of putting that belief into action through carrying out a new form of behavior. Although the behavior is the manifest element involved, we cannot understand its dissemination without reference to the belief. Yet the *same* relationship or need pattern may encourage a person both to believe and *not* to adopt the innovation. One may be told by a good friend (or the leader of his religious sect) that a new kind of fertilizer does grow bigger corn *but* that its use would ultimately ruin the soil (or violate a commandment from God). One may be told by a loved one that a disaster is approaching *but* that the best chance of survival is to stay put since attempting to escape would only increase the danger. One may need to believe that there are

[4] There may well be a parallel between this distinction in behavioral examples and "how sick" a person gets once his body "accepts" (i.e., does not fully repel) the germ. Since we are not attempting a full review of all the factors involved, however, we will not follow up this possibility.

great dangers in the world, but he may also need to believe in his own ability to face danger fearlessly.[5]

Thus, we have suggested that the dissemination of a behavioral innovation differs from the spread of a physically transmitted sickness in at least the following ways: (1) the element being disseminated is cognitive rather than physical; (2) the element may be transmitted through space and by means of a variety of social relationships; (3) "susceptibility" is a function of the need structures and cultural definitions of those "exposed" to the element, although situational factors may contribute significantly to these needs and serve to alter these definitions; (4) there is a less direct link between the element (the idea or belief) and the critical outcome (manifest behavior in keeping with the innovation); (5) the same kinds of factors operate to influence the acceptance of the belief and the adoption of the innovative behavior, but a given source of influence may operate in different ways with reference to these two outcomes.

SOCIAL DIFFUSION AND CONTAGION

We are now in a position to attempt a summary of the previous discussion in a series of postulates about the diffusion of a behavioral innovation similar to those with which we began. To simplify the statement of these postulates, we will refer to one who has accepted the underlying idea or belief as a "believer" and to one who actually carries out the behavioral innovation as an "adopter."

[5] The opposite may also be true. One may be influenced to carry out the behavior in question without actually accepting the belief. The farmer may begin to use the new fertilizer, or the doctor to prescribe the new drug, because all of the prestigious practitioners are doing so. Studies of crowd behavior have described cases of people who rush along with the crowd without knowing the cause of the excitement. One may engage in a public demonstration because of a need to be rebellious without accepting the beliefs of those who are leading the demonstration. Although it is important to emphasize this side of the picture, there is the danger of viewing the spread of a behavior as wholly unrelated to cognitive or motivational elements. We would submit that, although there may well be those who adopt the innovation without accepting the belief, an underlying belief is always involved, and the core of the diffusion is the result of the acceptance of that belief. We must recognize that there may be *other* reasons for some to adopt the behavior, but this should not lead us to deny the central role of a cognitive element in the process of dissemination.

Postulate 1. The probability of acceptance of the belief increases as the intimacy of a person's social relationships with those who believe increases. (If such relationships are segmental, the probability of acceptance will vary with the relevance of the belief to the life segment encompassed by the relationship.)

Postulate 2. The probability of acceptance of the belief increases as the number of persons known to have accepted it increases. (There are, however, counter forces in any situation which make universal acceptance unlikely.)

Postulate 3. The probability of acceptance of the belief increases as the level of prestige of persons known to have accepted it increases. (If a believer's level of prestige is higher in some specialized problem areas than in others, his prestige level in the area most directly related to the content of the belief will dominate.)

Postulate 4. The probability of acceptance of the belief increases with the degree of consistency between that belief and the established cultural definitions of the population of which the individual is a member.

Postulate 5. The probability of acceptance of the belief increases to the extent that the belief serves the needs of the person (whether these needs are a function of stable personality characteristics or situational determinants or both).

Postulate 6. The probability of adoption of the innovation increases to the extent the person becomes a believer. There will not be a perfect relationship here, however, because:

Postulate 7. The probability of adoption of the innovation increases as the intimacy of the social relationships between the person and adopters increases.

Postulate 8. The probability of adoption of the innovation increases as the number of persons known to have adopted it increases.

Postulate 9. The probability of adoption of the innovation increases as the level of prestige of persons known to have adopted it increases.

Postulate 10. The probability of adoption of the innovation increases with the degree of consistency between the action involved and other culturally approved forms of behavior in the population.

Postulate 11. The probability of adoption of the innovation increases to the extent that the behavior in question serves the needs of the person.[6]

These 11 postulates appear to apply best to cases of diffusion of a behavior pattern such as a technological innovation. When we consider the concept of contagion in relation to these postulates, they appear at first to be too orderly and systematic. The difficulty is evidently that the term "contagion," as distinct from "diffusion," normally refers to a more rapid dissemination of the pattern. This greater rapidity implies a less rational type of process, and it has been usual in discussions of contagion to suggest that the distinctions among sources of transmission included in these postulates are less relevant to contagion than to diffusion. Within the framework of these postulates, contagion is characterized by the greater significance of the needs of those persons involved. Contagion occurs in situations where the need is immediate and great. There is a strong need, shared by a number of people, to take action, but there is no clear definition of an appropriate act. When a seemingly appropriate act is suggested (and probably carried out by one or more of those experiencing the need), the blocked impulses to act are released and adoption of the suggested solution is rapid and widespread.

Redl (1949) has suggested that the original restraint in such cases is internally imposed by the actors due to their fear of the consequences of action in keeping with their needs, consequences which themselves may be internal (guilt) or external (punishment). The implication in his discussion is that the contagious act is already known and viewed as attractive by the actors, and knowledge (sight) of someone carrying out such an act serves to reduce the self-imposed restraints by making the act seem more acceptable. This certainly seems true in many cases, but it will generally be difficult to know the extent to which the restraint should be viewed as self-imposed. Thus, a more general statement of this position might be that contagion occurs in situations in which the need for action is great, where some barrier exists to prevent action in accord with the need, and where a seemingly suitable means of action is proposed

[6] Although all of these postulates are put in a single positive form, they should be understood to include the obverse of the statements made. Also, the parenthetical statements after Postulates 1, 2, 3, and 5 should be understood to be included in Postulates 7, 8, 9, and 11.

(usually through the example of one or more persons) which lowers that barrier.

Such a position predicts that rapid dissemination will occur where the need element is highly salient and the behavior of an adopter serves to lower the barrier which has prevented action to satisfy the need. Rapid dissemination might also be expected under other circumstances. For instance, even though the need element were not particularly high, one might expect rapid dissemination of a pattern once it had been adopted by a prestigious person (e.g., the admired Army sergeant whose manner of wearing his cap is copied by his men). Similarly, patterns which serve to symbolize the membership of individuals in various groups or categories which they define as significant are likely to be adopted rapidly (e.g., the "odd" hair and clothing styles adopted by adolescents). In the same way, the relationship between established cultural definitions and an innovation will influence the rapidity of dissemination (e.g., the difficulties faced in introducing technological innovations in traditional societies). All of the factors listed in the above 11 postulates, therefore, should be seen as relevant to the rapidity of dissemination of an innovation.

There is another dimension which should be considered, however, when we attempt to explain the differences in rates of diffusion, a dimension which is not reflected in our 11 postulates. Basically, the factors reflected in the postulates are all relevant to the ease with which an innovation (or the idea behind it) will be accepted once an individual is made aware of it. Situations vary, however, in the rapidity with which knowledge about an innovation (and its effects) may be disseminated. A major determinant of rapidity of dissemination of information is the distance between members of the collectivity. Perhaps the best way to denote such a variation would be to refer to "diffuse" and "compact" collectivities (Turner & Killian, 1957). In general, the more diffuse the collectivity, the more slowly will information travel and the more slowly will an innovation be disseminated. Obviously, the media of mass communications make this kind of statement debatable, but although these media are capable of transmitting information and are thus capable of reducing the "distance" between members of a collectivity and a central source of information, they do not reduce the distance between a given number and all other members of the collectivity. The immediacy of a crowd experience, for instance, cannot be duplicated by the mass media. This is in part a function of the rapidity of information flow among members in a crowd and in part a function of the flow of different kinds of knowledge than are communicable through the mass media—knowledge of other individuals' emotional arousal, their immediate response to shared experiences, and so on. Therefore, other things being equal, the compact collectivity is likely to facilitate the dissemination of intimate knowledge of members more rapidly and fully than the diffuse collectivity.

It has also been implicit in the preceding discussion that the effect of the action of innovators may have either or both of two different kinds of effects on those who know of their innovative behavior. The observation of such action may serve to increase the attractiveness of the behavior in question (by demonstrating that it is really possible, that it is enjoyable, that it is effective, that it is prestigious, and so on). On the other hand, as the discussion of Redl's analysis indicated, it may also serve to lower the barrier between the desire and the act. In the first case the innovator serves to increase the attractiveness of an act; in the second case he provides a means for carrying out an already attractive act. In the first case the observers become *motivated* to act by observing the innovator; in the second case they are already motivated and become *able* to act by observing the innovator.

We may now express these ideas in two further postulates which together with the greater relevance of needs in contagion help us to differentiate between diffusion and contagion.

Postulate 12. Rapidity of dissemination of the belief and/or the act will tend to be greater in a compact than in a diffuse collectivity.

Postulate 13. Knowledge of the behavior of adopter(s) (and its outcome) may serve either to heighten the attractiveness of the act or to lower the restraints from performing the act, or both.

In the pure case of diffusion, dissemination occurs in a diffuse collectivity. It depends more on social and cultural factors, and knowledge of the behavior of adopters serves to heighten the attractiveness of the act. In the pure case of contagion, dissemination occurs in a compact collectivity. It depends more on personal (need) factors, and knowledge of the behavior of adopters serves to lower preexisting restraints to performing the act. It is obvious, however, that these considerations do not permit a clear-cut differentiation between diffusion and contagion. Various combinations of these factors are possible. Rapid dissemination, based on heightened needs of the adopters, may occur in a diffuse collectivity. The spread of a pattern in a compact collectivity may be the result of the adoption of an innovator's act by a prestigious figure whose adoption of it makes it more attractive. Because of such complexities, we can only describe the characteristics of pure cases of contagion and diffusion while at the same time we must acknowledge the existence of various kinds of mixed cases.

HYSTERICAL CONTAGION

How does our view of hysterical contagion fit into this discussion? We have, of course, indicated throughout the previous chapters that the kinds of variables referred to in our discussion so far were operative in the example we studied. We have presented evidence of the significance of intimate associates (Postulates 1 and 7), of a "crowd effect" (Postulates 2 and 8) and of the importance of the personal characteristics of the women (Postulates 5 and 11). We also found that those who were most severely affected were the strongest believers (Postulate 6). We have suggested that the initial opinions of experts (Postulate 3) and the behavior of union stewards (Postulate 9) may have had an effect on the contagion. We have also suggested that the belief and the behavior in question were consistent with our cultural definitions of toxic insects and illness behavior (Postulates 4 and 10). Our data suggest that the compact nature of the collectivity in the dressmaking departments contributed to the rapidity of the spread of the symptoms (Postulate 12).

It seems reasonable, therefore, to view hysterical contagion as amenable to the same general kind of conceptualization as the diffusion and contagion of many other types of behavior in a population. Yet there are differences, and these need to be emphasized along with the similarities. The differences are most apparent, perhaps, with reference to Postulate 13. Implicit in Postulate 13 is the assumption that the behavior pattern which is disseminated through a population in both diffusion and contagion is one which is positively valued with reference to the belief involved. If one believes that nitrogen will help produce better crops, one's use of nitrogen is presumably an indication that he values better crops. In other words, the behavior in question may be assumed to have a positive value for the actor, a value which becomes meaningful by reference to the belief involved. This would be true even when the belief involved is a belief in a negative element in the environment. The proliferation of family bomb shelters is in response to the belief that nuclear warfare is a real threat, and the building of the shelter is positively valued by the believer as a means of accommodating to an environment defined in terms of that belief.

By definition, hysterical contagion occurs in response to a belief in a negative element in the environment, but that in itself does not differentiate it from diffusion and contagion as we have defined them. It is differentiated by the fact that the behavior which is the manifest content of hysterical contagion is not in any obvious way positively valued by the person who believes in the negative element. The behavior does not involve active coping with the problem but a passive collapse in the face of the problem. It is an indication of a failure to cope with a source of danger. In the usual case of diffusion or contagion in the face of danger, the actors "decide" to take some active part in the situation in an effort to bring it nearer to their own desires. In our example of hysterical contagion, however, those who became affected cases did not "decide" to faint or get sick because there was thought to be a poisonous insect among them. In fact, our data suggest that it was largely those people who could not decide to do anything about the threat who fainted or got so sick they required medical attention. Those who suffered the most severe symptoms tended to be people who could not admit that they *had* a problem and who did not know how to cope with it when it finally became obvious that they did have one. Evidently they did nothing until they collapsed under the strain. As in all cases of contagion, they had needs which were difficult to satisfy. The needs became objectified through the introduction of a belief in an external threat, a belief which was accepted because it fit their experiences of arousal. But given this belief, they were unable to cope with the threat defined by the belief, and "it" finally made them sick.

This view of hysterical contagion brings us back to a consideration of Postulates 5 and 11. Postulate 5 seems to be applicable to all cases of contagion, and we have suggested in our own example that the tension the women experienced made them receptive to a belief which explained their feelings. This was especially true for those women who could not admit that there was anything wrong with them or with their situation. The "external" sources of need, represented in our study by the measures of strain, increased both their discomfort and their need to understand it. The situation with Postulate 11 is not so clear, however. The women did not become sick because that behavior "served their needs" in anything like the way the behaviors involved in other cases of contagion serve the needs of the participants. They evidently got sick because they were unable to act in a way that would directly serve their needs.

In all cases of contagion, then, there tends to be a heightened arousal due to unsatisfied needs and a difficulty in need satisfaction. In some such situations there is introduced a belief which objectifies the source of difficulty and suggests a feasible means of combating it which can be used by those who are aroused. In others, there is introduced a belief which objectifies the source of difficulty in such a way that at least some of those suffering from the heightened state of arousal cannot take action to combat it. In the first case we would expect some form of behavioral contagion such as a crowd action. In the second case we would expect the contagion of some kind of symptoms which are the result of unresolved tension. In both cases, the tendency to accept the belief will be a function of the level of arousal, as suggested in Postulate 5. But in the first case the behavior which calls the event to our attention results from active attempts to cope with the threat, whereas in the second case the behavior that attracts our attention results from a *failure* to cope with the threat.[7]

With reference to Postulate 13, therefore, we must note that knowledge of others' having behaved in the relevant manner (e.g.,

---

[7] It has been suggested recently that another type of response to a threat may occur when coping is not possible: resignation to the inevitable (Forman, 1963). We suspect that the major difference between situations which lead to hysterical contagion and those which lead to resignation is that in the former a possible solution is known but forbidden while in the latter no solution is known. This difference will become more apparent from the later discussion.

getting sick) neither increases the attractiveness of the behavior nor makes it more possible for the observer to behave in that way which he would originally have chosen had it not been for some barrier. In contrast, in cases of hysterical contagion the knowledge tends to increase the sense of threat, thereby increasing the need to take *some other* action than that which is observed. In fact, if we specify the behavior in question as "getting sick," in no sense do the actors "choose" to carry it out. It evidently "just happens." The increased tension between the need to act and the lack of acceptable modes of action increases the likelihood that the observer will develop physiological symptoms which he will come to define as being like those he has observed. Unlike either of the conditions noted in Postulate 13, therefore, the need is heightened without the provision for a suitable means of coping with it. This leads to two further postulates which permit us to differentiate between hysterical contagion and contagion as we discussed it earlier.

Postulate 14. Evidence of others' failure to cope effectively with reference to the belief in a negative element in the environment increases the belief in that element and the need to find an effective means of coping.

Postulate 15. Heightened need for action without provision for effective action increases tension and the associated physiological symptoms which, if continued, will become socially disruptive.

There are two other matters which we view as relevant to placing our particular case into a more general context. First, it will be noted that we do not specify in Postulate 15 that the source of the threat will necessarily be used as an explanation of the physiological symptoms, even though this was the case in our study. We suspect that ours was a particularly "neat" case in which all of the pieces fitted together rather well. There are other such cases, however, where the malady of which the victims complain remains a mystery to all parties. There is simply a series of victims brought to the attention of the authorities. In these cases we would assume that there is a general source of tension (such as the work-related strains in our case) which becomes sufficiently severe and causes some persons to develop notable physiological symptoms without the invention of a consistent belief which objectifies the source of the difficulty. In still other cases, there may be a source of threat suggested which is such that individual victims could not be expected (e.g., the imminent collision of planets). The individual victims in such a case would again be viewed as either victims of an unknown malady (if others did not know of their belief in the imminent collision) or as victims of "nervous tension." In our case, not only did the negative element lend itself to the expectation of individual victims, it was also such that the best scientific knowledge could not challenge it without extended study. We thus suspect that it was a rather unusual case.

Although it is possible to argue persuasively that the behavior in question (getting sick) did not in any way "serve the needs" of the participants, it is also possible to challenge such a statement. If our interpretation is correct, the original tension experienced by the women came largely from the strain due to the job and to conflict between the job and home. The locus of their difficulty was certainly the plant, and the most obvious solution to their problem was rest. As we suggested earlier, it is possible to interpret the whole incident as a kind of "psychological strike" in which those most distressed by the situation managed both to retaliate against management and to get a respite from the strain of the work situation. It is possible, therefore, that their illness was not wholly dysfunctional with reference to the original source of their difficulties. More generally, it may be that hysterical behavior of this kind is more likely to occur when it provides a means (albeit a very indirect and unusual means) of coping with a situation which could not be coped with in more usual ways. Although we have no way of demonstrating such a function in the present case, we view it as a sufficiently likely possibility to suggest it as a focus of attention in further investigations.

HYSTERICAL CONTAGION AND EPIDEMICS

Let us now come full circle and reintroduce the concept of epidemic. We began with a rather strict definition of a medical epidemic as the dissemination of symptoms in a population by means of the spread of a toxic element. We argued that such an epidemic was different in several ways from the dissemination of a behavior pattern and turned to an examination of diffusion, contagion and hysterical contagion. Yet, in discussing hysterical contagion we necessarily find ourselves referring to symptoms and to socially disruptive behavior which bring the person to the attention of the authorities. We also find that it is not possible to refer to the individual who is involved in hysterical contagion as an "adopter." It is more relevant to view him as a "victim," to say that he was "stricken." The behavior involved in hysterical contagion is some kind of maladaptive behavior, behavior which shows that the organism is not functioning adequately.

In short, the manifest content of the physically transmitted medical epidemic and the case of hysterical contagion are often indistinguishable. In fact, the experts who were called into our case basically used hysterical contagion as a residual category when they could not find a toxic cause of the symptoms they observed. If it could not be demonstrated to be a "real epidemic," it must be "only hysteria." Certainly not all medical personnel would be this categorical, but the categorical perspective helps to make evident the similarity between the two pure types and suggests that a more careful analysis of any given case might reveal elements of both.

One of the points at which the two kinds of cases may be viewed as identical is the point at which the experience of symptoms becomes labeled and a plan of action is devised and carried out. In both the medical epidemic and the case of hysterical contagion, the significant manifest element is a series of persons complaining of symptoms who come to the attention of medical authorities. In both cases it is necessary for the victim to have an experience of discomfort, to define that experience as medically relevant, and to seek medical attention (or to behave so that others will seek it for him).

The differences between the pure physically caused epidemic and the pure case of hysterical contagion come before and after this point. Before it, the difference is in what "actually causes" the discomfort. In the pure physical epidemic case, the cause is some external toxic element which disrupts the bodily processes. In the pure hysterical contagion case, the cause is unresolved tension which leads to the unpleasant sensations. After the experience and the decision to seek medical aid, the difference between the two is a function of the ability of the experts to find a reasonable explanation for the discomfort. If an external toxic element can be found which is known to be capable of disrupting the bodily processes in the way manifest in the victims, it is likely to be defined as a physically caused epidemic. If no such cause can be found and/or if there seems to be a very dominant sense of unresolved tension among the population affected, it is likely to be termed a case of hysterical contagion.

The similarity of the manifest content of these two cases and the fact that both involve identical steps from the point of the experience of disturbance to the contact with the medical authorities lead us to stress the commonality of these two cases and to suggest that in the great majority of such cases there is reason to look for both physical and behavioral factors. This is particularly true since any increase in the incidence of a medically relevant disturbance is likely to become a social fact which has meaning to the population within which it occurs. Knowledge of such an increase should have an effect on those not (yet) affected. Assuming that the early cases have difficulties which others could conceivably develop, that the symptoms are relatively general or vague (headache, fever, stomach disturbances, etc.), and that the experts take the early cases seriously, several things are likely to happen. First, those who already have some minor physical upset (and we assume there are such cases at all times in any normal population) will be encouraged to define their ills as being the result of the newly announced ailment. Second, some of those who define their ills in this way will be motivated to seek medical attention, even though they might not have done so had not the "beginning of an epidemic" been reported. Third, the increase in the number of cases reported will increase the fear some persons will experience in the face of the threat that they too might be stricken. This fear, together with a heightened self-awareness, will increase the probability that they will experience some physiological upset which can be defined as due to the spreading illness.

We would expect this kind of process to occur whether or not there were a "real" toxic source of illness in the situation. In fact, given such a source, it is perhaps even more likely since the medical authorities will more clearly and effectively communicate the fact that there "really is" something to be concerned about. In our own case of the poisonous insect, the role of the official agencies of health investigation and control was undoubtedly very significant in this way because in the early stages they were not able to state with any confidence that there was *not* such a poisonous insect. The very seriousness and thoroughness of their investigation perpetuated the belief in the threat, even though it was intended to do the very opposite.

One can make the same statement on the other side of this dichotomy. Not only is there likely to be a behavioral element in any "real epidemic," but there is very likely to be a physical element in any case of hysterical contagion. It seems almost certain that some of the women who were victims of "the bug" were actually bitten by insects, and it may well be that some of them suffered a mild reaction to the bites. It seems equally likely that some of the women were suffering from other minor physical disturbances during the period in question (as well as the tension from the strain on the job). The introduction of the idea of a poisonous insect made it possible for such women to define their ailments in a common way and to seek medical assistance for them, although they might not have sought such aid had the flurry of cases not been occurring at that time.

We must conclude, therefore, that although it is possible to make an abstract distinction between a pure case of hysterical contagion and a pure case of a physical epidemic, any empirical case is likely to have elements of both. We have said that ours was probably as close to a case of a "pure behavioral event" as one could hope to find, but we must also acknowledge that it is not reasonable even in this case to rule out the possibility of "real" physically caused illness. The fact is that the term "epidemic" is correctly used to refer to any case in which there is an unusually rapid spread and high incidence of some form of bodily disturbance. In some of these cases the balance is undoubtedly very strongly on the side of some definable external toxic element's effect on a number of persons and in others (such as our case) the balance is undoubtedly very strongly on the side of the effect of some shared source of unresolved tension. But we would not expect to find cases that are purely one or the other.

CONCLUDING OBSERVATIONS

We need now to return briefly to the case of "The June Bug" in light of these comments. There is certainly evidence that this is a case of hysterical contagion, and our whole discussion of it has been predicated on the assumption that hysterical contagion was the central process involved. There is no doubt that it was the epidemic quality of the flurry of cases and the later "hysterical" interpretation of the event that brought it such wide publicity. Yet our discussion has suggested that hysterical contagion was only one of several processes which were probably going on at the same time even if we define it as a pure behavioral event. A full understanding of the event would require a specification and investigation of all of these processes. Although we can only speculate about some of them, it is important to recognize the probable complexity of the pattern which we have been able to view from only a limited perspective.

To sketch the various patterns which need to be combined it is necessary to broaden our perspective to include at least the whole plant as well as a more extended period of time than we have investigated. This is especially true for an understanding of the central belief in the case, the belief in a poisonous insect. Some of the early news items alluded to the fact that there had been complaints of insects for several weeks before the epidemic. Evidently during this time there had diffused rather widely in the population of the plant the belief that there was an uncommon number of insects and that they constituted at least a nuisance. It is within this context that the first few cases must be seen. As the symptoms and the knowledge of sickness spread, the link between this earlier belief and the immediate experience was made. The insect changed from a nuisance to a threat.

We must assume that in the face of this threat a number of different things began to happen, the most obvious and most central from our perspective being the rapid increase in reported symptoms. But there must have been other patterns of contagion going on at the same time. Undoubtedly in the face of this threat some of the women (with or without having experienced symptoms) evolved the solution of leaving the plant and there would presumably have been a contagious adoption of that solution. Others probably turned to officials in the plant for remedial action, and there would presumably have been a contagious move in that direction by some of the workers.

The increase of reported symptoms evidently understates the actual increase in symptoms—our self-defined affecteds attest to this. Given the experience of symptoms, a woman might or might not have become known to the medical authorities. She could have "clocked out of there," taken an aspirin, "talked it out" with a friend or her supervisor, *or* gone to the doctor. Except for the accidental discovery of the self-defined affecteds, our concern would have been exclusively with those known to the medical authorities. Even within that group, however, it proved useful to differentiate between those who went to the doctor on their own and those who fainted before they could find aid. A relevant aspect of this differentiation is the suggestion that there developed during the period of the epidemic a greater tendency to seek aid before being overcome. Thus, for those who did develop symptoms and could not cope with them in any other way, there evidently evolved an acceptable solution where one had not existed before. There was evidently a process of social facilitation in the use of this method of coping. In addition, there was also evidence that persons with milder symptoms were likely to report to the doctor in the latter part of the epidemic. This could be interpreted either as an indication of a heightened awareness of physiological disturbances and thus a tendency to define mild symptoms as significant, as an indication of a desire to cooperate with the officials by keeping them informed of even mild "attacks," or as a means of using a socially approved way of accomplishing some other goal (getting attention, going home, etc.).

This seems to mean that in any such case there are several processes of dissemination going on at the same time, all of which are interrelated but any one or combination of which may become the focus of attention: (1) the spread of a belief in a threat; (2) the spread of the experience of symptoms; (3) the spread of relatively unobtrusive methods of coping with the threat and/or the symptoms; (4) the spread of cases of collapse in the face of the threat and/or the experience of symptoms; (5) the spread of the solution to the experience of symptoms via seeking medical aid. Only the last three are likely to bring the process to the attention of outsiders, and, depending on the "unobtrusive" methods devised, it may be that only the last two will do so. All of these processes are to be expected whether the "cause" of the symptoms is "real" or "purely imaginary." In fact, we put these terms in quotation marks because we suspect that it is never possible to use them in such cases with complete confidence, and the social effects will be the same in any event.

References

Asch, S. E. Studies of independence and conformity. *Psychological Monographs*, 1956, 70(9).

Back, K. W., & Gergen, K. J. Idea orientation and ingratiation in the interview: A dynamic model of response bias. *Proceedings of the Social Statistics Section of the American Statistical Association*, 1963, 284–288.

Balint, M. *The doctor, his patient, and the illness*. New York: International Universities Press, 1957.

Barnett, H. G. *Innovation: The basis of cultural change*. New York: McGraw-Hill, 1953.

Bion, W. R. *Experiences in groups: and other papers*. New York: Basic Books, 1961.

Blumer, H. Collective behavior. In A. M. Lee (Ed.), *New outline of the principles of sociology*. New York: Barnes & Noble, 1951. Pp. 166–222.

Brown, R. W. Mass phenomena. In G. Lindzey (Ed.), *Handbook of social psychology*. Vol. II. Cambridge, Mass.: Addison-Wesley, 1954. Pp. 833–976.

Brown, R. W. *Social psychology*. New York: Free Press, 1965.

Cantril, H. *The psychology of social movements*. New York: Wiley, 1941.

Coleman, J. S. *Introduction to mathematical sociology*. New York: Free Press, 1964.

Coleman, J. S., Katz, E., & Menzel, H. The diffusion of an innovation among physicians. *Sociometry*, 1957, 20, 253–270.

Crowne, D., & Marlowe, D. *The approval motive*. New York: Wiley, 1964.

Devereux, G. Two types of modal personality models. In B. Kaplan (Ed.), *Studying personality cross-culturally.* Elmsford, N.Y.: Row, Peterson & Co., 1961. Pp. 227–241.

Dubos, R. *Man adapting.* New Haven: Yale, 1965.

Edwards, A. *The social desirability variable in personality assessment and research.* New York: Dryden Press, 1957.

Engel, G. L. *Psychological development in health and disease.* Philadelphia: Saunders, 1962. (a)

Engel, G. L. *Fainting.* (2nd ed.) Springfield, Ill.: Charles C Thomas, 1962. (b)

Festinger, L. Informal social communication. *Psychological Review,* 1950, 57, 271–282.

Forman, R. E. Resignation as a collective behavior response. *American Journal of Sociology,* 1963, 69, 285–290.

Funkenstein, D. H., King, S. H., & Drolette, M. E. *Mastery of stress.* Cambridge, Mass.: Harvard, 1957.

Grosser, D., Polansky, N., & Lippitt, R. A laboratory study of behavioral contagion. *Human Relations,* 1951, 4, 115–142.

Hoffer, E. *The true believer.* New York: New American Library, 1958.

Imboden, J. B., Canter, A., & Cluff, L. E. Convalescence from influenza. *Archives of Internal Medicine,* 1961, 108, 115–121.

Imboden, J. B., Canter, A., Cluff, L. E., & Trever, R. W. Brucellosis: III. Psychologic aspects of delayed convalescence. *Archives of Internal Medicine,* 1959, 103, 406–414.

Johnson, D. M. The "phantom anaesthetist" of Matoon: A field study of mass hysteria. *Journal of Abnormal and Social Psychology,* 1945, 40, 175–186.

Katz, E., & Lazarsfeld, P. F. *Personal influence.* Glencoe, Ill.: Free Press, 1955.

Katz, E., Levin, M., & Hamilton, H. Research on the diffusion of innovation. *American Sociological Review,* 1963, 28, 237–252.

Kerckhoff, A. C., Back, K. W., & Miller, N. Sociometric patterns in hysterical contagion. *Sociometry,* 1965, 28, 2–15.

Lang, K., & Lang, G. *Collective dynamics.* New York: Crowell, 1961.

Lionberger, H. F. Some characteristics of farm operators sought as sources of farm information in a Missouri community. *Rural Sociology,* 1953, 18, 327–338.

McDougall, W. *The group mind.* New York: Putnam, 1920.

Mechanic, D., & Volkhart, E. H. Stress, illness behavior, and the sick role. *American Sociological Review,* 1961, 26, 51–58.

Medalia, N. Z., & Larsen, O. N. Diffusion and belief in a collective delusion: The Seattle windshield pitting epidemic. *American Sociological Review*, 1958, 23, 180–186.

Miller, D. R., & Swanson, G. E. *Inner conflict and defense.* New York: Henry Holt, 1960.

Polansky, N., Lippitt, R., & Redl, F. An investigation of behavioral contagion in groups. *Human Relations*, 1950, 3, 319–348.

Redl, F. The phenomenon of contagion and "shock effect" in group therapy. In K. R. Eissler (Ed.), *Searchlights on delinquency.* New York: International Universities Press, 1949. Pp. 315–328.

Schachter, S. The interaction of cognitive and physiological determinants of emotional state. In L. Berkowitz (Ed.), *Advances in experimental social psychology.* Vol. I. New York: Academic Press, 1964. Pp. 49–80.

Schuler, E. A., & Parenton, V. J. A recent epidemic of hysteria in a Louisiana high school. *Journal of Social Psychology*, 1943, 17, 221–235.

Sherif, M. A study of some social factors in perception. *Archives of Psychology*, 1935, 27(187).

Smelser, N. J. *Theory of collective behavior.* New York: Free Press, 1963.

Swanson, G. E. Determinants of the individual's defenses against inner conflict: Review and reformulation. In J. C. Glidewell (Ed.), *Parental attitudes and child behavior.* Springfield, Ill.: Charles C Thomas, 1961. Pp. 5–41.

Szasz, T. S. *Pain and pleasure.* New York: Basic Books, 1957.

Turner, R. H., & Killian, L. M. *Collective behavior.* Englewood Cliffs, N.J.: Prentice-Hall, 1957.

Weider, A., Wolff, H. G., Brodman, K., Mittelmann, B., & Wechsler, D. *The Cornell index.* New York: The Psychological Corporation, 1948.

Welsh, G. S. Factor dimensions A and R. In G. S. Welsh & W. G. Dahlstrom (Eds.), *Basic readings on the MMPI in psychology and medicine.* Minneapolis: University of Minnesota Press, 1956. Pp. 264–281.

Wheeler, L. Toward a theory of behavioral contagion. *Psychological Review*, 1966, 73, 179–192.

Zeisel, H. *Say it with figures.* (Rev. ed.) New York: Harper, 1957.

Appendixes

A

COMPARISON GROUPS

The model of hysterical contagion which we have presented in Chapters 7–9 features the interplay of many variables. The intricate relation between the incidence of strain and inability to cope with it, the social definition of a situation in which it was possible to express symptoms in different ways, the personal background of the people involved, and the nature of the exciting incident contributed jointly to the spread of the contagion and to the different manifestations it took in the different women. An adequate test of this whole model in a factorial design, for instance, was, in the nature of the case, impossible; therefore, an intensive, careful analysis of the single incident was clearly the most available method in this case. We restricted ourselves, therefore, to explaining the different intricate patterns of behavior within a well-defined group. Some additional questions, however, can be treated only with the aid of comparison groups.

As we have said previously, we only defined the group which we studied as a socially meaningful unit after we first had a slightly broader definition of the population at risk. We decided to treat two additional groups, Negroes and the women outside the dressmaking departments separately on the basis of two criteria of the spread of the epidemic: seeking medical attention and reporting symptoms in the interview. By neither of these criteria did the epidemic spread in any significant way outside the dressmaking group so that these two other groups do not provide any significant contribution to the epidemic. This decision was also justified by the lack of sociometric links between the dressmaking departments and the other two groups.

There is still the question of belief in the epidemic. All workers in the plant were virtually certain to have heard of the epidemic, if only because the plant had been closed for fumigation. Let us turn first, therefore, to what we have called before "the pattern of lasting belief," and compare the extent to which they believed in physical causes for the epidemic. Table I shows the difference on two questions about their belief. On both questions, the two groups exhibit striking contrasts. The Negro respondents believed in the insect as much as, if not more than, the group among whom the

TABLE I
Beliefs About the Epidemic Among Population at Risk, Negroes and Nonsewing Room Cases

Questions and responses	Population at Risk (N = 408)* %	Negroes (N = 18) %	Nonsewing Room (N = 20) %
What do you think caused this to happen?			
Definitely an insect	33	50	30
Probably an insect	35	22	15
Don't know	20	22	33
Not an insect	11	6	20
Do you think that some kinds of people were more affected than others? In what way were they different?			
There was no difference	30	28	5
There were physical differences	22	30	15
Other (including "imaginative" and "nervous")	48	42	80

* This N of 408 represents the same definition of the population at risk as was used in Chapter 7.

epidemic occurred. The women who worked outside the room, on the other hand, showed more skepticism about the insect being the cause of the epidemic. This is shown by the answer to the direct question: What do you think caused this to happen? Sixty-eight percent of the population at risk said it was "definitely" or "probably" an insect. Among the Negro women we find 72 percent, a slightly higher proportion, giving the same answer, but among the women outside the big room only 45 percent, less than half, considered an insect the probable cause. Another question, which deals with the same topic in a different way, showed most striking differences from the women in the big room: Do you think that some kinds of people were more affected by this than others? and, if yes, In what way were they different? Only 1 of the 20 women outside the big room who were interviewed said there was no difference, 3 said there were physical differences, whereas the remainder gave politely skeptical responses, such as "imagination" and "nervousness." The last type of response was given by less than half of either the population at risk or the Negro pressers. We thus find two distinct patterns of belief in the groups who were not strongly affected by the epidemic. The women who were physically separated looked at the whole epidemic in a different way and disassociated themselves in their belief from the main group. Thus, we should not be surprised that they hardly showed any symptoms or went to the doctor about the symptoms. The Negro women, however, were physically close to the women at risk, they saw the epidemic themselves, and they saw the women being carried away. They expressed belief in the reality of the insect, but they still were hardly affected themselves. Thus, the social barrier was no hindrance to the spread of belief, but it effectively limited the spread of treated symptoms.

Of the different factors which we have stated as conditions for the occurrence of the epidemic, namely, strain with which the individual is unable to cope, personality disposition to experience illness, and the existence of a sociometric network, clearly the third condition distinguished both groups from the population at risk. There were hardly any sociometric ties between the white women working in the sewing room, the Negro women working there, and the women in the rest of the factory. The fact that the epidemic did not spread beyond this group which can be sociometrically defined gave us our original justification to restrict ourselves to this group as our population at risk. In addition, we can inquire now whether this group was different in other ways from either of the two other groups. Table II shows the comparison between the three groups on the relevant variables. The differences on the questions related to

TABLE II

Characteristics of Population at Risk, Negroes, Nonsewing Room Cases, and Control Plant Cases

Characteristic	Population at Risk (N = 408)* %	Negroes (N = 18) %	Non-sewing Room (N = 20) %	Control Plant (N = 135) %
Worked overtime at least two or three times a week	43	55	10	1
Do not mention supervisor as one to go to with a complaint	27	28	5	4
Provide half or more of family income	24	44	40	18
The section varies in output	30	39	5	50
It is wrong to stay home when not sick	72	94	80	70
Deny all symptoms	17	28	25	6
Had been sick during past several years	26	28	20	54
Had had to stay home because of sickness during past year	56	44	60	72
Had been taking medicine or pills recently	32	17	25	43
Describe health as "excellent"	21	11	15	23
Acquiescence	57	72	70	53

* This N of 408 represents the same definition of the population at risk as was used in Chapter 7.

strain are considerable, but the groups seem to be less distinguishable on the personality question. In general, on the strain questions the population at risk lies between the two other groups. The women outside the big room reported less strain. That is, they worked less overtime, were more likely to go to the supervisor, believed less that people varied in output than both of the other groups. This difference corresponds to the objective situation at the plant. These women dealt with more specialized and probably more highly skilled aspects of the production. This included the initial preparing of the material, dyeing, spinning, and other work of this kind. To other questions of this same kind, they show themselves to be more settled in the present situation. They are older and more likely to say that they would prefer to work at Montana Mills instead of keeping house. In spite of the fact that they get along better with the supervisor, they are also more likely to be union members. As shown in the table, they are less likely to believe that output varies between workers. Further, none of them believes that it is hard to keep up with this pace. Although they are major contributors to their families' income, they seem to be settled in a condition which they can handle (even union membership seems to be more a sign of belonging within a labor force than a question of strain), and in a working situation which they can handle easily. A reaction to strain, even legitimized as in the epidemic, seems to hold little attraction for them.

The Negro group, on the other hand, shows more strain than the population at risk: they work more overtime, they more often supply more than half of the family income, they see variation in output within their group. In effect, work takes more of their time, they need the income more, and they are under more strain to keep up the production. However, some other data show that they may not perceive a conflict situation. They feel only pressure to keep the job at any cost. Like the women outside the sewing room, they hope and expect to keep working. They also rate high on the scale of job satisfaction. We may surmise that the subjective situation at work was somewhat different from that of the population at risk. The Negro women needed the job badly, felt insecure in it, and therefore were not attracted in any way toward any situation which may have disrupted their job. An additional piece of evidence points in the same direction. As we saw before (p. 174), everybody in the population at risk who had been identified by others as having been affected acknowledged her part in the epidemic during her own interview. However, two of the Negro women were mentioned by other respondents as having been affected, but did not say so in their own interview.

In contrast to the consistent differentiation of the population at risk and the other two groups on strain, we find no striking differences in the personality patterns. The Negro group is slightly more inclined toward illness, that is, they are less likely to rate their health as excellent and are more likely to have been sick. However, they are less likely to have stayed home or taken medicine or pills. This agrees with the explanation that they are under a stress to work and would not jeopardize their job in any way. Correspondingly, they are slightly more likely to show symptom denial and more likely to say that it is wrong to pretend illness to stay home from work. The women outside of the big room show even fewer consistent differences in personality patterns. In one respect they are quite different from the population at risk. They are less likely to say that they have been sick, but are more likely to have stayed home because of illness. We might interpret this as due to higher job security.

The main conclusion which we can derive from the investigation of these additional groups is the great importance of the exact nature and strength of the strain to which the workers are responding. Within the same factory, subject to many of the same events, these two groups were apparently not sufficiently involved to become victims of the same hysterical contagion. The one group, the women outside of the dressmaking departments, were even so little touched by the epidemic that they were skeptical about the nature of the event itself. Their working situation was sufficiently different and superior so that the strain we have analyzed for the women at risk did not apply to them. They were under much less strain, so they could take a more objective view of the situation. The Negroes, on the other hand, were objectively under the same strain, held the same beliefs, and did not deny the reality of the epidemic. However, the other set of circumstances was missing. Because of their comparatively insecure situation and their social isolation, they were less apt to become involved.

The above discussion shows that the situation in this one plant was not homogeneous. It is possible that the strain affects only specific groups in the plant. However, in our whole study we have been able only to compare groups within one plant on several characteristics. We really do not know to what extent the relationships are typical for all the plants in the area or whether we are working with a very selected population. Some statements by the management led us to the conclusion that it was a peculiar group because it was a very new plant in the area and was forced to take some leftovers from the labor force. In addition, some of the conditions of managing the plant were shown in Chapter 5 to be somewhat unusual and may have contributed to the epidemic. A sample from another similar clothing manufacturing plant in the same area, not known to be unusual, will show the special conditions which Montana Mills might have had.

The last column in Table II shows the answers of the respondents in the control plant. On most of the measures of strain they show less strain than all three groups in Montana Mills. They work less overtime, name the supervisor as the person to go to for help, and are less likely to provide more than half of the family income. On the personality data they show more inclination toward illness, however. They experienced more illness in the last year, were more likely to have taken pills or medicine, but were more likely to rate their health as excellent. Some of these differences between Montana Mills and the control plant correspond to different plant organization. In general, in the control plant work was steady, without layoffs and with little overtime. On other questions about the work in the plant, the workers in the control plant rated their work lower: in contrast to Montana Mills they are less likely to say that their job is better than at other places, they see less intrinsic value in their work, and they are more likely to say that they would prefer to keep house and not work at the plant if they could do what they wanted. The general impression is that they felt freer in the interview to voice complaints and also to admit health troubles. The pattern may also indicate that they feel committed to the job at the present time, but do not see it as a permanent commitment.

We can interpret the difference between this group and the women in Montana Mills by saying that they are under fewer pressures which give them a trapped feeling. They accept the job as a means to get money which they want now (although it seems to be less necessary for the family). It is all right as far as jobs go, but it is not exceptional. Apparently they have taken extensive sick leave with satisfactory excuses, perhaps sometimes cynically, and do not feel excessive pressure. The work is there if they want it, neither too much—with overtime—nor having a danger of layoff. This in turn would provide less justification for a spectacular way of taking off during a peak production period.

We can look at the three groups besides the population at risk in the light of our discussion of the postulates of diffusion and contagion in Chapter 9. For the difference in belief of the two groups in the plant we might refer to the differences in prestige: the workers in the big room probably had less prestige than the ones outside, who were more skilled workers, while the white workers may have had prestige in the eyes of the Negro pressers. The difference in action, however, conforms best to Postulates 7 and 15. Neither the outsiders nor the Negroes had intimate ties with the affected. Also, neither group had a need for action, but the difference from the population at risk was in opposite directions, that is, the Negro workers faced too much risk by getting sick and thus this avenue was effectively blocked, while the workers outside the room were not under as much stress and lacked the original incentive. The control factory seems to be similar to this latter group. Although it must be admitted that we do not know what would have happened in the control factory if a woman had fainted, the fact still remains that no such incident did occur. The workers seem to be under less pressure and are able to express their complaints in other ways. One particular working condition is the same for the women outside the sewing room and those in the control factory, namely, the regularity of work. Neither group was exposed to overtime or layoffs. We might thus surmise that of all strain factors which increased tension, this was the most important.

B

INTERVIEW SCHEDULE:
INDUSTRIALIZATION AND
THE WORKER

Hello, I am _____, from the National Opinion Research Center. We are carrying out a number of studies of various kinds of plants all over the country to help in understanding the problems and satisfactions of both workers and management. One of the problems we are looking into is the matter of the health of workers. We were interested in talking to some of you here at Montana Mills for a number of reasons. First, this is a new plant with very modern machinery, air conditioning, and many other advantages. Second, it is part of a general pattern of industrialization of the South. And, of course, we are also interested in it because of some of the publicity the plant received recently.

Mainly, though, we are concerned with the general situation here in the plant and how those of you who are working here are getting along.

One thing I want to make clear, too, is that none of the things you may tell me will be reported to anyone else in the plant — to management, the union, or anyone else. We will, of course, give a report of the general findings to others in the plant, but

217

no one will be told about what any <u>individual</u> tells us. I doubt if you would have any worries on this anyway, but just in case you should, you can be sure that this is entirely confidential. Okay? Now ----------

1. How long does it take you to get to and from work? (one way)
    _____ Less than 15 minutes
    _____ 15–30 minutes
    _____ 30 minutes to an hour
    _____ More than an hour

2. Do you go alone or do you drive with other workers?
    _____ Alone
    _____ With others   Whom?_____
                               _____

3. How many people are in your family? (Household unit, including respondent)
    _____

4. How many of these work? (Including respondent)
    _____

5. Who is the chief breadwinner in your family?
    _____ Respondent is | Is his (her) job
    _____ Husband ──────────────→| steady, or is it
    _____ Father ───────────────→| seasonal?
    _____ Sister ───────────────→| _____ Steady
    _____ Other (Specify) ──────→| _____ Seasonal

6. What part of the family income comes from your wages? All, more than half, or less than half?
    _____ All
    _____ More than half
    _____ Less than half

7. How do you use your income? Is it just for you, is it pooled for the support of the family, or what?
    _____ Just for own use
    _____ Pooled for family support
    _____ Other (Specify)_____

8. How much difference would it make to you if you were unable to have this income?

_____ A great deal

_____ Some difference

_____ Not much

9. Is there any disagreement in your family on whether you should be working at Montana Mills? (Do some think you should and some think you shouldn't?)

_____ Yes ──────────→ | What's the disagreement about? (Who disagrees with whom on this? Who thinks you shouldn't? <u>Why</u> do they think you shouldn't?)

_____ No

10. Do you find that your work here interferes with some of your other activities? (Do you feel that you can't do as much of what you want to or should do outside the plant because you're working here?)

_____ Yes ──────────→ | What kinds of things does it interfere with? (Family, religion, recreation, housework, organized groups, etc.)

_____ No

11. Did you work elsewhere before coming to work here at Montana Mills?

_____ No ──────────→ | Why did you start working here?

Whose idea was it that you start working here?

_____ Her own

_____ Family member suggested it

_____ Friend suggested it

_____ Other person suggested it

_____ Yes ⟶

> Why did you change jobs?
>
> _____
>
> On the whole, how does this
> job compare with other jobs
> you've had? Is it better, about
> the same, or not as good?
> _____ This one is better
> _____ This one is not as good
> _____ Better in some ways,
>   worse in others
> _____ About the same
> (If better and/or worse:) What
> about this job is better (worse)?
>
> _____
> _____
> _____

12. How do you think others in your section feel about their
     job here? Do they think it is better, about the same, or
     not as good as jobs they've had before?
     _____ This one is better
     _____ This one is not as good
     _____ This one is better in some ways, worse in others
     _____ Some think it's better, some think it's worse
     _____ Don't know

13. When you think about your present job, what are the things
     about it that are good?

     _____
     _____
     _____

14. What are the things about it that are bad, or not so good?

     _____
     _____
     _____

15. How are the employees treated in this plant? The same
     as at most other places, better than at most, or worse
     than at most others?
     _____ The same as at most
     _____ Better ⟶
     _____ Worse ⟶
     _____ Better and worse ⟶
     _____ Don't know

> In what ways are they
> treated better (worse)?
>
> _____
> _____
> _____

NOTE TO INTERVIEWER: IN QUESTIONS 16-26 GET <u>FULL NAME</u> OF PERSONS MENTIONED.

16. A. Who are the people with whom you come into contact during the course of your work? _____

_____

ASK IF NOT CLEAR FROM Q. 16A:

    B. Who is your supervisor? _____
    C. Who is your steward? _____
    D. Who gives you your work? _____
    E. Who picks it up? _____

17. Do you take your lunch break by yourself, usually with the same people, or with whoever comes along?
    _____ Alone
    _____ Same people ——→ Who? _____ _____ _____
    _____ Whoever comes along ——→ Are there some people
                                        you see more than
                                        others? Whom?

                                        _____

18. On the whole, how well do the people in your section get along with one another?
    _____ Very well   _____ Okay, not bad
    _____ Poorly

19. How well do you like the people in your section? (most of them, on the whole)
    _____ Very much   _____ Okay, not bad
    _____ Don't like them

20. Comparing <u>your</u> section with <u>others</u>, are the people in <u>your</u> section better to work with, about the same, or do you think people in <u>other</u> sections might be better to work with?
    _____ Mine are better   _____ About the same
    _____ Others better   _____ Don't know

21. Of the people in your section, who is the person you admire most?

_____

22. Of the people in your section, who is the best worker?

_____

23. Who are your best friends in the plant?

_____   _____   _____

24. To whom would you turn for help if you had any personal problem in the plant?

_____

(If person outside plant mentioned:) Anybody in the plant?

_____

25. Is there anybody you think of who would want to turn to <u>you</u> first?
    _____ No
    _____ Yes ————————→ | Who?_____ |

26. If you had a complaint about your job, to whom would you go or to whom would you talk about it?
    _____ My supervisor

    | (If steward not men- |
    | tioned) Would you go to |
    | your steward? |
    | _____ Yes _____ *No |
    | _____ Don't know |
    | *If "No": Why not? |
    | |
    | _____ |
    | _____ |

    _____ No one
    _____ A friend, peer
    _____ Don't know

    _____ My union steward ——→

    | (If supervisor not men- |
    | tioned) Would you go to |
    | your supervisor? |
    | _____ Yes _____ *No |
    | _____ Don't know |
    | *If "No": Why not? |
    | |
    | _____ |
    | _____ |

27. How well does your supervisor understand your problems?
    _____ Very well
    _____ Okay, well enough, all right
    _____ Not very well, poorly
    _____ Don't know

28. How well do you think the others in your section think your supervisor understands their problems?
_____ Very well
_____ Okay, well enough, all right
_____ Not very well, poorly
_____ Don't know

29. How much do you have confidence and trust in your supervisor?
_____ Have a lot of confidence and trust
_____ Some, a little, sometimes
_____ Very little, none

30. How much do the others in your section have confidence and trust in your supervisor?
_____ They have a lot of confidence and trust
_____ Some, a little, sometimes
_____ Very little, none
_____ Don't know

31. How free do you feel about discussing important things about your job with your supervisor?
_____ Very free
_____ Some doubt, only at times
_____ Not at all free, won't do it

32. How would you rate your supervisor? Is he (she) strict, somewhat so, or is he (she) pretty easy-going?
_____ Strict
_____ Somewhat strict
_____ Easy-going
_____ Varies too much, he's (she's) too changeable
_____ Don't know

33. Would you say that he (she) treats everybody the same, or is he (she) strict with some and lenient with others?
_____ All the same
_____ Strict with some, lenient with others

I have here a number of statements. In each case you can respond to the statement in one of these four ways. (GIVE SUBJECT CARD WITH RESPONSES) You can Strongly Agree with the item, Agree with it, Disagree with it, or you may Strongly Disagree with it. I think we can do this best if you simply point to the answer that best describes how you feel about the state-

ment. Now for instance, how do you feel about this statement?
(Circle response given.)

34. Taking everything into account, things
    are better for us than they were for our
    mothers.   SA   A   D   SD

35. In general, there are more bad things
    than good things about my job.   SA   A   D   SD

36. Toward the end of the day, it often
    seems to me as if quitting time will
    never come.   SA   A   D   SD

37. The people I work with are a pain in
    the neck.   SA   A   D   SD

38. All things considered, it is better if a
    woman can stay home with her family.   SA   A   D   SD

39. The time spent at work does not inter-
    fere much with the things I really want
    to do.   SA   A   D   SD

40. I would not like to have my work week
    cut to 20 hours, even if my income
    stayed the same.   SA   A   D   SD

41. I don't care who I work with, as long
    as they don't bother me.   SA   A   D   SD

42. All in all, I am glad I have the job I
    have.   SA   A   D   SD

43. When you come right down to it, a
    worker's interests and those of man-
    agement are the same.   SA   A   D   SD

44. When I am at home, I often think about
    my friends at work.   SA   A   D   SD

45. The work I do is dull.   SA   A   D   SD

46. All in all, it would have been better if
    so many factories had not come into
    this area.   SA   A   D   SD

47. The people I work with are my best
    friends.   SA   A   D   SD

48. If I inherited a million dollars, I would
    still like to keep on doing the work I
    do now.   SA   A   D   SD

49. If you come right down to it, it doesn't
    matter to the worker how much profit
    the factory makes.   SA   A   D   SD

50. One of the best things about my work
    is the people I work with.   SA   A   D   SD

51. I would miss my job badly if I stayed away even for a brief vacation of more than a week.   SA   A   D   SD

52. I have never disliked anyone with whom I've worked.   SA   A   D   SD

53. Nobody would do the kind of work I do, if he didn't have to.   SA   A   D   SD

54. The time spent at work takes too much away from the things I really should do.   SA   A   D   SD

55. The people I would most like to visit me in my home are the people I work with.   SA   A   D   SD

56. I dislike my job.   SA   A   D   SD

57. All in all, it is good for our area that so much new industry has been built here.   SA   A   D   SD

58. A lot of people would like to trade their job for mine.   SA   A   D   SD

59. My job would be better if it weren't for the people I work with.   SA   A   D   SD

60. All things considered, it is better for a woman to work and bring income to her family.   SA   A   D   SD

61. I wouldn't take a better paying job if it would mean I would have to do different work than I do now.   SA   A   D   SD

62. Taking everything into account, our mother's times were better than ours.   SA   A   D   SD

63. Even if I had an entirely different job, I would like to do the kind of work I do now sometimes, just for fun.   SA   A   D   SD

Now, a few questions about one of the things that happened recently.

64. As you know, a number of people got sick here in the plant this summer, from an insect bite or something. Exactly, what did happen? (Get verbatim.)

_____

_____

_____

_____

_____

_____

65. Did anything like this happen to you?

_____ Yes ⟶ | Are you fully recovered from
_____ No | it now?
                | _____

66. Did this happen to anyone (else) in the plant whom you know well?

_____ Yes ⟶ | Who was that? [Get full
_____ No | name(s)]
                | _____
                | _____

67. About how many people in the plant do you figure this happened to?

    (GET ESTIMATE OF NUMBER AFFECTED)_____

68. What do you think caused this to happen? (Do you think it was an insect or something else?)

    _____

69. Do you think it could have been prevented in some way?

_____ Yes ⟶ | How could it have been pre-
_____ No | vented?
_____ Don't know | _____
                    | _____

70. Do you think that some kinds of people were more affected by this than others? (Do you think that it was more likely to happen to some people than to others?)

_____ Yes ⟶ | In what way were those who
_____ No | were affected different from
_____ Don't know | the others?
                    | _____
                    | _____
                    | _____

71. Do you think that whatever caused this is now taken care of, or do you think there is still a danger of it happening again?

_____ Still danger ⟶ | What could be done to pre-
_____ Taken care of | vent this from happening
_____ Don't know | again?
                         | _____

I'd like to ask you a few questions about your job.

72. First, is it a seasonal job, or can you count on working at least a full week all year?

_____ Seasonal ———→ | ASK BOTH QUESTIONS:
_____ Steady | A. If you should be laid off, how long do you expect to work before being laid off?
_____ Don't know ———→ |
| _____
|
| B. If you are laid off, how long would you expect to be without work? That is, how long would it be before you were asked to come back to work here?
|
| _____

73. When you were first hired at Montana Mills, did you expect your job to be seasonal?

_____ Yes ————————→ | How did you feel about it being seasonal?
_____ No |
_____ Didn't know then | _____ Liked it
| _____ Disliked it
| _____ Didn't care, didn't matter

74. Have you ever been laid off since you've worked at Montana Mills?

_____ Yes ————————→ | A. Did you know when you were laid off how long you would be out of work?
_____ No | _____ Yes
| _____ No
|
| B. How long were you out of work?
|
| _____
|
| C. Did you have any money put aside to help tide you over while you were laid off?
| _____ Yes, enough
| _____ A little
| _____ No

75. If you should be laid off in the future, do you have any money put aside to help tide you over?

_____ Yes, enough _____ A little _____ No

Now, how about the work you do on your job.

76. As far as your job is concerned, what's the thing you worry about the most? (Probe: Overtime, seasonal nature of the job, keeping up, keeping your job)

_____

77. Is the pace pretty much the same all the time on your job, or do you sometimes have to work harder or faster than you do at other times?

_____ Always pretty much the same
_____ Varies, is sometimes harder or faster

78. Compared with other people in your section, do you think you work faster, about the same, or do you work slower?

_____ Faster
_____ About the same
_____ Slower
_____ Don't know

79. Do you ever find yourself trying hard to keep up with the others?

_____ No, never have this problem
_____ Yes, sometimes do

80. What would happen if you got behind the others?

_____

81. If you make mistakes, do you have to do that work over again?

_____ No, never
_____ Sometimes ⟶
_____ Yes, always ⟶

Does that come out of your pay? Do you lose income when that happens?
_____ No
_____ Yes
_____ Sometimes

82. Compared with the others in your section, do you make more mistakes, about the same number, or do you make fewer mistakes?

_____ More _____ About the same
_____ Fewer _____ Don't know

83. In most plants there are people who work faster or slower than others. In your section, though, do most of the people turn out about the same amount of work as the others or is there a lot of variation?

    _____ Most about the same   _____ Much variation

    _____ Don't know

84. Are there any who usually turn out more than the other women?

    _____ No, all about the same

    _____ Don't know

    _____ Yes ——————→

> How do you feel about those who do this?
> _____ Doesn't matter one way or the other
> _____ I like them, think this is good
> _____ I don't like them, think this is bad
> How do others in your section feel about them?
> _____ They don't care one way or the other
> _____ They like them, think this is good
> _____ They don't like them, think this is bad

85. Are there any who usually turn out less than the other women?

    _____ No, all about the same

    _____ Don't know

    _____ Yes ——————→

> How do you feel about those who do this?
> _____ Doesn't matter one way or the other
> _____ I like them, think this is good
> _____ I don't like them, think this is bad
> How do others in your section feel about them?
> _____ They don't care one way or the other
> _____ They like them, think this is good
> _____ They don't like them, think this is bad

86. Do you think that some of the people here in this plant sometimes take off from work when they aren't sick, just to get a rest?

_____No   _____ Don't know   _____ Yes

87. Do you sometimes do this?

_____ No ——————→ | Do you think there is anything
_____ Yes ——————→ | wrong with this?
                                       | _____ No
                                         | _____ Don't know
                                         | _____ Yes   What? _____

(ASK QUESTIONS SEPARATELY FOR WEEKDAYS AND SUN-DAYS)

Now let's talk about working overtime.

88. About how many times in the last month have you worked overtime (during the week) (on Sundays)?

	During the week	Sundays
Every day		
Two or three times a week	_____	_____
Once each week	_____	_____
Once or twice a month	_____	_____
Not at all	_____	_____
Never (SKIP TO Q. 93)	_____	_____

89. Is working overtime (during the week) (on Sundays) the sort of thing you can refuse if you feel like it, or is it something that's expected of you and that's hard to refuse?

Can refuse	_____	_____
Can't, hard to refuse	_____	_____

90. Do you like working overtime (during the week) (on Sundays)?
    Like
    Dislike
    Like and dislike
    Indifferent

	During the week	Sundays
Like	————	————
Dislike	————	————
Like and dislike	————	————
Indifferent	————	————

91. Some people don't like working overtime (during the week) (on Sundays) because it interferes with other things they have to do or want to do. In your case how much does working overtime interfere with your:

	During the week	Sundays
Housework	_Much _Some _None	_Much_Some _None
Taking care of children	_Much _Some _None	_Much_Some _None
Being with your husband	_Much _Some _None	_Much_Some _None
Being with your friends	_Much _Some _None	_Much_Some _None
Going to church	_Much _Some _None	_Much_Some _None
Other(_____)		

92. Do any others ever complain about your having to work overtime (during the week) (on Sundays)? For instance:

	During the week	Sundays
Husband	_Yes _No	_Yes _No
Children	_Yes _No	_Yes _No
Friends	_Yes _No	_Yes _No
Others (_____)	_Yes _No	_Yes_ No

93. How do you feel about this: Would you rather work a straight work week <u>without</u> overtime, but <u>no</u> lay-offs during the year; or would you prefer <u>working overtime</u> but <u>being laid off</u> from time to time?

_____ Prefer steady work week
_____ Prefer overtime and lay-off
_____ Doesn't matter
_____ Don't know

94. How do you think others in your section feel about this? Do you think they would prefer to work a steady work week, or would they rather have overtime and lay-offs?

_____ Prefer steady work week
_____ Prefer overtime and lay-offs
_____ They don't care
_____ I don't know

95. A. How do you feel about working on Sunday? Do you think it is wrong?

_____ No   _____ Yes   _____ Objects, but for other reasons.

   B. Why do you feel that way?_____

   _____

96. Do you attend any particular church? Which one? (GET NAME OF SPECIFIC CHURCH, i.e., Ninth Street Primitive Baptist, not just Baptist)

   _____

97. About how often do you usually attend religious services?

_____ More than once a week
_____ Once a week
_____ Two or three times a month
_____ Three to twelve times a year
_____ Less than three times a year
_____ Never

98. Have you attended any religious revival meetings this summer?

_____ Yes ——————→ | What group sponsored it?
_____ No | _____

99. Does your church disapprove of working on Sunday?

_____ Doesn't belong to church
_____ No
_____ Yes

100. How has your general health been?
_____ Excellent
_____ Good
_____ Indifferent
_____ Bad
_____ Very bad

101. Have you been sick during the past several years?
_____ Yes
_____ No

102. Have you been in the hospital during the last few years?
_____ No
_____ Yes ———————→ | How many days? |
| _____ |
| Why? |
| _____ |

103. Have you had to stay at home because you were sick during the past year?
_____ No
_____ Yes ———————→ | How many days? |
| _____ |
| Why? |
| _____ |

104. Have you been taking any medicine or pills during the last few months.
_____ No
_____ Yes ———————→ | What? |
| _____ |
| What for? |
| _____ |
| Was it prescribed by a doctor? |
| _____ Yes _____ No |

Here is a list of statements of possible complaints people may have and how they feel about themselves. Can you tell me for each whether it is generally true for you or not. For instance, do you often. . . . (CIRCLE RESPONSE)

105. Do you often have bad pains in your eyes?   Yes   No
106. Do you often cry?   Yes   No
107. Are you hard of hearing?   Yes   No

108. Do you become scared at sudden movements or noises at night?   Yes   No

109. Are you often troubled with bad spells of sneezing?   Yes   No

110. Are you constantly keyed up and jittery?   Yes   No

111. When you catch a cold, do you always have to go to bed?   Yes   No

112. Do you suffer from asthma?   Yes   No

113. Do you have pains in the heart or chest?   Yes   No

114. Does every little thing get on your nerves and wear you out?   Yes   No

115. Do you suffer from frequent cramps in your legs?   Yes   No

116. Do you often suffer from an upset stomach?   Yes   No

117. Are you considered a nervous person?   Yes   No

118. Do your muscles and joints constantly feel stiff?   Yes   No

119. Must you do things very slowly in order to do them without mistakes?   Yes   No

120. Is your skin very sensitive or tender?   Yes   No

121. Does your skin often break out in a rash?   Yes   No

122. Do you suffer badly from frequent severe headaches?   Yes   No

123. Do you go to pieces if you don't constantly control yourself?   Yes   No

124. Do you frequently feel faint?   Yes   No

125. Do you often get spells of complete exhaustion or fatigue?   Yes   No

126. Does working tire you out completely?   Yes   No

127. Are your feelings easily hurt?   Yes   No

128. Are you frequently ill?   Yes   No

129. Are you constantly made miserable by poor health?   Yes   No

130. Do people usually misunderstand you?   Yes   No

131. Do people often annoy and irritate you?   Yes   No

132. Do you get nervous and shaky when the supervisor is watching you?   Yes   No

133. Are you scared to be alone when there are no friends near you?   Yes   No

134. Do frightening thoughts keep coming to you?   Yes   No

135. I find it hard to keep my mind on a task or job.   Yes   No

136. I have more trouble concentrating than others seem to have.   Yes   No

137. Sometimes my mind seems to work more slowly than usual.   Yes   No

138. I do many things which I regret afterwards.   Yes   No

139. I brood a great deal.   Yes   No

140. I very seldom have spells of the blues.   Yes   No

141. Life is a strain for me much of the time.   Yes   No

142. I feel tired a good deal of the time.   Yes   No

143. People often disappoint me.   Yes   No

144. I am easily embarrassed.   Yes   No

145. During the past year, how often were you bothered by:

    A. Nervousness

       _____ Very often
       _____ Fairly often
       _____ Not very often
       _____ Never

    B. Loneliness

       _____ Very often
       _____ Fairly often
       _____ Not very often
       _____ Never

146. During the past year would you have reported to the doctor if the following situations had arisen?

    A. You had been feeling poorly for a few days.

       _____ Certainly
       _____ Probably
       _____ Not very likely
       _____ Very unlikely

    B. You felt you had a temperature of about 100 degrees.

       _____ Certainly
       _____ Probably
       _____ Not very likely
       _____ Very unlikely

    C. You felt you had a temperature of about 101 degrees.

       _____ Certainly
       _____ Probably
       _____ Not very likely
       _____ Very unlikely

147. If you could do what you wanted, would you work here, keep house, or do something else?

_____ Work here

_____ Keep house

_____ Do something else ⟶ What? _____

_____

148. Where would you like most to live, on a farm, in a town or in a city?

_____ Farm

_____ Town

_____ City

Respondent's Name: _____

Date: _____ Time of interview: From _____ a.m.
                                                                              p.m.

                                                    to _____ a.m.
                                                                        p.m.

Index

Italicized numbers refer to theoretical or extended discussions of the concepts noted.